W9-CIR-044

BATMAN™

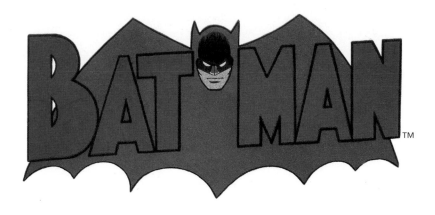

LONDON, NEW YORK, MELBOURNE,
MUNICH, AND DELHI

Editor Hannah Dolan
Additional Editors Pamela Afram, Neil Kelly, and Julia March
Editorial Assistant Emma Grange
Senior Designer Nathan Martin
Designers Clive Savage and Toby Truphet
Design Assistants Satvir Sihota and Rhys Thomas
Senior Designer and Brand Manager Robert Perry
Design Manager Ron Stobbart
Publishing Manager Catherine Saunders
Art Director Lisa Lanzarini
Publisher Simon Beecroft
Publishing Director Alex Allan
Senior Production Editor Jennifer Murray
Senior Production Controller Shabana Shakir

First published in the United States in 2012 by
DK Publishing
375 Hudson Street, New York, New York 10014.

10 9 8 7 6 5 4 3 2 1
001-184056-Jun/12

Page design copyright © 2012 Dorling Kindersley Limited.

Batman created by Bob Kane.

Copyright © 2012 DC Comics.
BATMAN and all related characters and elements are trademarks of and © DC Comics.
(s12)

DORL26842

All rights reserved under International and Pan-American Copyright Conventions. No part of this publication may be
reproduced, stored in a retrieval system, or transmitted in any form or by any means, electronic, mechanical, photocopying,
recording, or otherwise, without the prior written permission of the copyright owner.
Published in Great Britain by Dorling Kindersley Limited.

A catalog record for this book is available from the Library of Congress.

ISBN: 978-0-7566-9249-0

Colour reproduction by Altaimage, UK
Printed and bound in China by Hung Hing

The publisher would like to thank Laura Gilbert for her editorial assistance; Benjamin Harper and Josh Anderson
from Warner Bros. Consumer Products; Kevin Kiniry, Patrick Flaherty, Adam Schlagman, and Roger Bonas
from DC Entertainment; and John Wells for fact-checking the book.

Discover more at
www.dk.com

BATMAN

THE WORLD OF THE
DARK KNIGHT

WRITTEN BY
DANIEL WALLACE

Somerset Co. Library
Bridgewater, NJ 08807

Contents

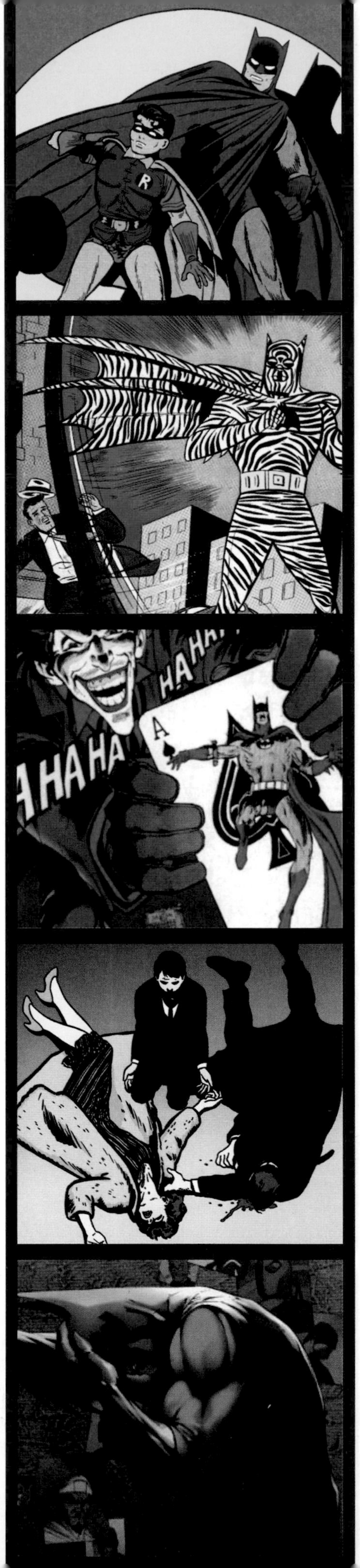
HA HA
AHAHA

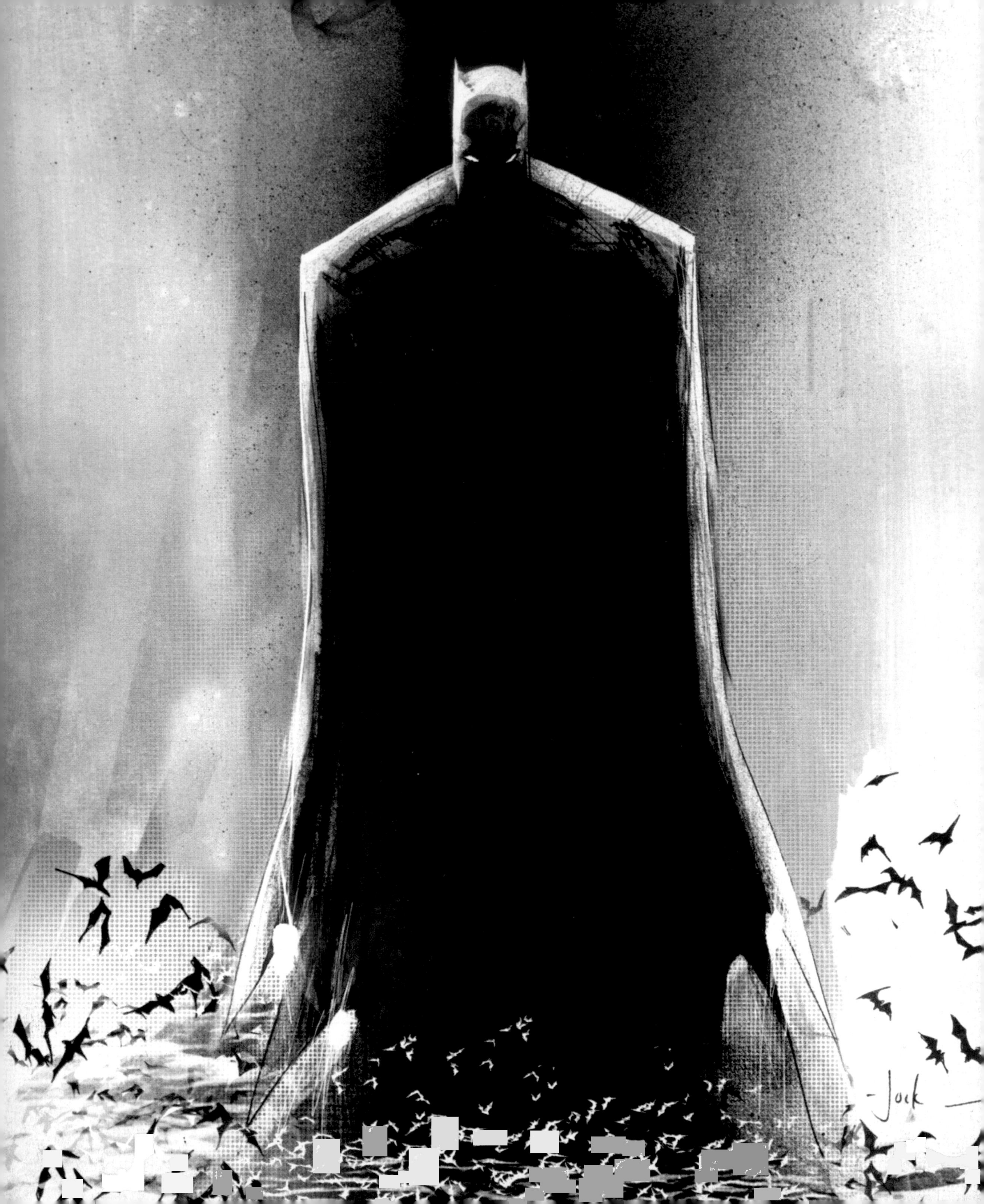
Jock

FOREWORD

I'll tell you a secret. The first time I saw the Batcave—saw it with my own eyes—I was terrified. It was 2010, I was writing my first issue of Batman, and I had just typed the words: "PAGES 8–9. A double spread of the Batcave, where we see…" And a chill hit me and I stopped typing. I was literally too scared to go on. Of course, I had a lot more writing to do that morning—descriptions of the Batcave itself, of the Batmobile, the dinosaur, the penny, the Joker card—but I just… couldn't. I actually got up and went to get a cup of coffee, suddenly worried I wouldn't be able to go any deeper into the cave, worried that I'd have to turn around and head back upstairs to the manor, call my editor and resign from the book.

What scared me, of course, was the sheer awesomeness of the cave itself. It stopped me in my tracks, and it made me reflect on how large Batman has loomed in my imagination over the years. Because in many ways Batman is the character that grew up alongside me. He was always my favorite. As a kid, I loved him in *Super Friends,* when he guest-starred alongside Scooby-Doo, and in other TV shows. Then as I got older I discovered the comics, the dark and gripping stories of the Denny O'Neil era. And of course, then came *The Dark Knight Returns* (my favorite comic of all time), *Year One, The Killing Joke…* The point is, at every age, there was always a Batman story I loved, one that spoke to me right then, one that made me want to write. And between the films and the comics coming out, it's still happening today, all the time.

Since being asked to write this foreword, I've thought a lot about why Batman is such a flexible character, why he endures so powerfully in so many different iterations. And in the end, my personal opinion is that Batman is enduring because he represents the hero in all of us—the hero we can all be, if we commit ourselves to a cause we believe in. Because the thing about Batman is, he has no superpowers; he's just a man—a man on an unshakable mission to do what he thinks is right, despite the odds, despite the punishment, the sacrifices, the pain… And yet through a sheer act of will, through his own dedication to justice—his dedication to preventing others from going through what he did in Crime Alley that terrible night—he has transformed himself into the most formidable hero of all time. After all, he lives in a world where men can fly and run faster than the speed of sound and yet, when the going gets tough, who do the other super heroes most often turn to for answers? Batman.

Of course, later on that morning that I was telling you about, I did put more words on the page, and I did go deeper in to the Batcave, where I met Bruce, sitting at his Batcomputer, eyes narrowed at a case on the screen. He might have even nodded hello. It was hard to tell. But come down for yourself and see. He's still here—always here. So I invite you, you standing there in the study—go ahead and turn the hands of the grandfather clock to 10:47, wait for the click, the creak of the secret panel swinging open, and step inside.

SCOTT SNYDER

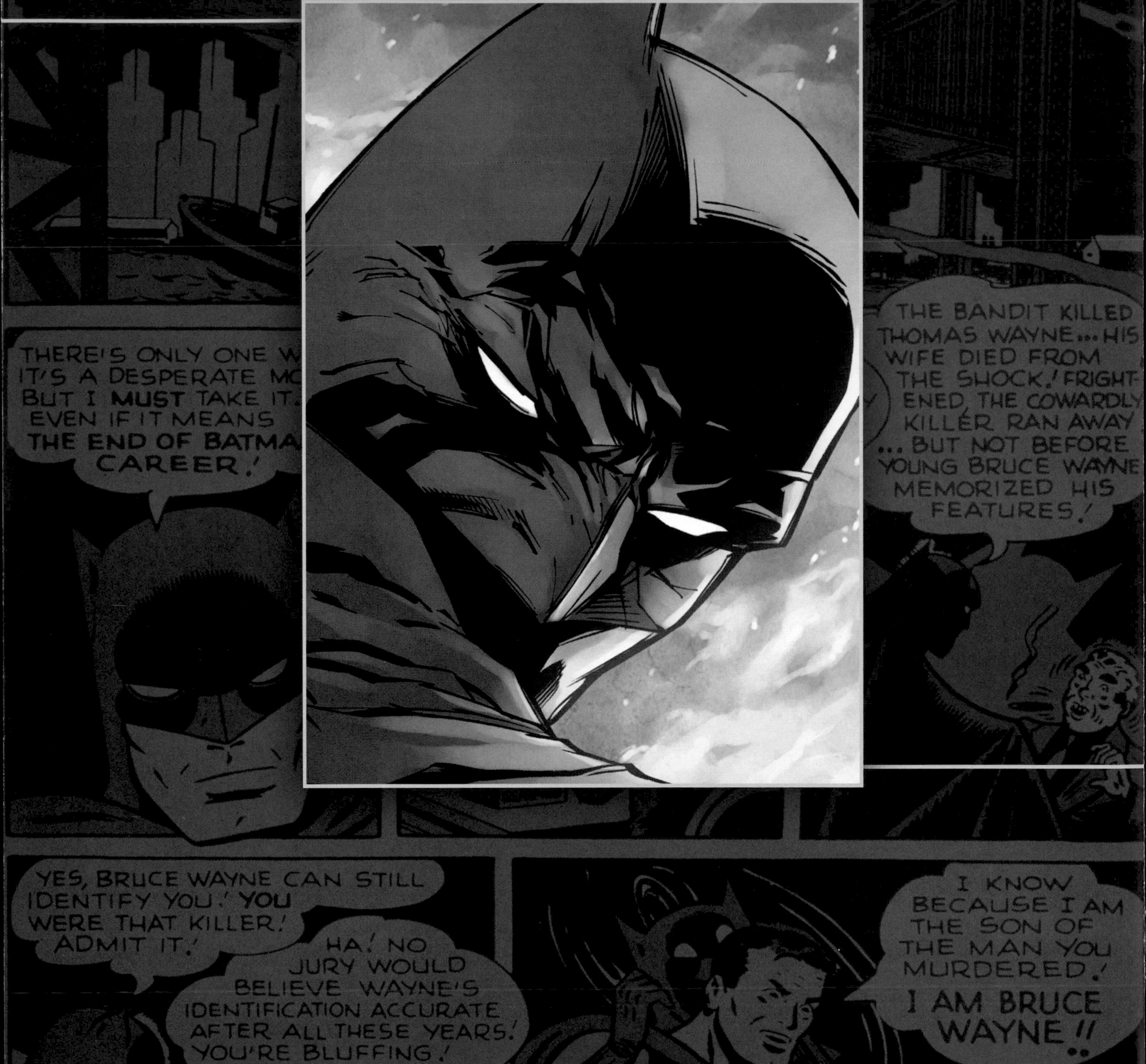
THERE'S ONLY ONE W
IT'S A DESPERATE MO
BUT I MUST TAKE IT.
EVEN IF IT MEANS
THE END OF BATMA
CAREER!
THE BANDIT KILLED THOMAS WAYNE...HIS WIFE DIED FROM THE SHOCK! FRIGHTENED, THE COWARDLY KILLER RAN AWAY ...BUT NOT BEFORE YOUNG BRUCE WAYNE MEMORIZED HIS FEATURES!
YES, BRUCE WAYNE CAN STILL IDENTIFY YOU! YOU WERE THAT KILLER! ADMIT IT!
HA! NO JURY WOULD BELIEVE WAYNE'S IDENTIFICATION ACCURATE AFTER ALL THESE YEARS! YOU'RE BLUFFING!
I KNOW BECAUSE I AM THE SON OF THE MAN YOU MURDERED!
I AM BRUCE WAYNE!!

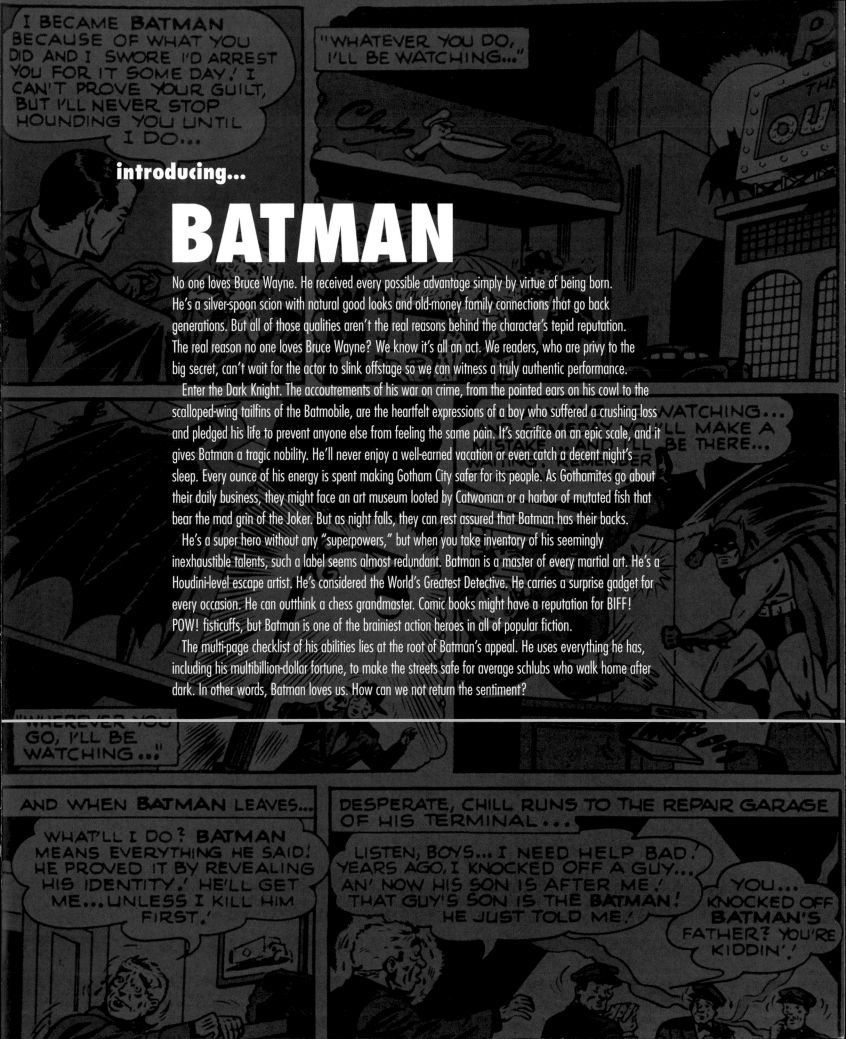

introducing...

BATMAN

No one loves Bruce Wayne. He received every possible advantage simply by virtue of being born. He's a silver-spoon scion with natural good looks and old-money family connections that go back generations. But all of those qualities aren't the real reasons behind the character's tepid reputation. The real reason no one loves Bruce Wayne? We know it's all an act. We readers, who are privy to the big secret, can't wait for the actor to slink offstage so we can witness a truly authentic performance.

Enter the Dark Knight. The accoutrements of his war on crime, from the pointed ears on his cowl to the scalloped-wing tailfins of the Batmobile, are the heartfelt expressions of a boy who suffered a crushing loss and pledged his life to prevent anyone else from feeling the same pain. It's sacrifice on an epic scale, and it gives Batman a tragic nobility. He'll never enjoy a well-earned vacation or even catch a decent night's sleep. Every ounce of his energy is spent making Gotham City safer for its people. As Gothamites go about their daily business, they might face an art museum looted by Catwoman or a harbor of mutated fish that bear the mad grin of the Joker. But as night falls, they can rest assured that Batman has their backs.

He's a super hero without any "superpowers," but when you take inventory of his seemingly inexhaustible talents, such a label seems almost redundant. Batman is a master of every martial art. He's a Houdini-level escape artist. He's considered the World's Greatest Detective. He carries a surprise gadget for every occasion. He can outthink a chess grandmaster. Comic books might have a reputation for BIFF! POW! fisticuffs, but Batman is one of the brainiest action heroes in all of popular fiction.

The multi-page checklist of his abilities lies at the root of Batman's appeal. He uses everything he has, including his multibillion-dollar fortune, to make the streets safe for average schlubs who walk home after dark. In other words, Batman loves us. How can we not return the sentiment?

THE BIRTH OF BATMAN

Batman was an instant sensation. His popularity helped to usher in the age of the comic book super hero.

Comic books were a new medium in the 1930s. Everyone was looking for ways to turn them into moneymakers. Some publishers simply reprinted comic strips taken from the nation's daily newspapers, but DC decided to make a big play for original content in the genres of humor and adventure. *Detective Comics* launched in 1937 with a focus on tough guys and private eyes, but it was a very different kind of hero who would give them their biggest hit. After issue #27's cover announced the "amazing and unique adventures of the Batman," Detective Comics—and DC as a company—would never be the same.

The new hero looked almost vampiric in his dark cloak, and he owed a debt to the grim pulp heroes of the era including the Shadow and the Spider. He became DC's second breakout star following Superman's debut in *Action Comics* the previous year. The non-superpowered, nocturnal Batman and the brightly colored Man of Steel couldn't be more different, but the two characters defined the polar extremes of the vast storytelling landscape offered by the super hero genre. DC spent most of the next decade filling in the middle ground with costumed heroes of every conceivable stripe.

Bob Kane and Bill Finger collaborated on Batman's creation, with Kane providing the art and Finger the scripting. Soon joined by inker Jerry Robinson, the team created nearly all of Batman's core elements—including Robin, the Batmobile, Gotham City, and Batman's bizarre Rogues Gallery—in just a few short years.

Bob Kane himself became a comic book character when he appeared on the pages of DC's Real Fact Comics #5 (1946). Readers were treated to a detailed tour of the Batcave with Kane playing the part of the tour guide.

Image labels: OLD BARN, WINCH, WINCH CHAIN, BAT PLANE, REINFORCED CONCRETE, WAYNE HOME, LAB, ELEVATOR, HANGAR, GARAGE, WORKSHOP

BOB KANE

Artist Bob Kane found work at the Max Fleischer animation studio during the 1930s but hoped to apply his illustration skills to the new medium of comics. After gaining experience at DC on the *Adventure Comics* feature "Rusty and His Pals," Kane came up with his own idea for a new super hero he thought could become as popular as Superman. He enlisted writer Bill Finger as his creative partner, and sold his Batman concept to *Detective Comics* editor Vin Sullivan. Under the terms of his deal, Kane received a byline on all stories. In 1943 Kane left comics to concentrate full-time on the Batman newspaper strip, but returned and remained involved with DC through the 1960s.

BILL FINGER

Writer Bill Finger met Bob Kane at a party and soon the two had struck a deal to collaborate as comics creators. During development of the Batman pitch, Finger refined Kane's concept for the hero. Out went a red costume and domino mask, and in came a cape, a blue-gray color scheme, and Batman's cowl with its trademark white eye-slits. Finger's scripts demonstrated a deep understanding of visual storytelling, and he emphasized Batman's potential as a detective by introducing Sherlock Holmes-style investigation to the stories. Soon made a DC staffer, Finger was instrumental in the development of many of Batman's best-known adversaries. He also helped develop the Golden Age version of the Green Lantern character with artist Martin Nodell.

JERRY ROBINSON

Jerry Robinson was just 17 years old and studying journalism at Columbia University when his artistic skills came to the attention of Bob Kane. Kane signed him on immediately as a comics inker and letterer. He and Bill Finger had just gotten Batman off the ground, and Robinson was able to contribute key concepts to the Dark Knight's legend during its developmental stage. Robinson is credited with illustrating a Joker playing card that led in part to the final design of Batman's arch-nemesis, and also with suggesting the name for Batman's sidekick, Robin. As Batman gained popularity, Robinson began to share inking duties on the comics with George Roussos, and when Bob Kane moved on to the Batman newspaper strip Robinson took over as penciller.

DETECTIVE COMICS
ISSUE #27

"As the two men leer over their conquest, they do not notice a third, menacing figure standing behind them. It is the Batman!"

MAIN CHARACTERS: Batman, Commissioner Gordon
SUPPORTING CHARACTERS: Lambert, Lambert Jr., Alfred Stryker, Steven Crane, Paul Rogers, Jennings
LOCATIONS: Commissioner Gordon's home, Lambert Mansion, Stryker laboratories, Wayne Manor

BACKGROUND

Detective Comics launched with the goal of telling stories about sleuths and private eyes—super heroes weren't in its mission statement. But after *Action Comics* delivered a breakout star in Superman, editor Vincent Sullivan hoped he could cause lighting to strike twice. *Detective Comics* #27 is where Batman began. Many of the building blocks of the Batman legend—including his double identity as Bruce Wayne, his relationship with Commissioner Gordon, and the white eye-slits of his pointed cowl—made their first appearances in this short, six-page story. Sandwiched between mostly forgotten figures like Buck Marshall and Cosmo the Phantom of Disguise, the dark-garbed vigilante pursued his own brand of justice and exhibited a cruel edge. Batman was both a super hero *and* a detective, and the newcomer soon pushed the other *Detective Comics* features out of the spotlight.

PUBLICATION DATE
May 1939

EDITOR
Vincent Sullivan

COVER ARTIST
Bob Kane

WRITER
Bill Finger

PENCILER
Bob Kane

INKER
Bob Kane

LETTERER
Bob Kane

The Story...

Danger and death traps abound as Gotham City gets its first taste of Batman, who solves a murder mystery by relying on fisticuffs and smart detective work.

News of a strange costumed "Batman" had all of Gotham buzzing when the wealthy scion Bruce Wayne decided to pay a social call to the home of his friend, Police Commissioner Gordon [1]. Their idle conversation was interrupted by a telephone call alerting Gordon to a gruesome discovery: Lambert, a chemical industrialist otherwise known as "the Chemical King," had been found stabbed to death in his home. Gordon sprang into action to investigate the crime scene while a seemingly bored Wayne almost reluctantly agreed to accompany him, remarking that the police case might prove an amusing diversion for the evening.

Over at the Lambert mansion [2], it became clear that the late tycoon had worked with three business partners—Steven Crane, Paul Rogers, and Alfred Stryker—any of whom may have had a motive to kill Lambert in order to secure control of the Apex Chemical Corporation. Lambert's son, who found his father after the gruesome attack, revealed that valuable business documents were missing from Lambert's safe [3]. Lambert's ex-partner, Steven Crane, then called Gordon to report a threat on his life and demand police protection. This imminent threat prompted Bruce Wayne to launch his own investigation into the case—in the fighting guise of the Batman!

He arrived too late to prevent Crane's murder [4], but Batman confronted the two assassins as they fled the scene, appearing from behind them in a dramatic rooftop reveal [5]. After knocking them out with his fists, the Dark Knight Detective drove off to investigate the two remaining businessmen with connections to Lambert—and it turned out they were already together! Paul Rogers had paid a visit to Alfred Stryker to warn him of the danger they were in, but Stryker revealed himself as the true villain behind the scheme.

Stryker's hulking manservant, Jennings, captured Rogers and hauled him into Stryker's science laboratory—a fitting lair for the man who would be the new "Chemical King"—placing his captive beneath a huge bell jar suspended from the ceiling [6]. As the jar lowered into place, the gloating goon announced that this act would spell Rogers' doom the moment the jar formed an airtight seal and flooded with poison gas [7].

Only seconds remained until the jar reached the floor, but suddenly Batman appeared at an open window. With a lunge he slid beneath the gas chamber, plugging the valve the instant it began to spray its vile toxin [8]. A powerful blow with a wrench shattered the glass and freed Batman, along with a grateful Rogers.

Stryker pulled a knife and tried to kill Rogers, but Batman effortlessly disarmed him [9], then revealed to both men all the evidence he had gathered about Stryker's plot. Desperate, Stryker pulled out a gun. Batman deflected a clumsy shot and countered with a punch to the face, sending Stryker tumbling over a railing into a vat of acid [10]. Batman delivered a grim eulogy as he watched the villain expire: "A fitting end for his kind."

The next day, Bruce Wayne visited Commissioner Gordon to hear the official version of the case. An unimpressed Wayne called Gordon's report of the horrific events a "lovely fairy tale" before taking his leave [11]. Wayne's act fooled Gordon, who had no reason to suspect that his idle socialite friend and Gotham City's strange new Batman were one and the same [12].

BATSUIT

Its pointed-ear silhouette strikes terror into the hearts of criminals everywhere, but the Batsuit is more than a tool of intimidation. Packed with microelectronics and shielded with Kevlar, it is the most advanced combat suit ever built.

ARMORD ALL OVER

The Batsuit offers Batman a powerful defense against fists, knives, and bullets—not to mention Mr. Freeze's ice blasts or the Joker's acid-squirting flowers. It is constructed of 15 micro-layers of Nomex-reinforced fabric, the innermost providing insulation against extremes of heat and cold. Covering the whole thing is a shell of triple-weave Kevlar.

Batman's cowl is made of Kevlar around a steel frame. Built-in electronics give Batman night vision, allow him to hear distant whispers or to shut out external sounds, and to transmit voice commands.

BECOMING A BAT

The most important layer of protection offered by the Batsuit is the effect that it has on startled victims. Dark colors and the cape's irregular outline provide perfect nighttime camouflage, so Batman can appear and disappear without warning. It's not surprising that some believe him to be a vampire or demon. Batman encourages such rumors, which intentionally bolster his reputation through the spread of psychological disinformation.

Armored gauntlets protect against knife strikes. The three sharpened prongs can cut ropes—and create an intimidating visage.

The cowl's ears contain an antenna and transmitter, which allow Batman to maintain constant contact with the Batcave's information resources.

Not all heroes have the spatial awareness to use a cape effectively as part of their costume. In the wrong hands, a cape can become unwieldy.

The bat-symbol on the suit's chest often serves as a target for enemy gunfire; consequently it carries the thickest layer of armor.

Smart armor reacts to pressure, remaining flexible while Batman is moving and becoming rigid when stabbed or crushed.

The outer layer of the Batsuit can be electrified with a charge of 200,000 volts to shock enemies who get too close for comfort.

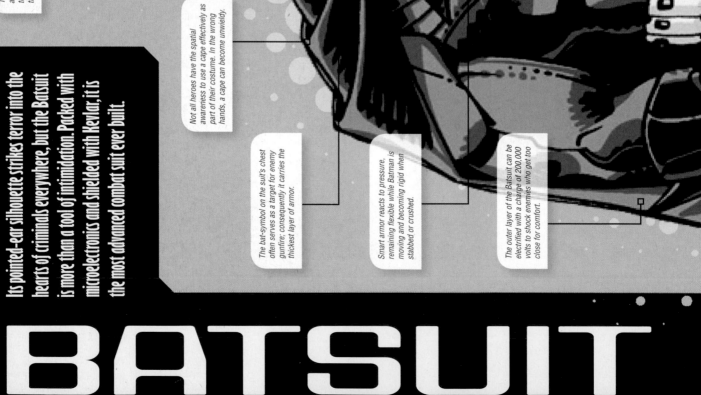

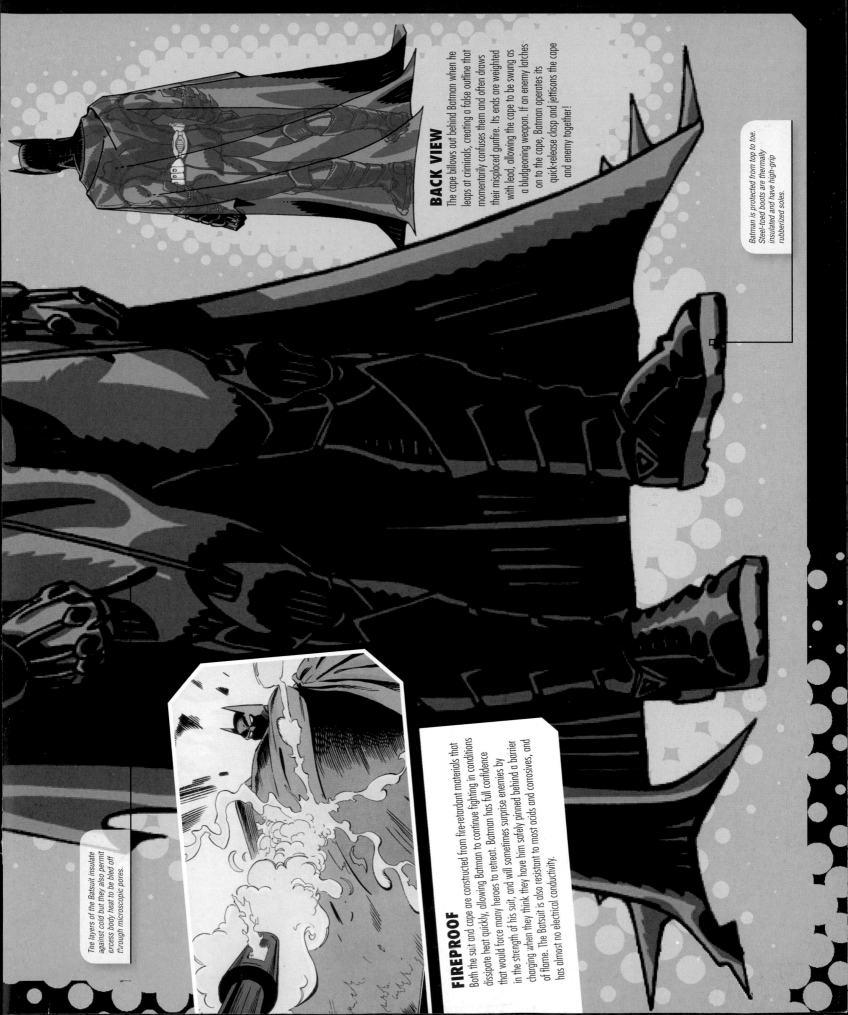

BACK VIEW

The cape billows out behind Batman when he leaps at criminals, creating a false outline that momentarily confuses them and often draws their misplaced gunfire. Its ends are weighted with lead, allowing the cape to be swung as a bludgeoning weapon. If an enemy latches on to the cape, Batman operates its quick-release clasp and jettisons the cape and enemy together!

Batman is protected from top to toe. Steel-toed boots are thermally insulated and have high-grip rubberized soles.

The layers of the Batsuit insulate against cold but they also permit excess body heat to be bled off through microscopic pores.

FIREPROOF

Both the suit and cape are constructed from fire-retardant materials that dissipate heat quickly, allowing Batman to continue fighting in conditions that would force many heroes to retreat. Batman has full confidence in the strength of his suit, and will sometimes surprise enemies by charging when they think they have him safely pinned behind a barrier of flame. The Batsuit is also resistant to most acids and corrosives, and has almost no electrical conductivity.

BATSUIT VARIANTS

While always remaining instantly recognizable, the Batsuit has gone through many changes over the years. Batman constantly updates it to take advantage of advanced materials and technology, or to provide protection from strange new enemies. Once superceded, older variants are rarely abandoned. Most are kept at the ready in the Batcave, or stored in vacuum-sealed cylinders for display in the trophy room.

ORIGINAL
Batman's first costume was a cloak and a gray bodysuit with an integral bullet-proof vest.

EARLY VARIANT
The stiff, winglike internal structure of this cape permitted Batman to glide for short distances.

1940S
Batman perfected his gadget-packed Utility Belt with this version of the costume.

1950S
Shorter ear points and a wider mask gave Batman a friendlier appearance.

1960S
Batman added a yellow oval around the bat-symbol to draw gunfire toward his ballistic chest armor.

1970S
A long, flowing cape helped Batman to disguise his silhouette when he lurked in shadows.

POST-KNIGHTFALL
After reclaiming his identity from Azrael, Batman adopted an all-black Batsuit.

NO MAN'S LAND
Batman introduced new armored materials into his suit while defending post-quake Gotham.

BATMAN INC.
As the Batman brand went global, Batman adopted an amalgam of his most familiar costumes.

MODERN SUIT
Batman's current Batsuit features sophisticated environmental and impact countermeasures.

TRAVELS THROUGH TIME

When an amnesiac Bruce Wayne was flung through time, instinct led him to fashion an outfit resembling the Batsuit in each era.

MAN-OF-BATS
Bruce battled with cavemen while wearing the skin of a giant bat as a prehistoric totem.

WITCH HUNTER
Dressed as a Puritan elder, Bruce investigated cases of alleged witchcraft in 17th century Gotham.

BLACK PIRATE
Bruce impersonated a swashbuckler to outwit the notorious Blackbeard, who mistook him for another pirate.

GUNSLINGER
In the Old West, Bruce faced down bounty hunters wearing an ensemble that featured a long black cape.

NOIR DETECTIVE
Hired to work on a case during an earlier decade, Bruce donned the outfit of a Gotham gumshoe.

FUTURE ARCHIVIST
Advanced nano-machines from the end of time called archivists turned Bruce into an augmented being.

ALTERNATIVE REALITIES

In branching timelines and on parallel Earths, Batman and his successors have demonstrated some unique spins on the traditional Batsuit.

DAMIAN WAYNE
In one possible future, Bruce's son Damian gained supernatural abilities including powers of instant healing.

KINGDOM COME
An aged Batman wore an armored suit to deal with a new age of heroes whose methods he found unethical.

JUSTICE
Batman teamed with his superpowered friends in the JLA to defeat the evil Legion of Doom.

BATMAN BEYOND
Batman passed the torch to Terry McGinnis in the alternate future setting of Neo-Gotham.

SPECIALIZED DESIGNS

Batman keeps a number of specialty Batsuits ready for use, while other have been worn just once, under unique circumstances.

WHITE LANTERN
The White Lantern ring of Life replaced Batman's usual costume with an all-white suit of blinding purity.

GREEN LANTERN
Batman has worn a Green Lantern ring and costume on more than one occasion, but only temporarily.

BLACK LANTERN
The Black Lantern ring of Death transformed a skeleton into a black-clad, undead Bat-horror.

SUIT OF SORROWS
Created during the Crusades, the Suit of Sorrows bestows great strength on those with pure hearts, like Batman.

RAINBOW BATSUITS
Batman wore a series of brightly colored costumes to draw attention away from an injured Robin.

ZEBRA BATSUIT
When a villain accidentally imbued him with energy, Batman saw his costume change to this striped variant.

SPECIALTY BATSUITS
Arctic, aquatic, slalom, desert, inferno, and other Batsuits are maintained in perfect condition in the Batcave.

ZUR-EN-ARRH BATSUIT
Left without his memory, Batman fashioned this multi-colored suit out of mismatched scraps.

OTHER BEARERS

Bruce Wayne isn't the only person to have put on the cape and cowl of Gotham City's most famous hero.

DICK GRAYSON
After Bruce Wayne's disappearance in time, the original Robin stepped into his shoes—and Batsuit.

JASON TODD
The second Robin went rogue and tried to become a new, better Batman using his own uncompromising methods.

TIM DRAKE
After meeting a grim future version of himself as Batman, Tim Drake vowed never to follow that path.

TWO-FACE
This bisected costume would have been Two-Face's if he had chosen to fill Batman's role.

HUGO STRANGE
This villain knows Batman's secret identity and has impersonated him more than once.

DOCTOR HURT
Claiming to be Thomas Wayne, Doctor Hurt appeared in Thomas's bat-themed masquerade costume.

AZRAEL
Jean Paul Valley became a new, dangerous Batman when Bruce Wayne suffered a back-breaking injury.

THE UTILITY BELT

As much a part of the Dark Knight's identity as his cape and cowl, the Utility Belt is a literal lifesaver. Over the years the simple pouches have given way to airtight, spring-loaded compartments, but the Utility Belt still fills the same multifunctional role.

ALWAYS PREPARED

Batman may have a specialized tool for any situation, but they would all be worthless if he couldn't get his hands on them at just the right moment. The Utility Belt is both a field kit and a mobile weapons locker, packing maximum power into a compact and wearable form.

SECURE CONSTRUCTION

Featuring solid components made from titanium, the Utility Belt is a triumph of user design. The belt balances ease of use with the ability to thwart unauthorized access, while using every centimeter of available space within a slim shape that lies flat against the body. The buckle features a complex lock which releases only after it registers a pre-programmed finger pattern. It also contains a tracking beacon and an explosive charge that can be triggered remotely to prevent the belt from falling into the wrong hands.

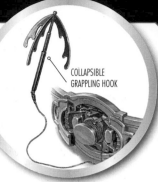

COLLAPSIBLE GRAPPLING HOOK

Earlier versions of the Utility Belt featured a jumpline reel within the buckle — this could be attached to a weighted hook and then thrown by hand.

REMOVABLE BUCKLE AND LOCKING MECHANISM

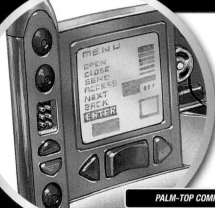

COMMUNICATIONS

One of the belt compartments can be removed to reveal a computer and digital communicator. The device responds to vocal and gestural commands, and possesses a backup touch screen and button array. Though Batman's cowl contains its own dedicated communication system, this device has the added functionality of holographic recording and three-dimensional playback.

PALM-TOP COMMUNICATOR

LIGHTS, CAMERA . . .

One of the belt's cylinders is a miniature camera, which can capture high-resolution video and still images in ultraviolet and infrared ranges beyond visual perception. All images are instantly uploaded and archived on the Batcomputer's servers. A powerful camera flash can also be used to blind attackers.

DIGITAL CAMERA

FOLDING BATARANGS

WEAPONS COMPARTMENTS

Several sections of the belt contain folding Batarangs or mini Batarangs, dispensed via spring-loaded ejectors. Titanium cylinders hold stacks of tear gas, smoke, and pellets designed to stun an assailant with a sudden flash-bang. One segment contains a magazine of anesthetic darts and a collapsible dart shooter. All of the belt's weapons compartments have quick-release covers that can be locked or unlocked with the swipe of a thumb.

MEDICAL KIT AND FIELD DRESSINGS

FIELD EQUIPMENT

All remaining space in the Utility Belt is allocated to general and mission-specific field equipment. Common items include a first-aid kit containing a wide spectrum of antidotes for various toxins, an oxygen rebreather, a tiny lock pick, and an acetylene torch capable of cutting through the hull of a battleship. When facing specialized foes Batman might choose to carry flamethrowers, defoliants, electromagnetic pulse generators, or even rare substances like Kryptonite.

ANYTHING BUT GUNS

The trauma of his parents' murders left Batman with an aversion to firearms. In Batman's view, guns are often carried by crooks who harm innocents with their indiscriminate fire. But even a well-aimed gun will take a life, and a fundamental principle of Batman's crusade is his "no killing" rule. The Batarangs and other custom tools require considerable skill to wield, but are designed only to incapacitate their targets. Batman's inner circle have all been trained in their use.

BAT-GRENADES

An entire room of enemies can be subdued with a single Bat-grenade. These single-use devices have many tactical applications, including bringing down large structures through controlled explosions and disorienting a crowd of enemies with a concussive blast. Grenades have timers that vary from five seconds to 40 minutes, or they can be activated remotely via radio signal. Large canister grenades can be rolled into rooms or affixed to doorframes where they are triggered by a tightening activation cord. Small pellet grenades can be thrown by the handful or stuck to a wall with a dab of contact cement.

FIRING PIN ATTACHED TO A PULL CORD

CONCUSSION GRENADE

WEAPONS

Batman's arsenal of non-lethal weapons isn't for amateurs. Each device requires the strong arm and careful aim of a seasoned expert.

EXPLOSIVE PELLETS

EXPLOSIVE PELLETS

These hardened gelatin spheres break upon impact, releasing concealing smoke screens or irritants like tear gas. Other pellets are packed with flash-bang charges that temporarily leave foes deaf and blind. The pellets are carried within impact-resistant cylinders on Batman's Utility Belt to prevent accidental explosion.

BAT-CUFFS

AEROSOL SPRAY

AEROSOL SPRAYS

Depending on the mission, any number of hand-held aerosol canisters might be clipped to Batman's Utility Belt. Knockout sprays also induce temporary amnesia. Supercooled sprays freeze electronics and render adhesives brittle. Tracking sprays tag targets with infrared paint, which Batman can detect through the filtered lenses in his cowl. Any aerosol canister can be placed freestanding in a room and set for timed release.

BAT-CUFFS

With a stranded-metal cable core surrounded by sapphire-impregnated nylon, these restraints are too strong to be broken by any human being, save those who possess superpowers.

HARD-IMPACT BATARANG

SPINNING BATARANG

LIGHTWEIGHT FOLDING BATARANGS

CUTTING BATARANGS

BATARANGS

Batman's signature weapon is the Batarang, a bat-shaped throwing tool usually cast from a hardened steel alloy. Though the name is derived from the Australian boomerang, not all Batarangs are designed to return to Batman's hand. Some are modeled on throwing knives, darts, and even flying discs. Hard-impact Batarangs can knock foes off their feet, while the micro-serrated edges of cutting Batarangs will slice a jumpline in half. Mini Batarangs have many sharp points and are thrown like Japanese shuriken.

GRAPNEL

Batman uses a handheld grapnel gun to navigate Gotham's rooftops. Its compressed CO_2 launcher fires a projectile — typically a grappling hook, Batarang, or wall-penetrating dart — attached to a reel of de-cel monofilament jumpline which can hold up to 400 lbs. Once the projectile has latched onto its target, the reel rapidly retracts and pulls Batman up to his new vantage point in mere seconds. It is a definitive tool for Batman, allowing him to swing silently between Gotham's towers. In emergencies, the explosive punch of the grapnel gun can also be used to knock armored enemies off their feet.

PENETRATING DART

The grapnel gun assembly is often tipped with a wall-penetrating dart featuring a smart-acceleration drill bit. Upon impact, internal microcircuitry instantly detects the composition of the surrounding surface, then spins to secure firm anchorage in metal or masonry.

MICRO-DIAMOND DRILL BIT

FINGERLIGHT

Batman's cowl contains vision-enhancing lenses but his Utility Belt also stores miniature spotlights for precision work. This light can be clipped to a finger or the end of a tool, providing 10,000 micro-candela LED power in a wide or a focused beam. It can also bathe areas in undetectable infrared, or project a laser beam when targeting or measuring distances.

FOCUSED BEAM

GADGETS

Batman is one of the smartest people on Earth, and has both the tools and the training to deal with almost anything. His gadgets have been custom-built to his exact specifications.

MOBILE COMPUTER

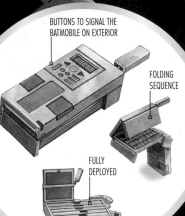

BUTTONS TO SIGNAL THE BATMOBILE ON EXTERIOR

FOLDING SEQUENCE

FULLY DEPLOYED

Communication links in the Batsuit constantly connect with the Batcave's servers, but Batman carries a portable data center when he doesn't have (or can't risk) a two-way connection. Waterproof, shock-resistant, and signal-shielded, the computer unfolds to reveal a simple keypad interface and a shatterproof display screen. The bare-bones design makes the mini-computer nearly impossible to break, and the unit is capable of using vocal, gestural or holographic interfaces.

CRIME SCENE KIT

Batman's detective work usually needs to be completed before the G.C.P.D.'s investigators arrive. A miniature crime scene analysis packet on his Utility Belt contains a fingerprinting kit, a DNA analyzer, several sterile sample bags, a chromatograph to identify substances within a testing sample, and a multi-spectrum environmental recorder.

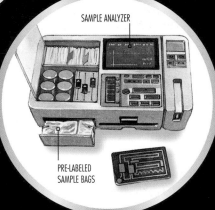

SAMPLE ANALYZER

PRE-LABELED SAMPLE BAGS

TOOL KIT

Each tool in this tightly packed sleeve fits into a powered, universal drive unit inside the handle. Drill bits and tool points of various sizes are included, along with wire cutters or strippers and electronic lock pickers.

DRILL BIT ENGAGED

BINOCULARS

Batman's multifunction binoculars offer high-resolution digital viewing in conventional, low-light, infrared, and ultraviolet modes. The binoculars can capture both still-frame and video footage, and the data can be uploaded to the Batmobile or Batcave.

GAS MASK

The gas mask covers the lower half of Batman's face to create a positive seal with the Batsuit and offer 100 percent protection against environmental toxins. With the addition of an oxygen cylinder, Batman can survive underwater or in a vacuum.

FACE SHIELD DEPLOYED

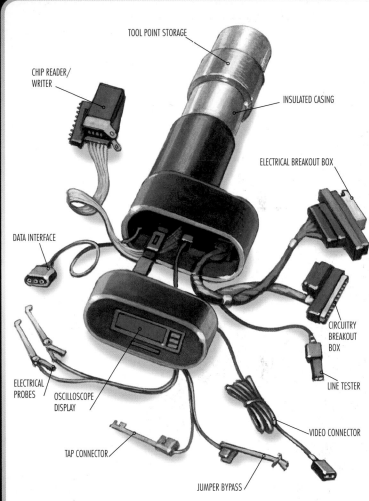

TOOL POINT STORAGE

CHIP READER/ WRITER

INSULATED CASING

ELECTRICAL BREAKOUT BOX

DATA INTERFACE

CIRCUITRY BREAKOUT BOX

ELECTRICAL PROBES

OSCILLOSCOPE DISPLAY

LINE TESTER

VIDEO CONNECTOR

TAP CONNECTOR

JUMPER BYPASS

UNIVERSAL TOOL

This single piece of field equipment allows Batman to perform various types of electronic wizardry. It contains line taps, electrical bypass jumpers, power and communication line analyzers, connectors for standard audio or visual and computing interfaces, and breakout boxes for linking with non-standard electrical configurations. On the rare occasion the universal tool can't get the job done, Batman can direct the Batcomputer to hack into Gotham City's data grid.

THE → BATCAVE

During daylight hours bats nest amid the stalactites.

Ceiling ports—quick-launch access for the Batplane.

The Joker's unmistakable calling card.

An information hub displays selected readouts.

The Batcave is also used as a garage. Various Batmobiles and vehicles built for specialized functions sit fueled and ready on a mechanized platform. The Batcave's concealed entrance also connects to Gotham's hidden network of tunnels, and the platform can rotate to move any vehicle into position. Batman, Robin, and Alfred are all skilled mechanics.

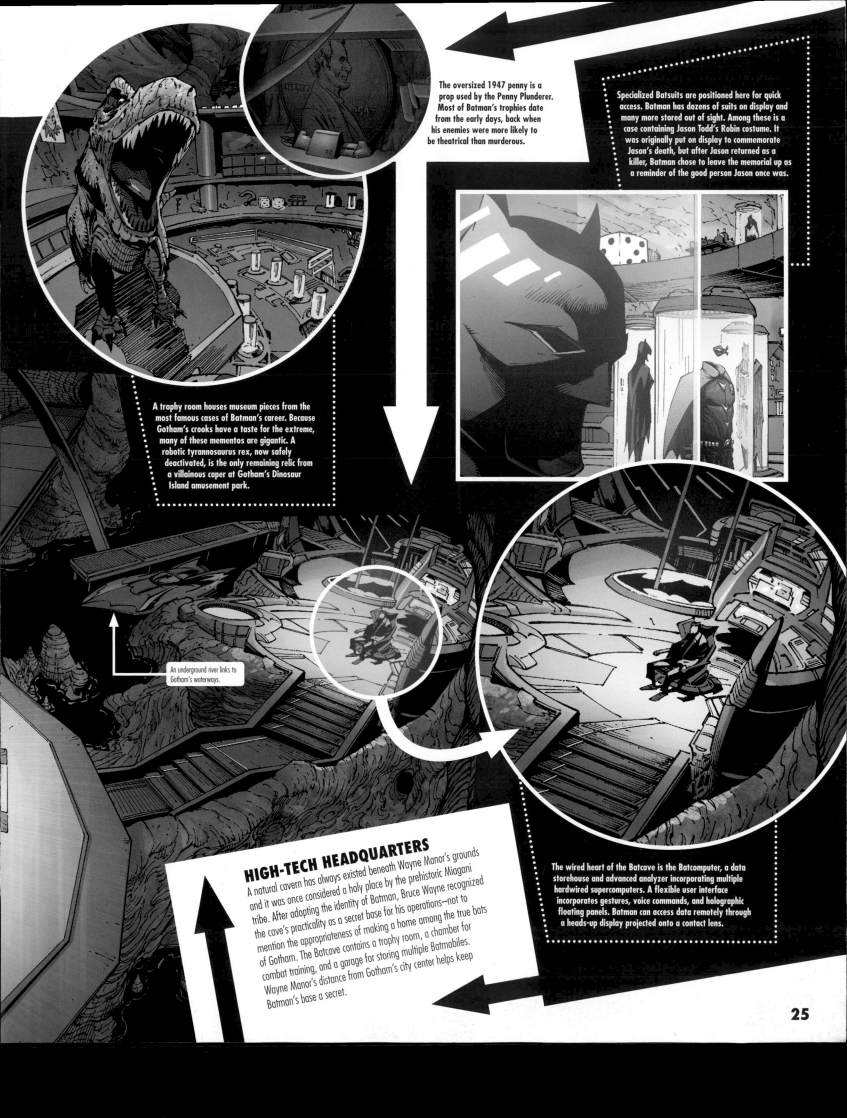

The oversized 1947 penny is a prop used by the Penny Plunderer. Most of Batman's trophies date from the early days, back when his enemies were more likely to be theatrical than murderous.

Specialized Batsuits are positioned here for quick access. Batman has dozens of suits on display and many more stored out of sight. Among these is a case containing Jason Todd's Robin costume. It was originally put on display to commemorate Jason's death, but after Jason returned as a killer, Batman chose to leave the memorial up as a reminder of the good person Jason once was.

A trophy room houses museum pieces from the most famous cases of Batman's career. Because Gotham's crooks have a taste for the extreme, many of these mementos are gigantic. A robotic tyrannosaurus rex, now safely deactivated, is the only remaining relic from a villainous caper at Gotham's Dinosaur Island amusement park.

An underground river links to Gotham's waterways.

HIGH-TECH HEADQUARTERS

A natural cavern has always existed beneath Wayne Manor's grounds and it was once considered a holy place by the prehistoric Miagani tribe. After adopting the identity of Batman, Bruce Wayne recognized the cave's practicality as a secret base for his operations—not to mention the appropriateness of making a home among the true bats of Gotham. The Batcave contains a trophy room, a chamber for combat training, and a garage for storing multiple Batmobiles. Wayne Manor's distance from Gotham's city center helps keep Batman's base a secret.

The wired heart of the Batcave is the Batcomputer, a data storehouse and advanced analyzer incorporating multiple hardwired supercomputers. A flexible user interface incorporates gestures, voice commands, and holographic floating panels. Batman can access data remotely through a heads-up display projected onto a contact lens.

BATMOBILE

Batman's famous ride is sleek, jet-propelled, and as strong a tank. New versions of the Batmobile are rolled out frequently, but all of them sport an ominous, bat-winged profile to announce the arrival of the Dark Knight.

TORTURE CHAMBER

The Batcave's wind tunnel is ideal for testing the Batmobile's aerodynamics but when its side panels open, the real fireworks begin. Machine guns, flamethrowers, acid jets, and high-intensity lasers attack the Batmobile from every angle to expose weaknesses in its armor. The Batmobile's carbon-fiber body is protected by an outer layer of ceramic fractal armor that repels projectiles and deflects concussive force. Even the Batmobile's windshield is bulletproof, and the vehicle's tires are gel-filled and reinforced with Kevlar.

Panels explode away when ejector seats are triggered.

Smoke-screen grenades.

LEADING EDGE
The Bat insignia on the hood serves as a steel-reinforced battering ram. The vehicle's grill is also made of a metallic weave containing graded diamond particles.

Retractable winch has 1,300 feet of cable on its reel.

The nose contains an advanced tactical radar jammer.

STATE-OF-THE-ART ENGINE
The Batmobile rides on impact-resistant hydraulics and has a valve train exhaust system. Its lightweight engine produces a tremendous amount of power, but still manages to be just slightly larger than those found in conventional automobiles.

NON-LETHAL OFFENSE
An arsenal of tools is stored here to slow down or deter foes without causing serious injury; retractable cannons can fire tear gas canisters, concussion grenades, tire-piercing caltrops, adhesive sprays, or Teflon lubricant slicks.

UNDER THE HOOD
The Batmobile is driven by a 1,200 horsepower jet turbine. Within the vehicle's nose is a sensor suite containing a landsat videomapper, a radar imager, and an infrared headlight mode, permitting Batman to engage in "blind driving" even when the Batmobile's windshield has been polarized for full opacity.

A police-band radio monitors transmissions from the G.C.P.D., while omni-directional microphones controlled from the dashboard allow Batman to conduct remote surveillance when parked.

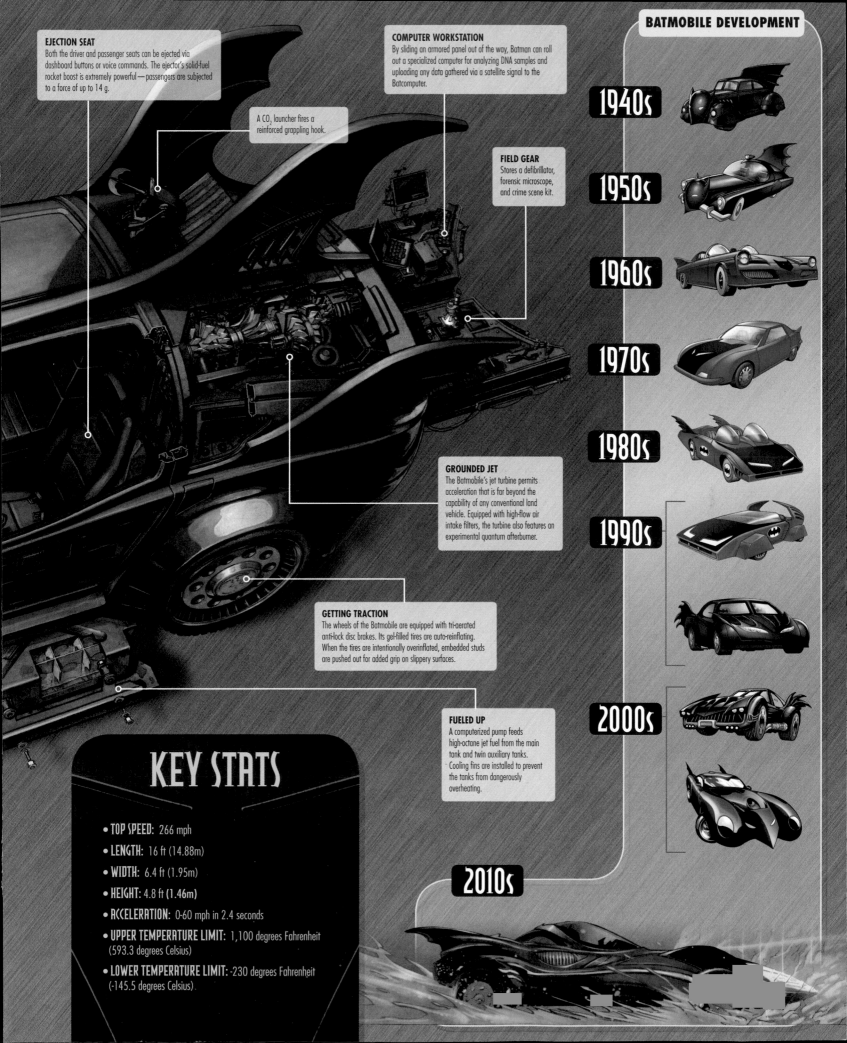

EJECTION SEAT
Both the driver and passenger seats can be ejected via dashboard buttons or voice commands. The ejector's solid-fuel rocket boost is extremely powerful — passengers are subjected to a force of up to 14 g.

A CO_2 launcher fires a reinforced grappling hook.

COMPUTER WORKSTATION
By sliding an armored panel out of the way, Batman can roll out a specialized computer for analyzing DNA samples and uploading any data gathered via a satellite signal to the Batcomputer.

FIELD GEAR
Stores a defibrillator, forensic microscope, and crime scene kit.

GROUNDED JET
The Batmobile's jet turbine permits acceleration that is far beyond the capability of any conventional land vehicle. Equipped with high-flow air intake filters, the turbine also features an experimental quantum afterburner.

GETTING TRACTION
The wheels of the Batmobile are equipped with tri-aerated anti-lock disc brakes. Its gel-filled tires are auto-reinflating. When the tires are intentionally overinflated, embedded studs are pushed out for added grip on slippery surfaces.

FUELED UP
A computerized pump feeds high-octane jet fuel from the main tank and twin auxiliary tanks. Cooling fins are installed to prevent the tanks from dangerously overheating.

KEY STATS

- **TOP SPEED:** 266 mph
- **LENGTH:** 16 ft (14.88m)
- **WIDTH:** 6.4 ft (1.95m)
- **HEIGHT:** 4.8 ft (1.46m)
- **ACCELERATION:** 0-60 mph in 2.4 seconds
- **UPPER TEMPERATURE LIMIT:** 1,100 degrees Fahrenheit (593.3 degrees Celsius)
- **LOWER TEMPERATURE LIMIT:** -230 degrees Fahrenheit (-145.5 degrees Celsius)

BATMOBILE DEVELOPMENT

1940s

1950s

1960s

1970s

1980s

1990s

2000s

2010s

BAT-VEHICLES

The Batmobile might rule the streets, but Batman can't corral crime in all its forms until he covers land, air, and sea. Luckily, the resources at WayneTech are at his disposal and he can commandeer a range of experimental vehicles that will never be declassified for civilian use. The Batplane and the Bat-Sub allow the Dark Knight to keep pace with superpowered colleagues like Superman or Aquaman, while the Batcycle and other nimble rides provide the maneuverability the Batmobile lacks. Each unique vehicle bears a blue or black color scheme and sharp-tipped edges — trademark design elements that wordlessly announce Batman's arrival.

BATPLANE

Batman maintains a squadron of Batplanes, from speedy interceptors to massive cargo carriers that sit in a secret hangar. Almost all Batplanes are capable of vertical takeoffs and landings and bear dynamic camouflage to evade sensors. The Batplane has a highly advanced autopilot which responds to remote voice commands.

The cockpit can be ejected in an emergency.

Wings are lined with anti-icing units.

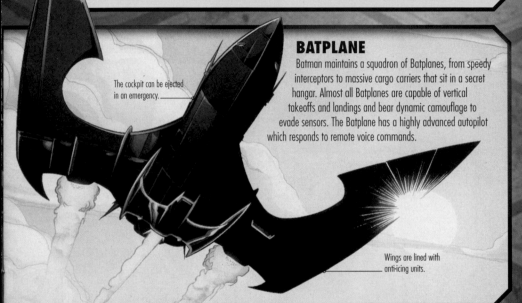

Struts are braced with Kevlar for added tensile strength.

BAT-GLIDER

Batman can't fly like an actual bat but his glider provides the next best thing. This lightweight and responsive glider can be used for silent drifting between rooftops, or — when its twin engines are attached — for a single-person powered flight. In case of an unexpected landing in Gotham Harbor, it is outfitted with an emergency flotation device. Without its engines, the glider is small enough to be stored in a shoulder-slung case.

BAT-COPTER

Because the Batplane is capable of vertical takeoff and stationary hovering, the helicopter is no longer as important as it was at the start of Batman's career. However, its whisper-quiet rotor and rooftop-mapping sensors make it a consistently effective tool for nighttime patrols. Batman and Robin have found that this vehicle is best used in tandem, with one of them using their bird's-eye view behind the controls as the other tracks a fleeing suspect down Gotham's alleyways.

Panoramic canopy provides a wide field of view.

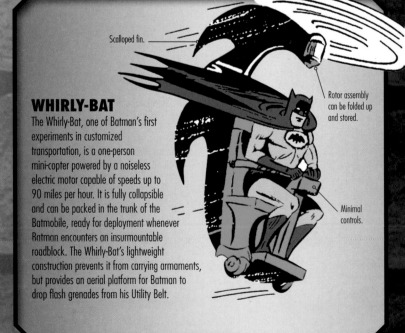

Scalloped fin.

Rotor assembly can be folded up and stored.

WHIRLY-BAT

The Whirly-Bat, one of Batman's first experiments in customized transportation, is a one-person mini-copter powered by a noiseless electric motor capable of speeds up to 90 miles per hour. It is fully collapsible and can be packed in the trunk of the Batmobile, ready for deployment whenever Batman encounters an insurmountable roadblock. The Whirly-Bat's lightweight construction prevents it from carrying armaments, but provides an aerial platform for Batman to drop flash grenades from his Utility Belt.

Minimal controls.

BATCYCLE

The Batcycle can go places that the Batmobile can't. This custom-built street motorcycle has a 786cc liquid-cooled engine and a sleek profile for roaring through narrow gaps in traffic. The Batcycle's computer-controlled gyroscopic stability system helps it stay upright during high-speed weaving. Though Batman presents a bigger target to his enemies on the Batcycle, the vehicle's front cowling and windscreen are completely bulletproof. A variant of the Batcycle is the Bat-Pod, a minimalist two-wheeled motorcycle that can be stored inside the Batmobile and ejected while the larger vehicle is still in motion.

Puncture-proof racing tires for road traction.

BATBOAT

The Batboat carries an arsenal of non-lethal weapons including hull-puncturing homing torpedoes, controlled-explosion depth charges, and a harpoon gun. Outrigger pods can turn the Batboat into a high-speed hydrofoil capable of speeds up to 150 miles per hour. Although the Batboat is fully sealed and capable of submerging, it carries its own dedicated submarine as well as a Bat-Jetski for quick intercepts.

A pneumatic grapnel can latch onto other ships or serve as an anchor.

BAT-SUB

This submersible is typically carried aboard the Batboat but can be launched directly from the Batcave via Gotham's interconnected waterways. The submarine is equipped with floodlights and sonar-mapping software for navigating Gotham Harbor's murky waters. It carries six hours of air with an additional 12 hours in its emergency tanks. An airlock provides access to the water, which Batman can explore with customized scuba gear or his submersible scooter.

ATV

As the urban Batcycle can't handle rocky ridges or soggy muck, the short-range ATV is carried on the Batplane for use in such situations. While it does have a cumbersome design, it sacrifices speed for superior four-wheeled stability and all-terrain access.

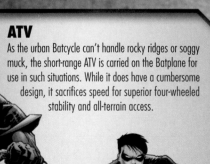
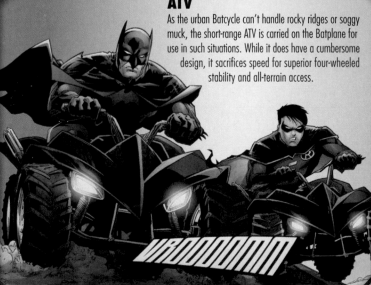

VROOOOMM

BAT-JETSKI

Carried onboard the Batboat, the Bat-Jetski fills a similar role to the Batcycle in aquatic environments. At night its small size makes it hard to spot from enemy lookouts. Batman's Jetski can easily outmaneuver larger boats and reach a top speed of 95 miles per hour.

ORIGIN

The shocking, senseless murder of his parents by a common street mugger gave young Bruce Wayne a burning sense of purpose. He channeled his survivor's guilt into a career battling crime, in a disguise that struck fear into evil hearts—a bat!

Their evening at the movies had just ended, but the Wayne family needed to cross Gotham's notorious Crime Alley on their way home. A mugger demanded cash and shot Thomas and Martha Wayne when they resisted. Young Bruce could do nothing to stop it.

BECOMING THE BAT...

LEAVING GOTHAM

KIRIGI—NINJA MASTER

HENRI DUCARD

Haunted by what he had witnessed, and wracked with guilt over his inability to act, Bruce vowed that no one would suffer the same fate that he had. As heir to the Wayne family fortune, he had both power and privilege—yet those advantages didn't prevent Thomas and Martha Wayne from dying in a flash of gunpowder. Bruce knew he couldn't bring them back, but with the right resources at his disposal he could make the streets safe again.

He knew it wasn't enough to simply fund the police—not in a city as dangerous and corrupt as Gotham. Instead, Bruce decided to take the fight directly to those who challenged law and order, avenging his parents every time he saved a life and every time he put a crook behind bars.

Bruce Wayne left Gotham to undertake the training he would need to carry out his one-man campaign. He studied languages and psychology at Cambridge University and the Sorbonne. He meditated in the mystic Tibetan city of Nanda Parbat and lived among the Ghost Tribes of the Ten-Eyed Brotherhood in Africa. In Korea he learned the art of the ninjutsu under Master Kirigi. From the world-class manhunter Henri Ducard he gained the secrets of tracking targets by the clues they left behind. Bruce absorbed every ounce of instruction, but remained troubled by the amoral stance of his tutors. Most of them cared only for the technique itself, and didn't concern themselves with how their students might apply it. After years of globe trekking, Bruce had honed his body and mind to near-perfection. It was time to return home.

Though he had become an expert martial artist and criminologist, Bruce dressed in simple street clothes on his first patrol. Unimpressed, the thugs fought back. Bruce knew he could tame the city only when his mere reputation was enough to demoralize his foes. He must be a frightening figure, someone who struck from the shadows and saw every secret. Inspired by a bat crashing through a window in Wayne Manor, Bruce seized on the notion of creating a mysterious "Batman" to strike fear in the hearts of the cowardly and the superstitious. Tales of the Batman spread. Soon, the swirling cape and pointed cowl were enough to frighten the guilty into confessing their darkest crimes.

"I must be a creature of the night. Black, terrible——a bat!"

AN INDOMITABLE WILL

Batman does not possess superhuman powers, but his absolute determination and strength of will make him nearly unstoppable.

GENIUS INTELLECT

All of Batman's most amazing feats, from his combat mastery to his detective prowess, are the products of a brilliant mind. His unique mental gift is the ability to learn and retain the secrets of many disciplines simultaneously, from which he is able to understand the bigger picture.

• TECHNICAL QUALIFICATIONS: Batman's nearly photographic memory allows him to recall instantly any technical manual he has read. He has expertise in fields as diverse as computer programming, electrical repair, and bomb disposal.

• LANGUAGES: Batman can understand dozens of world languages, including Russian, French, German, Japanese, Cantonese, Turkish, Arabic, and Swahili. He also knows phrases in extraterrestrial tongues, such as Kryptonian.

• MASTER TACTICIAN: Batman's most powerful weapon is his ability to read his enemies and anticipate their next moves. This gives him an edge in anything from personal combat to planning long-term strategic campaigns.

• ESCAPOLOGY: From the writings of Houdini and hands-on instruction from escape artist Mister Miracle, Batman has learned to free himself from straightjackets, handcuffs, locked trunks, and other traps within seconds.

• PILOTING/DRIVING: Batman is an expert in offensive driving, performing quick-reverse J-turns and nudging other vehicles into fishtailing spins. He is also a skilled motorcycle rider and hydrofoil driver. In the air, Batman can pilot military-grade jet fighters, attack helicopters, and even low-orbit space shuttles.

• TRACKING/DETECTING: Under the tutelage of French investigator Henri Ducard, Batman learned how to shadow suspects from a distance, how to scrutinize environments and objects for clues, and how to find fugitives who have gone off the grid and vanished from public records.

• DISGUISE: Batman knows that a successful disguise is more than just a change in appearance. He can alter his voice, stance, and mannerisms, and mimic dozens of regional accents. Alfred Pennyworth, formerly a British stage actor, has been known to give him pointers.

PSYCHOLOGY

Fear is what separates Batman from other super heroes. Fear is why he adopted the identity of a bat, and why criminals often surrender at the mere sight of his swirling cape. Batman exploits his reputation to squeeze information out of underworld contacts, but he isn't above using force when necessary. Roughing up a suspect gets quick results, and suspending them from the top of a skyscraper with nothing more than a batrope around their feet is even better. Scare tactics like these have spread Batman's terrifying reputation far and wide.

MATCHES MALONE

This mid-level crook maintains a low profile in Gotham's underworld. However, the real Matches Malone died years ago — and the current holder of that name is actually Batman in disguise! By assuming the identity of a preexisting villain whose backstory stands up to scrutiny, Batman has gained inside information on Black Mask, Two-Face, and other crime kingpins. "Matches" has a nondescript and easily forgettable appearance, with his only quirk being the matchstick that he constantly keeps between his teeth.

THE WORLD'S GREATEST DETECTIVE

Batman's shift isn't over when he returns to his home base. Deep within the Batcave is a forensics laboratory that would be the envy of any police force. The Batcomputer can perform heavy data crunching or hack into protected public records, and Batman stays connected to its systems while he is out in the field so he can make on-the-spot analyses of his surroundings. For more thorough results, however, Batman insists on bringing samples back to the Batcave and running tests there.

Batman is trained to look for the unexpected, and often discovers clues that previous investigators have missed.

CRIME-FIGHTING TECH

The Batcave is stocked with the most advanced investigative equipment in the world. The tools at Batman's disposal include:

- Fume/particulate analyzer
- Gunpowder and explosive residue analyzer
- Forensic microscope
- Chemical spectrometer
- Multiband light-source projector
- Latent print development chamber
- Tire track and footprint impression kits
- Indented writing restoration tools
- Serial number restoration gel
- Global G.P.S. tracking system
- Facial composite software
- Autopsy investigation tools
- Electronic surveillance and line tap detectors
- Narcotic reagents and chromatography test kits
- Florescent invisible detection powder

ALWAYS WATCHING...

The Batcomputer is connected to the internal networks of the C.I.A., Interpol, the covert operations agency Checkmate, and most of the world's governments. To gain a better perspective on global trouble spots, Batman designed and launched the Brother Eye surveillance satellite, but he destroyed it when it grew dangerously self-aware.

STAYING ON TOP

Batman's skills are legendary, but if he doesn't keep himself in top condition he'll quickly lose them. Gotham's guardian maintains an exhausting daily regimen that keeps him ahead of the pack.

FIGHTING STYLE

Although Batman has endeavored to become an expert in every continent's top martial arts disciplines, he has chosen to combine his talents to create a highly personal combat style that comprises several core arts. The distance separating Batman from his opponent is what usually dictates which combination of abilities he will use first.

"THE MOST DANGEROUS MAN ALIVE."

LONG/MEDIUM RANGE
Shotokan Karate
Capoeira (Brazilian martial arts)
Savate (French kickboxing)

CLOSE RANGE
Western Boxing
Muay Thai (Thai boxing)
Wing Chun Kung Fu
Okinawan Goju-Ryu Karate
Panantukan (Filipino martial arts)

GRAPPLING
Judo
Brazilian Jiu-Jitsu
Sambo Wrestling (Russia)

WEAPONS
Fencing
Kobudo (Japanese weaponry including the Katana longsword, bo staff, nunchaku, sai and tonfa)
Escrima (Filipino stick fighting)
Kali (Filipino knife fighting)

MARKSMANSHIP
Batman is a skilled shot with all categories of firearms, though he has sworn never to carry one or to use one against another living being. He is also an expert with projectile weapons such as bows, crossbows, and blow guns.

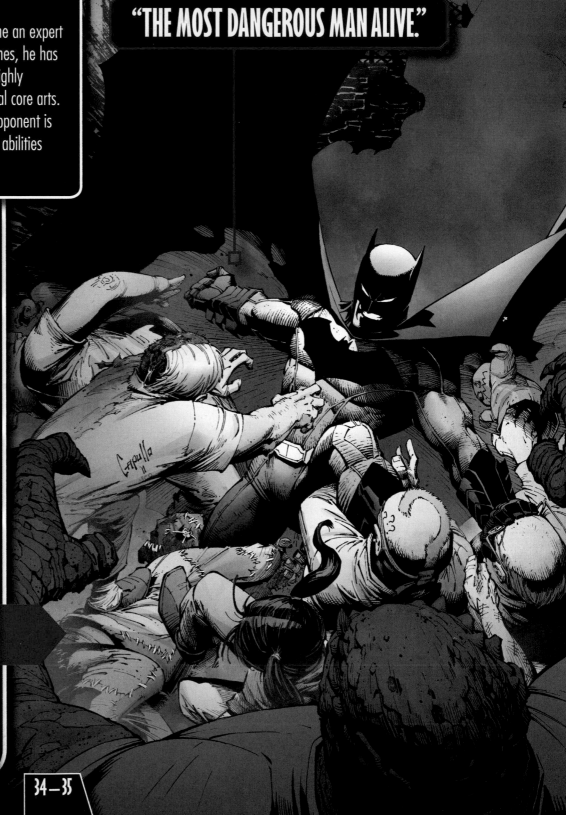

TRAINING*

Batman patrols Gotham every night—at a minimum this provides an intense cardio and upper-body workout with rope swinging and parkour-style acrobatics. But patrolling doesn't provide the full workout he requires. Back at the Batcave, the Dark Knight engages in short but intense sessions that focus on building endurance, maintaining muscle, or practicing combat routines. Batman varies his schedule daily to give his body enough time to recover from the previous workout. These sessions are interspersed with restorative SWS (slow-wave sleep) naps throughout the day.

SPARRING

Former professional boxer Ted Grant, better known as Wildcat, taught Batman the sweet science of bare-knuckled pugilism. Batman toughens his fists by working a punching bag, and he also practices his footwork against Robin. Sparring, however, is the one area that does not require much gym practice. Batman gets to put his skills to practice throwing punches at Gotham's many crooks each night.

MONDAY

MORNING: Five-mile run, one-hour upper body strength conditioning.
MIDDAY: One-hour circuit training session, 20 minutes punching bag.
EVENING: Weapon training, 30 minutes swimming, power yoga, or tai chi.

TUESDAY

MORNING: One hour climbing wall, 30 minutes lower body strength conditioning.
MIDDAY: One hour circuit training, 30 minutes punching bag.
EVENING: Martial arts technical practice.

WEDNESDAY

MORNING: Five-mile run, 30 minutes punching bag session.
MIDDAY: 30 minutes circuit training, one hour overall strength conditioning.
EVENING: A light sparring session (if a partner is available).

THURSDAY

MORNING: 30 minutes jumping rope, one hour circuit training.
MIDDAY: One hour power lifting, 30 minutes kettlebell training.
EVENING: One hour punching bag, 30 minutes yoga session.

FRIDAY

MORNING: Five-mile run, one hour upper body strength conditioning.
MIDDAY: 30 minutes circuit training, one hour heavy sparring session (if a partner is available).
EVENING: One-hour swimming, yoga, or tai chi.

SATURDAY

MORNING: One-hour swim, 30 minutes upper body strength conditioning.
MIDDAY: One-hour parkour training, 30 minutes sparring session (if a partner is available).
EVENING: One hour circuit training.

SUNDAY

MORNING: 10 mile run followed by stretching.
EVENING: Technical training e.g. target practice.

DIET

Batman eats a variety of high-protein, high-calorie foods for immediate energy and as fuel for his hard-working body. He spreads his calorie intake throughout his waking hours so he's always ready to go. Batman isn't obsessive about his diet and often goes off-menu to enjoy Alfred's special meals or to take part in a business luncheon as Bruce Wayne. He never drinks alcohol, and secretly substitutes ginger ale for champagne at social functions.

BREAKFAST: Oatmeal, a banana, two boiled eggs, orange juice or green tea.

MID MORNING: Tuna, four rice cakes with peanut butter.

LUNCH: Grilled chicken, jacket potato, steamed vegetables, vitamin and essential oil supplements.

AFTERNOON SNACK: Cottage cheese, oatmeal crackers, fruit.

DINNER: Grilled chicken, fish or steak, steamed vegetables, rice or pasta.

BEFORE BED: Protein shake.

HYDRATES CONSTANTLY BY DRINKING PLENTY OF WATER

* Only to be undertaken by genuine Batmen.

PHYSICAL ATTRIBUTES

STRENGTH

Batman's body might be 210 lbs of toned muscle, but he doesn't prioritize weight training above an all-over approach to fitness. Matched with honed combat techniques, he is able to put maximum power behind each blow and knock out opponents twice his size. Because Batman often needs to carry others—be they rescued hostages or handcuffed crooks—his lifting strength is considerable.

ENDURANCE

Stamina is arguably Batman's secret weapon. Others may match him in strength or speed, but they often grow tired and drop their defenses. Batman's training includes runs and swims of up to an hour at a time. When he's on a mission, short meditative breaks allow him to rejuvenate his body and mind.

REFLEXES

Batman's incredible reflexes are the result of the mental training he received in the monastery of Nanda Parbat and the ninjutsu skills taught by Master Kirigi. He's so fast he can snatch an arrow mid-flight.

AGILITY

Gotham's rooftops provide practical instruction in urban agility, with nightly patrols requiring a mix of leaping, tumbling, balancing, and rope swinging. Dick Grayson, who was a circus acrobat before he became Robin, has taught his mentor a thing or two about the high-wire arts. When Batman pairs agility with strength, he can take down targets with devastating force.

DURABILITY

The Batcave has some of the most advanced medical equipment in the world courtesy of Wayne Biotech, and Alfred has been trained as a battlefield medic. In his career, Batman has been shot, stabbed, burned, and frostbitten. Killer Croc has snapped his ribs and Bane has broken his back. Despite Alfred's protests, Batman always returns to duty before he has fully healed.

He is a man of few words, but when Batman speaks, villains listen. The Dark Knight knows that criminals are a cowardly and superstitious lot, and he has honed a psychological approach to intimidation that is just as effective as a punch or a kick.

"I made a promise on the grave of my parents that I would rid this city of the evil that took their lives. I believe someday I will make good on that promise."

"I don't enjoy fear. But I've learned to respect it."

"I believe in Jim Gordon. I believe in Harvey Dent. I believe in Gotham City."

"They say that when you kill a man you not only take away what he was, but all he will ever be."

"I hardly even knew my parents as people. But suddenly I knew the world. It was hard and cold and dark and lawless. Its face was fierce and bestial. The only face I had with which to glare back at it… was utterly inadequate."

"I've escaped from every conceivable deathtrap. Ten times. A dozen times."

"Criminals, by nature, are a cowardly and superstitious lot. To instill fear into their hearts, I became a bat."

"Deep down, Clark's essentially a good person… and deep down, I'm not."

"One day, there will be no pain, no loss, no crime. Because of me, because I fight. For you. One day, I will win."

"If detective work were easy, everyone would be doing it."

"Days. Months. Years, spent memorizing the finite ways there are to hurt and break a man."

"I chose this life. I know what I'm doing. And on any given day, I could stop doing it. Today, however, isn't that day."

"The first person I ever revealed my identity to was Dick Grayson. I wanted to make a difference in his life, the way, if my parents had lived, they would have made a difference in mine."

"He tried to use Gotham's legends against me. But I'm the only legend this city needs."

"Dick saw being Robin as a thrill. It's probably why he outgrew it. Jason saw Robin as a game. It's probably what got him killed."

"Think clean thoughts, chum."

"Sometimes it's only madness that makes us what we are."

GREAT ESCAPES!

"I've escaped from every conceivable deathtrap. Ten times. A dozen times."
– Batman

Batman's mind and body are both honed to perfection. With the physical and mental working in synchronization, the Dark Knight can pick any lock and fight his way free from the strongest of snares.

When gangsters heard Batman describe an "inescapable" death trap he'd dreamed about, they built it for real—then took bets on whether he would survive! Batman jammed the machine gun as the chamber filled with water, and escaped through a hole in the wall.

BATMAN VS. BODY TRAP

The Joker's goons fired strange webbing at Batman and Robin, which wrapped around their torsos and grew tighter as they struggled. Robin couldn't breathe and was fading fast. Batman entered a state of meditative calm to relax his muscles, sloughing off the constricting material and cutting Robin loose with a Batarang.

BATMAN VS. WOLVES

While working on the Mad Monk case, Batman found himself cornered by a pack of wolves. He hit them with a cloud of knockout gas and entangled one with a Batarang line, but another sank its fangs into his leg. Batman tried blasting the wolf with pepper spray and blinding it with his cape before he finally gained the upper hand.

BATMAN VS. BURIAL

Doctor Hurt and the agents of the Black Glove had beaten Batman, and as their final act of triumph they buried him alive. Batman slowed his breathing and focused his muscle movements, which allowed him to break the coffin's lid and methodically make his way up through the loose layer of dirt that marked his shallow grave.

BATMAN VS. DROWNING

The Scarecrow flooded a Gotham sewer tunnel, and Batman remained behind to save the mayor from the rising waters. In search of an exit Batman swam through the passageways using his rebreather, and when it expired he pressed on with only the air in his lungs. Close to death, Batman at last found a hatch and escaped with the mayor to higher ground.

BATMAN VS. SCORPION VENOM

In a swordfighters' duel with Rā's al Ghūl, Batman stepped too close to a desert scorpion and it stung his heel. Left to die on the burning sands, Batman kept his strength up until Talia al Ghūl could deliver an anti-venom antidote in the form of a kiss. Batman, exhausted but defiant, challenged Rā's al Ghūl to a rematch.

BATMAN VS. ROLLER COASTER

Inside a Guatemalan cavern, the Joker tied Batman's arms and placed him on top of an amusement-park train — with an innocent victim lying directly in its path! Batman snatched a stalactite to cut his bonds, then hurled a Batarang at the engine's front wheels. The train jumped the track, sparing the Joker's hostage at the very last instant.

BATMAN VS. THE G.C.P.D.

Trapped in the cellar of a condemned building and surrounded by a squad of hostile police officers, Batman used a blowgun to render several of them unconscious. To cover his escape Batman summoned thousands of bats using an ultrasonic transmitter hidden in his boot.

BATMAN VS. SUPERMAN

Even though Poison Ivy had brainwashed Superman and turned him against the Dark Knight, Batman never lost his head. Reasoning that even a mind-controlled Superman wouldn't use deadly force against a friend, Batman subdued him with hypersonics, electrocution, and low-dosage Kryptonite until Catwoman could distract him and break the spell by putting Lois Lane in danger.

WEARING A MASK

Those who know Batman well agree that his true personality is that of the grim, unsmiling Dark Knight, while the Bruce Wayne in the newspaper headlines is merely a role. Bruce is a skilled actor, assuming other identities (such as the crook Matches Malone) when the need arises.

KEEPING SECRETS

His parents' murders are a matter of public record, so to preserve his anonymity, Batman crafted Bruce Wayne's personality to be the complete opposite of the terrifying Dark Knight. Bruce makes occasional appearances at Wayne Enterprises for interviews or to attract new investors, but leaves the daily running of the company to his employees so he can pursue his "playboy" lifestyle.

KEY DATA

FULL NAME Bruce Wayne

OCCUPATION Businessman, philanthropist

WEAPONS/ POWERS/ ABILITIES Genius intellect, vast wealth and technological resources, powerful political connections

AFFILIATIONS Wayne Enterprises, Batman, Inc.

RELATIVES Thomas and Martha Wayne (parents, deceased); Dick Grayson (adopted son); Jason Todd (adopted son); Tim Drake (adopted son); Damian Wayne (biological son)

FIRST APPEARANCE DETECTIVE COMICS #27 (May 1939)

> "A brighter, better Gotham is just one dream away!"
>
> BRUCE WAYNE

BRUCE WAYNE

Bruce is well-liked and knows when to turn on the charm. With a single speech he can win over a roomful of hostile investors.

Who is Bruce Wayne? Many would describe him as a bored playboy, heir to a rich fortune. None realize it is all an act. The deaths of his parents changed Bruce, and his true personality is indistinguishable from the deadly serious demeanor of the Batman.

Dick Grayson, Tim Drake, and Damian Wayne are seldom asked to appear in the intense public spotlight.

Bruce maintains his after-hours image as a nightclub-hopper by recklessly flashing his money—while carefully sipping non-alcoholic champagne.

Nobody would suspect the hands-on role Bruce has assumed to ensure that the loss he suffered is never experienced by others.

IN THE PUBLIC EYE

The fun-loving side of Bruce Wayne died years ago, after a mugger's bullets ended the lives of his parents. However, Batman requires the Wayne family's wealth to continue his crime-fighting crusade, and he therefore maintains the Bruce Wayne playboy façade at nightclubs, yacht races, and gallery openings where the exploits of a handsome billionaire bachelor always get covered in the *Gotham Gazette*.

The Wayne family's real estate and R&D firm is one of Gotham's largest employers, and the Batcave and other technological wonders are possible only through below-the-line withdrawals from Wayne Enterprises' operating budget. In his role as company head, Bruce Wayne meets with investors and directs projects where he believes they will do the most good for the city. His associated charity, the Wayne Foundation, is dedicated to the memory of his parents and pledged toward the reduction of violent crime in Gotham.

Bruce has been romantically linked to a string of beautiful women, including Vicki Vale, Silver St. Cloud, and Jezebel Jet, with all of his dalliances providing gossip fuel and free publicity for Wayne Enterprises. Bruce has never married, but he has four sons, all of whom have filled the role of Robin. He legally adopted Dick Grayson, Tim Drake and Jason Todd, while Damian Wayne is his biological son with his lover Talia al Ghūl.

The Waynes have a long history in Gotham City, with Wayne Manor's ownership going back generations. His family's elite social standing is one reason why Bruce felt comfortable revealing to the public his private funding of Batman's activities and his formation of the international superteam Batman, Inc. This partial confession has diverted suspicion of his double identity and allowed Batman to hide in plain sight.

Alfred Pennyworth is Bruce Wayne's right-hand man. He ensures that Bruce never blows his cover.

WAYNE MANOR

A STATELY HOME

The ancestral home of the Wayne family has stood on Gotham's northern slope for generations, at the center of what is now the wealthy Crest Hill area of Bristol Township. The mansion is far too large for the few people who currently live there, but Bruce Wayne sometimes opens the gates to welcome hundreds of partygoers to charity auctions and masquerade balls. Within Wayne Manor are treasures acquired through generations of wealth, including rare paintings, antique weapons and suits of armor, and historic documents dating back to Gotham's founding. Beneath the manor lies the Batcave, which is accessed through a secret passage hidden behind a grandfather clock. The grounds of Wayne Manor also house garages, gardens, and horse stables.

HISTORY

Originally built for Bruce Wayne's ancestor Darius Wayne during the 1800s, the manor forms a distinctive "W" shape when viewed from above. The cave beneath the manor grounds has existed since prehistoric times, and was formerly sacred ground for the Miagani tribe and the location of a pirate's treasure stash. After Darius Wayne, the ownership of the manor remained in family hands. It passed to Alan Wayne in the early twentieth century, and eventually to Thomas and Martha Wayne, then their son Bruce. After Bruce Wayne launched his career as Batman, he gave Wayne Manor a radical but largely invisible upgrade. The subterranean cavern became the high-tech Batcave, while the mansion received a state-of-the-art sensor web to keep Bruce Wayne and family butler Alfred Pennyworth alerted to unwelcome visitors. Wayne Manor went unoccupied for a brief time when Dick Grayson left for college, with Bruce and Alfred temporarily relocating to a penthouse apartment in the city. After an earthquake rocked Wayne Manor and caused extensive damage to its foundations, Bruce rebuilt his home adding new features to make it even more secure.

Bruce Wayne's childhood memories of Wayne Manor were mostly happy, but in one incident he fell into a pit connected to the vast subterranean network under the manor. The screeching bats he encountered left him shaken.

The forefathers of the Wayne family are placed in chronological order in the portrait hall. They include witch hunter Nathaniel Wayne, Revolutionary War hero "Mad" Anthony Wayne, and Bruce's great-great-grandfather Judge Solomon Wayne.

Though it has been rebuilt and improved, Wayne Manor still bears Gothic elements from its original designs and nods to the Scottish and Norman roots of the Wayne family.

Windows are bulletproof and wired with motion sensors.

SECURITY

Wayne Manor is the first line of defense for the Batcave. Its surveillance and security systems are among the best in the world, and even a ninja death squad has little hope of breaching the manor if the security grid is active. Gargoyles and other pieces of ornamental statuary conceal radar sensors and heat-imaging scopes, and every inch of the grounds is bathed by motion sensors and biometric detectors that set off silent alarms when triggered. Non-aggressive deterrents include nausea-inducing sonic projectors, while more extreme measures include net traps and a taser charge that electrifies the entire lawn. Wayne Manor is shielded from electronic surveillance by an electromagnetic bubble.

- **Proximity motion detectors**
- **Interior silent alarms**
- **HIAD (Human Identification At a Distance) sensors**
- **Voice-activated taser lawn**

CATACLYSM

When a magnitude 7.6 earthquake shook Gotham, it left Wayne Manor in ruins. Within the city limits, criminals ran wild as the government implemented a civilian evacuation and, subsequently, an armed blockade. Bruce Wayne was preoccupied with keeping the peace as Batman, but he invested in the swift reconstruction of the manor as a symbol of Gotham's inevitable return.

THE BATCAVE

A grandfather clock conceals the entrance to the Batcave. When its hands are turned to 10:47, the time of Thomas and Martha Wayne's deaths, a door behind it unlocks. The Batcave can also be reached via access vents or secret hatches in the sewer tunnels.

Retractable floodlights can turn night into day.

Radar and biometric sensors are concealed from view.

The mansion's foundations are reinforced against tectonic shocks.

Wayne Manor

Main level

Sub-levels 1–7

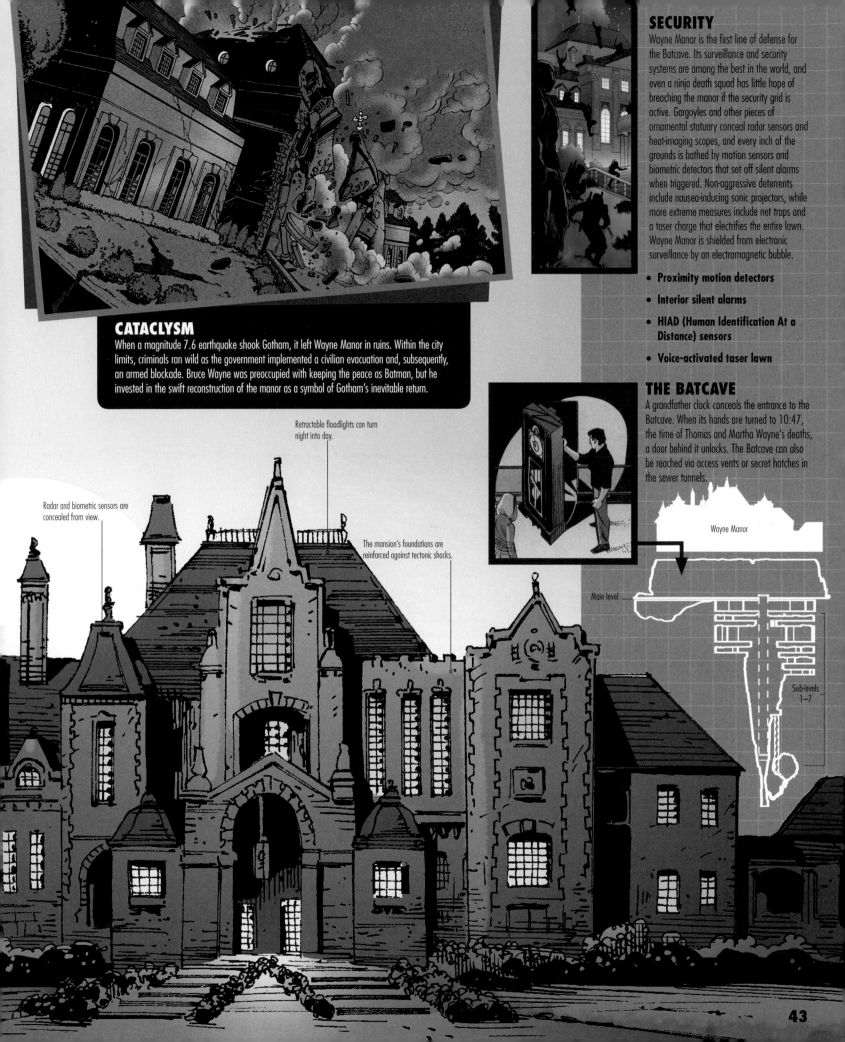

WAYNE ENTERPRISES

Gotham's most famous corporation not only bears the Wayne family name, it also supplies Bruce Wayne with the money and technology he requires to carry out his crime-fighting crusade. Wayne Enterprises is a diverse and profitable company, active in dozens of countries and involved in everything from real estate to biotechnology. Bruce is both CEO and chairman but he has little impact on day-to-day operations beyond starring in interviews. As Batman, he makes use of advanced Wayne Enterprises prototypes to keep the Batcave fully stocked.

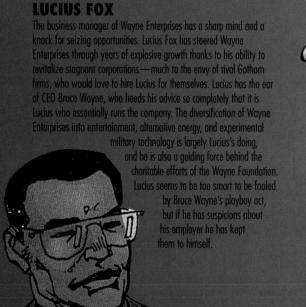

AS OLD AS GOTHAM

Traditions run deep in Gotham City. Waynes have made their homes on this site since the 1600s, with the first Wayne merchant house arising soon after. The 1800s saw the incorporation of Wayne Shipping, and transatlantic commerce soon made the family fantastically wealthy. Bruce Wayne is the latest Wayne to serve as the head of the family company. Unlike his father, Thomas—who worked mainly as a physician—Bruce seems to have made Wayne Enterprises his only responsibility.

LUCIUS FOX

The business manager of Wayne Enterprises has a sharp mind and a knack for seizing opportunities. Lucius Fox has steered Wayne Enterprises through years of explosive growth thanks to his ability to revitalize stagnant corporations—much to the envy of rival Gotham firms, who would love to hire Lucius for themselves. Lucius has the ear of CEO Bruce Wayne, who heeds his advice so completely that it is Lucius who essentially runs the company. The diversification of Wayne Enterprises into entertainment, alternative energy, and experimental military technology is largely Lucius's doing, and he is also a guiding force behind the charitable efforts of the Wayne Foundation. Lucius seems to be too smart to be fooled by Bruce Wayne's playboy act, but if he has suspicions about his employer he has kept them to himself.

A HANDS-OFF CEO

Bruce Wayne has a brilliant mind but lacks the necessary time to devote his efforts to the advancement of Wayne Enterprises. Instead he places his trust in Lucius Fox and makes brief appearances in the executive offices, where he reinforces his employees' suspicions that their boss would rather be golfing than working. Yet Bruce is disarmingly likeable, and his role as the head of the traditionally family-run company is reassuring to potential investors.

As a well-known public figure, Bruce Wayne attracts a lot of attention, which he then uses for his advantage. At a press conference at Wayne Manor, he announced an ambitious plan for Wayne Enterprises and its construction and real estate subsidiaries. A holographic projection displayed his vision for a revitalized downtown business district.

COMPANY DIVISIONS

WAYNE TECHNOLOGIES

More commonly called WayneTech, this division of Wayne Enterprises spearheads research into microcomputers, robotics, and holography, with many of its projects highly classified. It is rumored that WayneTech secures alien devices left behind by advanced cultures—such as Darkseid's Fourth World gods—and reverse-engineers them for commercial applications. WayneTech has many rivals in this field, including Lex Luthor's LexCorp.

WAYNE BIOTECH

A giant in Gotham City's healthcare industry, Wayne Biotech spends billions in research and development on cures for illnesses, and its success in sequencing the human genome was a breakthrough in understanding many types of hereditary disease. Together with its sister company Wayne Medical, the division leads efforts to train hospital personnel in specialized care. As Batman, Bruce Wayne relies on the Wayne Biotech databases to help him identify strange toxins, such as those cultivated by Poison Ivy.

WAYNE AEROSPACE

Wayne Aerospace is a leading manufacturer of private jets and commercial airliners, but is best known for its role as a supplier of experimental aircraft to the U.S. military and NASA. A top-secret "skunkworks" operation within Wayne Aerospace develops prototype aerial vehicles that are years ahead of the curve, with these breakthroughs often appropriated by Bruce Wayne in the design of new Batplanes. The division has a major West Coast rival in Ferris Air, the employer of Hal Jordan—otherwise known as Green Lantern.

WAYNE SHIPPING

One of the oldest subsidiaries of Wayne Enterprises, the shipping division operates a fleet of international cargo freighters that carry manufactured goods and mined metals. The credibility of Wayne Shipping gives Bruce Wayne virtually unlimited access to the warehouse docks of Gotham Harbor, where he can keep an eye on the city's smuggling and drug-running rings.

WAYNE CHEMICALS

The chemical division of Wayne Enterprises is responsible for manufacturing medicines and vaccines developed by Wayne Biotech. It also works closely with its sister divisions Wayne Pharmaceutical, Wayne Botanical, and Wayne Oil, and maintains a robust research and development department dedicated to finding new industrial uses for chemicals. The advanced spectrochemical analyzers invented by Wayne Chemicals have helped Batman identify the components of the Scarecrow's fear gas so that he can synthesize antidotes.

WAYNE FOUNDATION

The Wayne Foundation is the charitable arm of the Wayne family empire and provides food, shelter, and medical care for the least fortunate of Gotham's citizens. The Thomas Wayne Foundation helps operate free clinics throughout the city, while the Martha Wayne Foundation is active in the arts and culture scene and provides housing and educational assistance to the homeless. By lessening poverty and hopelessness, Bruce believes he can build a foundation for long-term success in a way that far exceeds the reach of Batman.

GOTHAM CITY

GOTHAMITE PRIDE

This great city has a rich but checkered history. Often overshadowed by nearby Metropolis, Gotham has suffered a series of bad breaks in recent years. Yet it remains a hub of industry and culture whose citizens are protected by Batman's constant vigilance.

GOTHAM'S HISTORY

Founded in the early 1600s, Gotham City started off as a Puritan community that quickly became the target of many accusations of ritual witchcraft. Rumors of the occult never strayed far from Gotham, and as the city grew so did the stories of evil and madness that dwelt there. Soon Gotham City had acquired a frightening reputation that wasn't helped by its proximity to dens of murder like Slaughter Swamp.

Gotham's distinctive skyline began to take shape in the 1800s, when Judge Solomon Wayne led a Gothic Revival movement that gave the city a wealth of flying buttresses and leering gargoyles. Solomon's son Alan Wayne, a rumored associate of the secret society called the Court of Owls, also headed many architectural projects up to the 1920s Art Deco era. Gotham's most distinctive landmarks from both these periods survived the recent earthquake and the No Man's Land quarantine that followed, and now share space with the shining edifices of glass and steel erected by Wayne Enterprises.

The city houses both the fantastically wealthy and the desperately poor. Tension between the two classes has led to incidents like the fatal mugging that orphaned young Bruce Wayne. In recent years, crime and corruption have sent Gotham into decline. For a symbol of this decline look no further than Amusement Mile, where decaying roller coasters and abandoned carnival games provide an eerie backdrop for criminal scheming. Yet Gotham's business district is a haven for high-end boutiques and art galleries, and the Gotham Knights baseball team pack season ticket holders into a multimillion dollar sporting complex. Robinson Park is famous for its world-class botanical gardens.

So much money concentrated in such a small area has lured common crooks and costumed villains alike, and a prison industry arose out of necessity. The notorious Arkham Asylum houses those judged to be criminally insane, while Blackgate Penitentiary is a maximum-security facility on a tiny island.

1 Crime Alley
2 Arkham Asylum
3 Wayne Manor
4 The Drake Household
5 Brentwood Academy
6 Gotham County Underwater R.R. Tubes
7 Old Gotham
8 Robert Kane Memorial Bridge
9 Amusement Mile
10 Rogers Yacht Basin
11 Robinsville

12 Cape Carmine
13 Sprang Bridge
14 Sprang River
15 New Trigate Bridge
16 Aparo Park
17 Old Steam Tunnel
18 Brown R.R. Tubes
19 Gotham Water District Tunnel
20 Novick Tunnel
21 Peterson R.R. Tubes
22 Vincefinkel Bridge
23 Gotham River

24 Gotham Light & Power
25 Archie Goodwin International Airport
26 Mooney Bridge
27 Dixon Dock
28 James Gordon's House
29 Tricorner Yards
30 Robinson Park
31 The Reservoir
32 Wayne Botanical garden
33 Finger River
34 City Hall District

35 City Hall
36 Gotham Superior Courthouse
37 G.C.P.D. Headquarters
38 The Clock Tower
39 Wayne Tower
40 One Gotham Center
41 Blackgate Isle
42 Cathedral Square
43 Grant Park
44 Miller Harbor
45 Monolith Square
46 The "C" Building

47 Aparo Expressway
48 Port Adams
49 Knights Dome Sporting Complex
50 Ranelagh Ferry
51 One Port Trinity Place
52 Von Gruenwald Tower
53 R.H. Kane Building
54 Surh Complex
55 Kubrick District
56 Vauxhall Opera Shell & Indoor Concert Center

G.C.P.D. HEADQUARTERS

The downtown HQ of the Gotham City Police Department is called "Gotham Central" by the officers who work there. Atop the G.C.P.D building sits the Bat-Signal, which alerts Batman to emergencies that require his intervention. Under the leadership of Commissioner James Gordon, the G.C.P.D. has established close ties with Batman—something that is not always popular among the detectives of the Major Crimes Unit.

ARKHAM ASYLUM

This terrifying madhouse has become a second home for the Joker, Two-Face, and many other mass murderers. Arkham's security is a critical public concern, yet appears to be sadly lacking. Escapes by inmates are common. The entire facility has been destroyed and rebuilt more than once, each time quickly falling back into its old patterns.

CRIME ALLEY

This street once carried the name as Park Row, until the random murders of Thomas and Martha Wayne, two of Gotham's leading citizens. The G.C.P.D.'s failure to solve the case led to the street being nicknamed "Crime Alley," and contributed to the erosion of the public's confidence in the powers-that-be. Every year on the anniversary of his parents' deaths, Batman visits Crime Alley to honor their memories and renew his vow to help the unfortunate.

GOTHAM HARBOR

The murky waters of Gotham Harbor are a scene of constant activity, with freighters arriving at its docks at all hours of the day and night. The international import and export business is a huge part of the city's economy, but it also provides cover for the extensive weapons smuggling and drug trafficking that enriches the city's costumed villains, criminal gangs, and organized crime families.

ROBIN

> "If there's one thing I've always been sure of, it's that Batman will need a Robin, and Robin will need a Batman."
>
> ALFRED PENNYWORTH

As the Dark Knight's squire, Robin fills a vital role in Batman's life. Many have worn the Robin costume in the years since Dick Grayson first coined the name, and Batman and Robin continue to live up to their public nickname: the Dynamic Duo.

JASON TODD

Jason Todd first met Batman when he was caught trying to steal the Batmobile's tires—and their relationship has been a tempestuous one ever since. For a time, Jason adventured as the second Robin, but his rebellious nature made him a problematic partner for Batman. He met a brutal end when the Joker took his life in a time-bomb blast after a vicious beatdown. Jason later returned due to the reality-warping effects of the Infinite Crisis, now possessing the cruel edge of a killer and still carrying a grudge against Batman for failing to prevent the Joker's act.

DICK GRAYSON

Dick Grayson proved that Batman's fight against crime didn't need to be a lonely one. Already a star acrobat as a child, Dick became an orphan the day a gangster sabotaged his parents' high-wire act—all because their employer, Haly's Circus, refused to pay protection money. Bruce Wayne took the boy into his home, and soon the two were a crime-fighting double act, with Gotham headlines heralding the sensational exploits of the Caped Crusaders. When he grew from a boy to a man, Dick found a new identity as Nightwing, but he left Batman with a firm belief in the power of a partner.

STEPHANIE BROWN

Raised by second-rate crook the Cluemaster, Stephanie Brown first became a costumed super hero in order to foil her father's criminal schemes. As the Spoiler, Stephanie formed a close relationship with Tim Drake that put her into the Batman family's orbit. She became the fourth Robin during a drawn-out gang war in Gotham, which culminated in her apparent death at the hands of Black Mask. However, Stephanie survived the attack and she recuperated from her injuries in Africa before returning to Gotham for a brief stint as Batgirl. Stephanie has since become the Spoiler once again.

DAMIAN WAYNE

Bruce Wayne didn't even know he had a son until he met tcn-ycar-old Damian Wayne face-to-face. The child of Bruce and Talia al Ghūl, Damian grew up in the care of the League of Assassins and received genetic augmentation to make him the perfect fighting machine. Batman took Damian under his wing to curb his violent impulses. During a period when Bruce was believed to be dead, Dick Grayson took over as Batman and made Damian the new Robin. Now that Bruce has returned, the pairing of Batman and Robin is truly a family act.

TIM DRAKE

Tim Drake figured out the secret: Batman and Robin's real identities! Following the death of Jason Todd, Tim grew so concerned that the increasingly unhinged and withdrawn Dark Knight needed a new squire that he volunteered himself to become the third Robin. Later, when Captain Boomerang murdered Tim's father and made him an orphan, Tim found a new home in Wayne Manor as Bruce Wayne's adopted son. As Robin, Tim led the Teen Titans and proved himself in combat and as a detective. He has since gone solo as Red Robin now that Damian Wayne has assumed his former role.

ALFRED PENNYWORTH

"Perhaps taking the night off might be in order, Master Bruce?"

ALFRED PENNYWORTH

Visitors to Wayne Manor are more likely to meet Alfred Pennyworth than the actual man of the house, Bruce Wayne. The Wayne family's butler secretly provides support for Batman's crime-fighting operation and keeps the Dark Knight in business.

DECADES OF SERVICE

Alfred cleans Batman's costume after a night of crime fighting in preparation for his next patrol.

Alfred has been there since the beginning. After Bruce lost his mother and father in a tragic mugging, the loyal butler became his surrogate father. He abetted in the legal wrangling that prevented Bruce from being placed with other relatives or in foster care. As a young boy and now as Batman, the Dark Knight has always regarded Alfred as the only person other than Commissioner Gordon whose opinion he trusts without reservation.

Alfred worries for Bruce's safety, but he has accepted the importance of Batman's mission and does everything in his power to secure Bruce's well-being. Alfred stitches his wounds, repairs his uniform, and brings plates of sandwiches down to the Batcave whenever Bruce is working late. Alfred's dry wit often softens his disapproval of the Dark Knight's more extreme impulses, and he keeps Batman grounded by reminding him of the bonds that truly matter.

As Batman opened his lair to others, Alfred became their mentor, too. Dick Grayson, Jason Todd, and Tim Drake all grew up under Alfred's watchful eye, and even Damian Wayne has set aside his arrogance and warmed to the man he calls "Pennyworth." Other super heroes who know Batman's secret identity, including Superman, have the utmost respect for Alfred.

In his public role, Alfred runs the Wayne household, keeps Bruce's schedule, and arranges for public benefits to be held at the manor. His knowledge of the home and its grounds is second to none. Alfred has the highest security clearance within Batman's hierarchy—higher even than any of the Robins—and with the touch of a button he can activate defenses that turn Wayne Manor into a fortress.

For Bruce Wayne's public duties, Alfred ensures Bruce always makes a good impression.

Food, drink, and medicine are among the necessities that Batman would be likely to neglect if Alfred didn't deliver them to the Batcave.

Of all the Robins Alfred has mentored, the latest—Batman's son Damian Wayne—has tested Alfred's patience the most.

One of Alfred's primary duties at Wayne Manor is to convince curious Gothamites that nothing is amiss, despite Bruce Wayne's frequent absences.

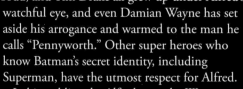

Other than Batman, no one knows more about the Batcave's complex computer systems and vehicle pool than Alfred.

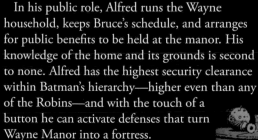

Restocking a Utility Belt with smoke grenades or stitching a torn glove are all in a day's work for Alfred. He is always on hand for repairs at the end of Batman's long evenings of crime fighting.

KEY DATA

FULL NAME Alfred Pennyworth

OCCUPATION Butler, mechanic, surgeon, repairman

WEAPONS/ POWERS/ ABILITIES Armed and unarmed combat training, skilled actor

AFFILIATIONS Outsiders, Batman Inc.

RELATIVES Jarvis Pennyworth (father, deceased), Wilfred Pennyworth (brother), Daphne Pennyworth (niece)

FIRST APPEARANCE BATMAN #16 (April–May 1943)

Alfred is at all times impeccably dressed, honoring the butler tradition begun by his father in his home country of England.

Batman's gear is what keeps him alive and his identity secret, so he trusts no one with its care other than Alfred.

Alfred's fingerprints, voice pattern, and retinal scans grant him secure access to Batman's equipment in Wayne Manor and the Batcave.

CLEAR-HEADED CALM

Nothing rattles Alfred. The multitalented butler can repair Batman's vehicles, deal with armed intruders inside the Batcave, or treat multiple rib fractures sustained by Master Bruce during a night on patrol.

RAISING A SON

Bruce became an orphan while still a boy, and Alfred stepped in to become his father figure. When Batman was believed killed during the events of the Final Crisis, Alfred faced the terrible task of burying Bruce's body and saying goodbye to the man he had loved as a son.

COMMISSIONER GORDON

"I've got a friend coming who might be able to help. Should be here any minute."

COMMISSIONER GORDON

If Batman is Gotham's strength, Jim Gordon is the city's soul. The resolute commissioner of the Gotham City Police Department is Batman's ally in the war against crime, and a rare person of integrity within a justice system notorious for its corruption.

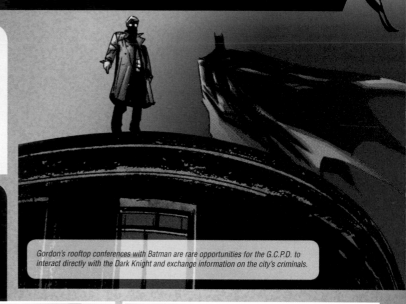

Gordon's rooftop conferences with Batman are rare opportunities for the G.C.P.D. to interact directly with the Dark Knight and exchange information on the city's criminals.

James Gordon is an ordinary man in a city of many maniacs, and the public face of the G.C.P.D.

MAKING A DIFFERENCE

James Gordon thought he had seen everything during his time on the Chicago police force until his transfer to Gotham City. Afflicted with the triple curse of street crime, institutional rot, and a class of costumed super-villains, Gotham needed a champion. Quite unexpectedly, it got two.

As Lieutenant Gordon fought for reform within a crooked police department, a vigilante dressed as a bat emerged to battle the villains the police wouldn't touch. But the people in power didn't like it one bit. The G.C.P.D. received orders to arrest the Batman. Gordon stood alone in his defense of the hero, but soon even Batman's worst detractors had to admit he got things done. In time, the G.C.P.D. installed the Bat-Signal on the roof of its headquarters and Gordon became the commissioner of police. When summoned by the Bat-Signal's spotlight, Batman refused to speak to anyone but Gordon.

Commissioner Gordon's partnership with Batman left little time for a homelife, which took its toll on his loved ones. After divorcing his first wife Barbara, he married G.C.P.D. detective Sarah Essen. But Gordon

Gordon's worklife ended his marriage to Barbara Gordon, but G.C.P.D. detective Sarah Essen understood the pressures of life on the force.

When tempted to kill the Joker, Gordon held back—and helped convince Batman to do the same.

suffered his greatest loss when she was shot and killed by the Joker. His adoptive daughter Barbara was there to help him shoulder the burden.

Though he has earned the right to retire from the force many times over, James Gordon is too committed to Gotham City to abandon it.

Gordon's devotion to duty always comes first, even when he is forced to go up against members of his own family. Gordon's only son, James Jr., emerged as a serial killer, forcing his father to arrest him and send him to Arkham Asylum.

TAKING A STAND

You can always count on James Gordon to do the right thing, not the popular thing. This has earned him Batman's respect, but also attracted the scorn of Gotham politicians who prefer the old ways of quiet bribery. Gordon's enemies always know where to find him, making his courage perhaps even more remarkable than Batman's.

Gotham's weather is harsh and unpleasant, so Commissioner Gordon is rarely seen without his trademark beige trenchcoat.

HAZARDOUS DUTY

Commissioner Gordon has been shot, beaten, stabbed, and kidnapped during his time on the force, but he shows no signs of slowing down. For a Gotham cop it's all part of the job.

KEY DATA

FULL NAME *James W. Gordon*

OCCUPATION *Police Commissioner*

WEAPONS/ POWERS/ ABILITIES
Weapons training, unarmed combat training, logical detective mind

AFFILIATIONS *Gotham City Police Department*

RELATIVES *Barbara Kean Gordon (first wife), Sarah Essen Gordon (second wife, deceased), Barbara Gordon (daughter), James Gordon Jr. (son), Roger C. Gordon (brother, deceased), Thelma A. Gordon (sister-in-law, deceased)*

FIRST APPEARANCE DETECTIVE COMICS #27 (May 1939)

GOTHAM CITY POLICE DEPARTMENT

The Gotham Central building's offices are overcrowded and understaffed. Most G.C.P.D. officers prefer to spend their time pounding the pavement.

STREETS OF GOTHAM

Batman can't be everywhere at once. The men and women of the Gotham City Police Department attempt to keep the peace in their hometown by dealing with everything from purse-snatchings to super-villain rampages. Once riddled with corruption, the G.C.P.D. cleaned up its act under the leadership of Police Commissioner James Gordon. The Bat-Signal sits on the roof of the downtown headquarters—a structure also called Gotham Central—ready to light up the night sky when the Batman's help is required. However, the detectives of the Major Crimes Unit (M.C.U.) consider it a point of pride to solve cases without the need for Batman's intervention.

BATTLING BUREAUCRACY

When a robbery or homicide is believed to have been committed by a costumed villain, the case is usually kicked up to the Major Crimes Unit. The team's hard-working detectives are put at great risk every day, but still have to deal with the frustrations of paperwork and red tape.

SPECIAL UNIT

The G.C.P.D.'s Quick Response Team (Q.R.T.) is trained in hostage rescue and counterterrorism. Its members carry heavy weapons and wear body armor. Prior to the appointment of Commissioner Gordon, the Q.R.T. was ordered to capture Batman.

JAMES GORDON

James Gordon battled his way to the top of the G.C.P.D., opposed at every step by a crooked mayor and a corrupt cop culture bred by his predecessor, Commissioner Loeb. As the new commissioner, Gordon brought in a crew of handpicked detectives. He also forged strong ties with Batman, but because the Dark Knight is technically an unsanctioned vigilante, a non-city employee has been assigned the task of switching on the rooftop Bat-Signal to summon Batman. Gordon briefly resigned as commissioner to make room for Michael Akins but has since returned to the job.

COMMISSIONER MICHAEL AKINS
Akins took over as police commissioner during Jim Gordon's time away from the job. He was uncomfortable with the close link between his department and Batman.

SERGEANT JACKSON DAVIES
A good-hearted police sergeant working the second shift on the Gotham City streets, Davies is well respected within the M.C.U. for his expertise and practical advice.

DETECTIVE HARVEY BULLOCK
Infamously fond of cigars and donuts, Harvey Bullock is a sloppy dresser but an excellent cop. He is fiercely loyal to Commissioner Gordon.

DETECTIVE JOSEPHINE MACDONALD
"Josie Mac" MacDonald has metahuman psychic abilities that allow her to read inanimate objects. She keeps her powers a secret from her colleagues in the G.C.P.D.

DETECTIVE ROMY CHANDLER
Detective Chandler partners Detective Marcus Driver. Her smart investigative work allowed the G.C.P.D. to arrest the arsonist villain Firebug when he attacked Gotham.

LIEUTENANT RON PROBSON
Lieutenant Probson supervised the detectives of the Major Crimes Unit until the Joker killed him during a violent struggle in a G.C.P.D. interrogation room. He ran a tight ship and was nicknamed "the Probe."

DETECTIVE CRISPUS ALLEN
Crispus Allen is a perfectionist who insists on completing every case he is assigned. The fact that some rank-and-file G.C.P.D. officers think the M.C.U. is made up of elitists is a sore spot with Detective Allen.

DETECTIVE MARCUS DRIVER
After losing his partner in a super-villain standoff, Marcus Driver only grew more attached to his role within the G.C.P.D. He has little patience with Gotham's costumed characters, and views every case as an opportunity to outshine Batman.

CAPTAIN MAGGIE SAWYER
Captain Sawyer formerly headed the Special Crimes Unit (S.C.U.) in Metropolis, tasked with containing the public threat posed by Superman's foes. Her experience has served her well in Gotham as the now-leader of the Gotham M.C.U.

DETECTIVE RENEE MONTOYA
Renee Montoya worked alongside Detective Crispus Allen. She survived a kidnapping ordeal when Two-Face took a romatic interest in her. She is now known as the costumed hero The Question.

FRIENDS & ALLIES

Batman has plenty of enemies, but help is never far away. From famous faces to top-secret operatives, everyone has a place in Batman's network.

SUPERMAN

The last son of the dying world of Krypton, Superman grew up in the care of a kindly Kansas couple and now masquerades as *Daily Planet* reporter Clark Kent. The Man of Steel is one of Batman's oldest and closest friends despite their differing approaches to crime fighting. While Batman may be the brains behind the Justice League of America, it is Superman who is the team's public face. Both heroes are inspirations to the many others who have followed in their wake.

WONDER WOMAN

No mere super hero, Diana carries the blood of the Greek gods in her veins. She is the daughter of Queen Hippolyta from the mystical land of Themyscira—known as Paradise Island by outsiders—where the all-female Amazons maintain a proud warrior culture. After leaving her home and arriving in Man's World, Diana took the name Wonder Woman. Alongside Superman and Batman, Wonder Woman is the third member of a trinity that unofficially leads the super hero community.

AZRAEL

The centuries-old Sacred Order of Saint Dumas selected Jean-Paul Valley to become their avenging angel Azrael, submitting him to psychological conditioning and sending him out to assassinate the wicked. Jean-Paul reformed under Batman's influence, and even took Batman's place after Bane broke the hero's back. But he eventually went too far, becoming overly violent, and Batman had to reclaim his role by force. After Jean-Paul's apparent death, Michael Lane debuted as the newest Azrael.

BLACK CANARY

Dinah Lance is a second-generation super hero and the current head of the Birds of Prey. An expert martial artist, she has the superpowered ability to vocalize a concussive, ultrasonic Canary Cry. Black Canary and Green Arrow are frequently a passionate item, although both of them are so stubborn that their relationship is often on the rocks. Black Canary has always been an ally of Batman's, even though her responsibilities to the Birds of Prey come first.

DEADMAN

Circus aerialist Boston Brand was murdered while performing in front of a packed house, but the goddess Rama Kushna gave him a second chance at life by resurrecting him as a ghost. As Deadman, he existed in a spectral form that couldn't be seen by others, yet he possessed the power to take over anyone's body for a short time. Batman and Deadman have teamed up surprisingly often—after Deadman demonstrated his abilities with enough detail to overcome Batman's natural skepticism.

GREEN ARROW

Multimillionaire Oliver Queen gained unerring skill with a bow and arrow while stranded on a desert island and forced to hunt to survive. After returning to Star City and becoming the Robin Hood-inspired Green Arrow, he helped found the Justice League of America and was also a member of the Outsiders. Green Arrow is romantically linked with Black Canary and is a longtime friend of Green Lantern's, but he doesn't always get along with Batman. The Dark Knight, however, knows he can always count on Green Arrow to speak his mind.

HUNTRESS

On a parallel Earth, the Huntress is Helena Wayne, the grown daughter of a married Bruce Wayne and Selina Kyle. In a former timeline, however, the Huntress emerged from the aftermath of a mob hit, when a young Helena Bertinelli swore revenge on the rival family that had gunned down her mother and father. As the crossbow-toting Huntress, Helena Bertinelli became a member of the Justice League of America and the Birds of Prey, as well as an occasional member of Batman's inner circle.

LESLIE THOMPKINS

Dr. Leslie Thompkins is a regular fixture in Gotham City's Crime Alley, where her humanitarian efforts are the district's sole bright spot. She runs a free clinic that provides treatment for the homeless, inspired by the long-ago murders of Thomas and Martha Wayne and the orphaned boy she comforted on that day. Leslie eventually learned of Bruce Wayne's Batman career, and counsels him against giving in to the darker side of his nature, while constantly worrying that she has not been a good enough role model for him.

SPOILER

Raised by the second-string villain the Cluemaster, Stephanie Brown set out to sabotage her father's crimes as the masked hero Spoiler. She caught the attention of Tim Drake and soon found herself running with Batman's crew, even becoming the fourth person to take on the role of Robin. Black Mask seemingly murdered Stephanie, but she survived and secretly recuperated in Africa under the care of Dr. Leslie Thompkins. After a stint as Batgirl, Stephanie has returned to her identity as Spoiler.

ZATANNA

Zatanna is one of the world's most powerful users of magic, with the ability to reshape matter or make objects appear out of thin air by reciting phrases backward. She is primarily a nightclub entertainer, not a crime fighter, but she answers Batman's call whenever a case requires mystical assistance. During her time with the Justice League of America, Zatanna used her abilities to erase the memories of criminals, an incident that irreparably damaged Batman's trust in her and also changed his whole attitude to the JLA.

BLACK LIGHTNING

An Olympic-level athlete with the power to unleash electrical bolts, Jefferson Pierce won fame as the costumed hero Black Lightning. At Batman's request he was one of the founding members of the Outsiders, and he helped Batman take out the Brother Eye satellite during the Infinite Crisis. Black Lightning has also held a high-ranking post in the U.S. government and served with the Justice League of America. His daughter Thunder was on the roster of Batman's recent Outsiders lineup.

CREEPER

Jack Ryder earned minor celebrity status as a television talk-show host, but exposure to an experimental mutagen changed his body chemistry and allowed him to transform into the nightmarish Creeper. While in his altered state, Ryder gained enhanced strength and agility, but lost his ability to think rationally. Though he is always unpredictable, the Creeper is usually one of the good guys. Just the same, Batman relies on him only when other options are unavailable.

ONYX

Instruction at the Ashram Monastery and a career with the League of Assassins gave Onyx nearly unbeatable martial arts skills and expertise in wielding close-quarters weapons. Onyx teamed up with fellow vigilante Orpheus during Gotham's War Games, when gangs were pitted against each other, but she failed to keep him safe from Black Mask. She later encountered Jason Todd as the Red Hood, but rejected his offer to join his no-mercy crusade against gangs and drugs.

HAROLD

A technological genius, Harold Allnut was originally hired to build terrifying machines for the Penguin until Batman took him in. Harold looked after the Batmobile and designed new Bat-gadgets. His physical deformities and inability to speak left him vulnerable to the temptations of Hush, who cured Harold's disabilities in exchange for information on Batman. When Harold had a last-minute change of heart, Hush silenced him forever with a bullet.

ORPHEUS

Gavin King was a talented dancer and martial artist committed to making a difference in the fight against poverty and prejudice. Outfitted with a hi-tech stealth suit, he kept order in Gotham under the name of Orpheus, enjoying Batman's indirect support. During the War Games incident and the gang infighting, Orpheus prepared to play the central role in bringing Gotham's gangs under Batman's control. Instead he was ambushed and killed by Black Mask.

"This is bigger than I am. And it's bigger than you are."
— Batman

Earth's greatest protectors possess power on the scale of gods, from the Flash's ability to run at near-lightspeed to Aquaman's influence over every creature in the sea. Batman is the only non-superhuman to earn a place among these icons, yet he is the one that the others follow when things get rough. Intelligence and a tendency to be prepared make Batman the Justice League of America's secret weapon.

JUSTICE LEAGUE OF AMERICA

The timeline-shaking events of Flashpoint reset the Justice League's origins, bringing its seven core members together during an invasion by Darkseid and the Fourth World armies of Apokolips. Batman led the counterattack, reigning in the team's loose cannons and directing newcomers.

JUSTICE'S ENEMIES

When its members fight as one, the Justice League of America can be almost invincible. But Earth has plenty of super-villains, and they have often ganged up in the hope of tearing apart the team that has caused them so much misery. The Joker, Lex Luthor, and the Cheetah led the Injustice League Unlimited, with membership largely consisting of villains hoping to take shots at their lifelong enemies. Gorilla Grodd joined to take a swing at the Flash, and the alien bounty hunter Fatality turned her anger toward Green Lantern.

JLA

A fresh alien assault, this time from the shape-shifting White Martians, reunited Batman, Superman, Wonder Woman, Aquaman, and the Martian Manhunter under a new JLA that also included the next-generation versions of the Flash and Green Lantern. With the world under a telepathic spell and his colleagues captured, Batman stood alone against the White Martian invaders. The Dark Knight deduced his enemies' true natures and infiltrated their Antarctic base, deploying their one weakness—fire—to topple their takeover bid.

ORIGINAL LEAGUE

Prior to the Flashpoint event, the Justice League of America originally pulled together to thwart the extraterrestrial Appellaxians and the space going echinoderm called Starro. Fighting alongside fellow founding members Superman, Wonder Woman, the Flash, Green Lantern, Aquaman, and the Martian Manhunter, Batman provided the team high-tech gear and the computing resources of the Batcave. The Justice League operated from a hidden cavern in Happy Harbor, Rhode Island, before relocating to a space station in planetary orbit.

TEAM PLAYERS

Batman might act like a solo agent, but he has always been willing to enlist help from others, from Robin to the Batman Family. The most famous super squads on the planet have counted the Dark Knight on their roster, and many teams only came into existence under Batman's authority.

JUSTICE SOCIETY OF AMERICA

Before the Flashpoint event and on an alternate world called Earth-2, Batman and Superman spent World War II as reserve members of the Justice Society of America. Alongside Golden Age heroes like the Sandman, Hourman, the Spectre, and Doctor Fate—as well as the original versions of Green Lantern, Hawkman, the Flash, and the Atom—the Justice Society of America battled the Axis powers as the Justice Battalion alongside the American armed forces and on the orders of President Franklin D. Roosevelt himself. Batman's history with the team was erased after the Crisis on Infinite Earths, but Earth-2 has since been brought back into existence.

BATMEN OF ALL NATIONS

As soon as Batman had made his mark in Gotham, a number of global heroes followed his lead. France's Musketeer, Italy's Legionary, Argentina's Gaucho, Australia's Ranger, England's Knight and Squire, and the Native American Man-of-Bats all counted themselves within the loosely affiliated Batmen of All Nations. The heroes first assembled to learn detective tips from Batman, and regrouped many years later on an island where the mysterious Doctor Hurt ran them through a series of death traps.

BATMAN INCORPORATED

With the Batmen of All Nations providing the template, the Dark Knight built his own international team, country by country. Batman, Inc. has brought "Batman franchises" to nations including Japan, France, Russia, and the Democratic Republic of Congo. Only time will tell whether extending the power of the Bat brand to other heroes will dilute Batman's own presence, or prove to have repeatable symbolic power.

THE OUTSIDERS

The first team created solely to serve Batman's interests, the Outsiders are covert agents who handle jobs that fall outside the range of public super hero institutions like the Justice League of America. Now that Batman Incorporated is up and running, Batman has reinvented the Outsiders as a small squad able to tackle specific assignments on behalf of Batman, Inc. Led by Red Robin, its members include Halo, Looker, Metamorpho, Katana, and Freight Train.

CATWOMAN

Bruce Wayne's Batman identity is much closer to his "true" personality than the manufactured playboy exterior he wears in public — and therefore Catwoman might be the woman who knows him best of all. The two have shared a flirtatious attraction ever since they debuted as Gotham adventurers. Catwoman is a thief, but since her crimes seldom harm the truly needy, Batman is willing to overlook her outlaw status from time to time.

VICKI VALE

Vicki Vale is a photojournalist for the *Gotham Gazette* who shared an early fling with Bruce Wayne. Following a stint as the host of the television talk show *The Scene*, Vicki returned to the *Gazette* to investigate rumors of Bruce's mysterious disappearance in the wake of the Final Crisis. Bruce soon returned to the public eye, but Vicki's keen investigative sense allowed her to deduce his secret identity. She has chosen to keep her knowledge of Batman's double life to herself.

BATMAN'S LOVE LIFE

Batman keeps himself at an emotional distance from even his closest friends, making the passionate connection of romance a rare thing indeed. Yet several women have grown close to Bruce Wayne over the years, and a few of them have successfully penetrated his defenses and learned to love Batman, too.

JEZEBEL JET

As a supermodel, Jezebel Jet had a celebrity status equal to Bruce Wayne's. After she won Bruce's trust, he opened up to her about every detail of his life, even giving her a tour of the Batcave. However, Jezebel planted doubts in Bruce's mind about his sanity, and was finally revealed to be an undercover agent of Doctor Hurt's evil Black Glove organization. A vengeful Talia al Ghūl later targeted Jezebel for elimination.

SASHA BORDEAUX

Sasha Bordeaux worked for Bruce Wayne as his bodyguard, which put her in a position to uncover his secret Batman identity. She also fell in love with him, but a budding romance between Sasha and Bruce was cut short when both were held as suspects in the murder of Vesper Fairchild — another of Bruce Wayne's love interests. Eventually cleared of all charges, Sasha accepted a high-ranking position within the counterinsurgency team Checkmate, receiving a new identity and cybernetic implants.

VESPER FAIRCHILD

Radio host Vesper Fairchild met Bruce Wayne when he was a guest on her talk show, and the two became an item. Vesper later pursued a career as an investigative journalist, but when her work brought her too close to discovering his alter ego, Bruce cut Vesper out of his life entirely. Soon after, Bruce discovered Vesper dead on the floor of Wayne Manor. The G.C.P.D. arrested Bruce as the primary murder suspect and it took months for Batman's operatives to identify the real killer.

JULIE MADISON

One of Bruce Wayne's first loves, Julie Madison often found herself the target of villains who had designs on her family's fortune. She was briefly Bruce's fiancée but his unexplained absences drove them apart. She left Bruce without ever learning his Batman secret, and adopted the stage name of Portia Storme to pursue an acting career.

SHONDRA KINSOLVING

Gifted with superhuman empathic and healing abilities, Shondra Kinsolving was a physiotherapist who took on Bruce Wayne as a patient. Bruce had been suffering from exhaustion, and he and Shondra grew close during their sessions. Their romance was interrupted when Shondra's brother exploited her abilities for evil and she experienced a mental breakdown. Shondra recovered, but she moved on without Bruce Wayne.

TALIA AL GHŪL

As the head of killing organization the League of Assassins, Talia al Ghūl is without a doubt Batman's deadliest paramour. A decade ago, a liaison between the two resulted in the birth of a son, Damian Wayne — though Talia kept the boy's existence a secret from his father. She recently brought Damian into Bruce's life and often uses him as a pawn to gain leverage over her "beloved." Talia's ambition is even greater than that of her father Rā's al Ghūl's, and she will settle for nothing less than world domination.

SILVER ST. CLOUD

Silver St. Cloud, a socialite and high-class Gotham event coordinator, quickly learned Bruce Wayne's secret identity — but the truth split them apart. Ultimately, Silver couldn't bear living with the knowledge that every night Bruce faced death as Batman, and she broke off their romance. She returned much later to renew their connection, but experienced a brutal attack at the hands of the costumed assassin Onomatopoeia.

SUPER SANITY

Some psychologists at Arkham Asylum believe the Joker's madness may be a coping mechanism, allowing him to reinvent himself to fit the changing times. Over the years, the Joker has evolved from a harmless trickster into a deranged mass murderer.

It's no dye—the Joker's hair was left permanently green by his chemical bath! The same fluid made his skin turn ghastly white.

Flowers tucked into the Joker's lapel are not just for decoration—they are often disguised acid squirters or gas sprayers.

The Joker's distinctive, comedic look is made up of a purple jacket with tails, a clashing yellow shirt, and a knotted green tie.

HOME AGAIN

The Joker's stays in Arkham Asylum do nothing to rehabilitate him. Instead, he seems to treat them as temporary vacations that let him regain his strength in preparation for his next crime.

KEY DATA

REAL NAME *Unknown*

OCCUPATION *Professional criminal*

WEAPONS/ POWERS/ ABILITIES
Electrified joy buzzer, acid-squirting flower, exploding cigar, "bang"-flag harpoon gun, unarmed combat skills, brilliant criminal mind

AFFILIATIONS *Injustice League*

RELATIVES *None confirmed*

FIRST APPEARANCE BATMAN #1 *(Spring 1940)*

The Joker never misses a chance to be violent. The pointed toes of his shoes sometimes conceal pop-out knife blades.

"I'm not mad at all. I'm just differently sane."

THE JOKER

THE JOKER

Gotham City seems to breed theatrical villains, but the Joker has a killer act to top them all. The Clown Prince of Crime is Batman's arch-enemy. Never locked up for long, the Joker is always eager to spread his stylish mix of mirth and mayhem.

Batman has free access to Arkham Asylum in order to conduct interrogations.

The Joker has a complicated relationship with his jester-like love interest Harley Quinn, but she always returns to his arms.

GETTING THE JOKE

Colorful and chaotic where Batman is dark and driven, the Joker is the perfect foe for someone who has dedicated his life to keeping Gotham's madness at bay.

No one knows the Joker's origin or even his real name. Some claim he started out as a failed stand-up comedian driven to desperation by the death of his wife. While robbing a chemical plant as the criminal Red Hood, he fled from the Batman and tumbled into a bubbling vat. When he emerged his skin was chalk-white, his hair shocking green, and his sanity a thing of the past.

The Joker escapes from Arkham Asylum with ease. His crimes are grandiose and imaginative, and usually involve fun items given deadly twists—an acid-squirting flower, for example, or an amusement park that he has transformed into a giant death trap.

Nearly everyone close to Batman has suffered from the Joker's evil. He beat Jason Todd, the second Robin, to death (although he would later be resurrected). He shot Barbara Gordon in the spine, sidelining her Batgirl career for years. And he murdered Sarah Essen, the wife of Police Commissioner James Gordon. Every crime hurts Batman, but he will never cross the line that separates him from killers like the Joker.

Batman and the Joker seem to be locked in an inseparable struggle—one that the Joker views as nothing more than a game. The Joker frequently reinvents his persona in response to Batman's own changes. He became a clownish prankster during the era of the gung ho Batman Family, and a sadistic torturer only after Batman had grown increasingly grim. No other super hero seems to hold the Joker's interest for long.

Feared by Gotham's fellow criminals, the Joker is loved by just one—his delusional sidekick Harley Quinn. With Batman as his straight man, the Joker has vowed to keep the people of Gotham laughing—even if it kills them!

Some say the Joker was once just an ordinary guy who felt forced to turn to crime to provide for his pregnant wife.

Joker Venom leaves its victims with a ghoulish grin, announcing the Joker's involvement.

The decaying infrastructure of Gotham's Amusement Mile is the Joker's favorite haunt.

The Joker's murders are sometimes cruelly personal. He coldly shot Sarah Essen, wife of Commissioner Gordon.

The Joker is a deadly combatant when armed with knives or razors—something that often surprises Batman.

ROGUES GALLERY

TWO-FACE

Harvey Dent was an idealistic Gotham City district attorney until a mob informant threw a vial of acid against the side of his head. The trauma caused him to become Two-Face, who viewed the world through the polar opposites of order and chaos. Two-Face's crimes always involve the number two, and he makes important decisions by flipping a scarred silver dollar and choosing the path of good or evil based on which side lands face-up. Attempts have been made to repair his facial scarring, but none of these have cured his insanity; although he has briefly returned to his Dent persona, he has ended up simply destroying one side of his face and becoming Two-Face once again.

CATWOMAN

Batman's relationship with Selina Kyle has always been complicated. As the costumed Catwoman, Selina has an eye for expensive treasures — especially if they have a cat theme — and she has no qualms about stealing them. Stealthy and agile, Catwoman is also a skilled martial artist. Batman can't condone her criminal side but he is still drawn to her flirtatious playfulness. Killing is against Catwoman's own moral code, and her main targets for thievery at the moment are mobsters and gangsters. Armed with a whip and ten face-scratching claws, Catwoman often helps the Dynamic Duo but she can never truly be trusted.

THE RIDDLER

Edward Nigma, also known as the Riddler, is arguably the second-best detective in the world after Batman himself. Motivated by the desire to prove his own cleverness, he earned his reputation by staging robberies and leaving the clues in plain sight. In so doing, he dared the police to catch him — and proved himself their intellectual superior when they could not. This compulsion has resulted in him being repeatedly imprisoned in Arkham Asylum. Batman is the only person who can always solve the Riddler's puzzles, and sometimes the two of them work together to solve perplexing cases. The Riddler has also been associated with the Secret Society of Super-Villains.

MR. FREEZE

Dr. Victor Fries could have been a world-class scientist if his wife Nora hadn't contracted a terminal disease. Victor attempted to freeze her in cryogenic stasis until a cure could be found, but an accident left her trapped between life and death. It also changed Victor's body chemistry so that he could no longer survive outside a sub-zero environment. Now, as the emotionless Mr. Freeze, he wears a life-sustaining cryo-suit and stalks the city, stealing diamonds for his personal collection and money to fund his cryogenic research. Armed with his deadly freeze gun, he is also a ruthless killer, turning his luckless victims into blocks of ice.

When it comes to crime, Gotham City is like no other place on Earth. Ever since Batman took down the Falcone family and other traditional criminal kingpins, a growing legion of colorful super-villains have fillled the gap. Many of the worst offenders are also mentally unstable, ensuring that Arkham Asylum does a brisk business. Whether he's dealing with an obsessive mastermind, a costumed lawbreaker, or a mutated freak of nature, Batman always has his hands full.

POISON IVY

A close encounter with biological toxins transformed biochemist Pamela Isley into the plant/human hybrid known as Poison Ivy. She can control plants with her thoughts and can turn humans into mind-numbed slaves by infecting them with spores. Poison Ivy's goal is to protect the natural world from those who would harm it, but her methods are too extreme for Batman. She has spent much of her life imprisoned in Arkham Asylum for the criminally insane, and has been a member of the Gotham City Sirens, the Injustice League, Injustice Gang, the Secret Society of Super-Villains, and the Suicide Squad. Her only human friend is Harley Quinn.

THE PENGUIN

Mocked as a child for his short stature and beak-like nose, Oswald Cobblepot embraced the nickname "Penguin" when he made his mark in Gotham's criminal underworld. Known to the public as the owner of the Iceberg Lounge nightclub, the Penguin secretly has a hand in gambling, gunrunning, stolen goods, and other illicit industries. He is also a former member of the Injustice League. The Penguin is obsessed with birds and is rarely seen without an umbrella. Unlike many of the Dark Knight's adversaries, the Penguin is sane and has the impeccable manners of a gentleman. He is a useful source of information, providing Batman with tips that enable him to foil the plots of the Penguin's rivals.

BANE

Bane grew up inside the walls of a prison on the island nation of Santa Prisca. Serving time for his own father's acts of rebellion against the island's corrupt government, Bane was brutalized by his experience. His aggression made him a perfect test subject for the experimental Venom steroid. With tubes pumping Venom directly into his bloodstream, he gained vastly increased physical strength and broke out of the prison. Fascinated by Batman, Bane set his sights on challenging and defeating him. He hatched a plot that only ended when he broke Batman's back. Although Batman eventually recovered, Bane remains one of his most intimidating foes. Bane was once associated with the Secret Six.

RĀ'S AL GHŪL

Also called the Demon's Head, Rā's al Ghūl is the founder of the League of Assassins. His avowed aim is to restore the Earth's ecological balance by killing most of the planet's inhabitants. His favored method of assault on the world's population is the use of a biological weapon, such as a genetically engineered virus. He has lived for centuries as a result of periodic immersions in the Lazarus Pits, pools of rejuvenating chemicals that restore the dying to life. Rā's al Ghūl is an expert swordsman and accomplished martial artist. He is also the father of Talia al Ghūl, and the grandfather of the fifth Robin, Damian Wayne (Talia's son with Batman).

ROGUES GALLERY

SCARECROW

Dr. Jonathan Crane is trained in the psychology of fear, a subject he learned well during an unhappy childhood that was dominated by playground bullies. As an adult he studied phobias in a clinical setting, and developed a gas to activate the fear centers in the brains of its victims. Dressing up in rags and calling himself the Scarecrow, Crane forces the people of Gotham to face their worst nightmares. His fear toxin make his victims hallucinate, so that they believe that their worst phobias have come to life. The Scarecrow can also resort to physical combat, using a style called "violent dancing," based partly on boxing and the crane style of kung fu. He was once an associate of the Injustice Gang.

KILLER CROC

Killer Croc was born Waylon Jones, a child afflicted with a strange, progressive condition that triggered the emergence of primitive evolutionary traits in his genetic code. Over time he grew to resemble a massive crocodile, developing pebbly skin, a tooth-filled snout, a powerful tail, and a tough protective hide. Taking the name Killer Croc after finding work wrestling alligators, he realized his superhuman strength could help him become a powerful, wealthy figure in Gotham's crime scene. Prone to fits of bestial rage, Croc was responsible for the murder of Joseph and Trina Todd, an act that inspired their adoptive son Jason to take up the role of the second Robin.

HUSH

The bandages covering his face hide the fact that Hush is Tommy Elliot, Bruce Wayne's friend since childhood. As a boy, Tommy attempted to murder his wealthy parents by cutting the brake lines in their car. His father perished in the crash, but Thomas Wayne intervened to save Tommy's mother. Furious with the Wayne family for ruining his plot to inherit the Elliot family's fortune, Tommy swore revenge. He grew up to become a gifted neurologist and plastic surgeon, but the desire for vengeance remained. As the devious criminal Hush, he is a master strategist and manipulator, consumed by a desire to kill the Batman and ruin the life of his boyhood friend, Bruce Wayne.

CLAYFACE

Many Clayfaces have taken shape over the years, but all of them exhibit the ability to reshape their muddy, protoplasmic bodies into a variety of forms. They have also all shared a common enemy in the form of the Dark Knight, who is always the first line of defense against their criminal activities in Gotham. In combat, a Clayface creature can turn his appendages into hammers and hooks, and he can even survive being torn apart or blasted to bits. The mud monster also has enough control over his shapeshifting to temporarily impersonate other people. Clayface has been associated with the Injustice League and the Anti-Justice League, as well as the Secret Society of Super-Villains.

"BACK OFF, B-MAN! YOU WANT MISTER J, YOU GOTTA GO THROUGH ME!"

Harley Quinn

HARLEY QUINN

Hopelessly devoted to her boyfriend, the Joker, Harley Quinn is a cheerfully deranged costumed villain. A qualified psychologist and Olympic-level gymnast, Dr. Harleen Quinzel originally fell in love with the Joker while working on his case at Arkham Asylum. Ditching her career for a life of crime, she created her own costumed persona, adapting her own name and wearing the costume of a medieval jester—a harlequin. Harley stays loyal to "Mister J" even when he treats her poorly, and is close friends with Poison Ivy. She has been a member of the Secret Society of Super-Villains, the Secret Six, and the Gotham City Sirens.

BLACK MASK

Most of Gotham's underworld is controlled by Black Mask. Roman Sionis was the first to carry the name, having suffered a disfigurement that left him looking like a living skull. A ruthless, sadistic criminal, he ran his underworld organizations like a highly efficient business. When he moved against the members of Batman's inner circle, he tortured the fourth Robin, Stephanie Brown, who later died of the severe injuries inflicted upon her. Catwoman eventually shot and killed Sionis, and Dr. Jeremiah Arkham—the insane administrator of Arkham Asylum—became the new Black Mask. He uses the asylum inmates as soldiers in his battle for supremacy in Gotham's underworld.

KILLER MOTH/CHARAXES

One of Gotham City's more bizarre villains, Killer Moth modeled himself on Batman—instead of a bat, he used the image of a moth as the theme for his criminal persona. The Secret Society of Super-Villains member wears a winged suit and carries a cocoon gun capable of immobilizing his targets. Barbara Gordon trounced Killer Moth in her first outing as Batgirl, and the villain's defeats have only grown more numerous since then. One incarnation of Killer Moth was granted powers by a demon named Neron and he was transformed into the mutated moth-monster Charaxes. Following Charaxes' death, his successor carries out his nefarious schemes wearing a classic moth-inspired costume.

TALON

In a Gotham City that exists on an alternative, parallel Earth, an old nursery rhyme warns of the "Court of Owls." However, few realize that the term refers to a secret society that controls the city behind the scenes. An assassin for the Court of Owls—an evil version of the Justice League—Talon is the apprentice to Owlman, a villanous equivalent of Batman. The Robin-like sidekick wears an owl-inspired battle suit and carries edged weapons and throwing knives. Talon was transported to Batman's universe by his lover, Duela Dent. The pair briefly joined the Teen Titans, fighting for the forces of good. Duela was later murdered, and at present Talon's whereabouts are unknown.

SOLOMON GRUNDY

The supernatural menace Solomon Grundy came into being more than a century ago, after the body of Cyrus Gold sank into the murk of Slaughter Swamp and emerged as a shambling, undead monster. With tremendous strength and no ability to feel pain, Grundy is a nearly unstoppable bundle of animal instincts with almost no guiding intelligence. Each time he is destroyed, a new incarnation is reborn in the swamp, making Grundy essentially immortal.

CAIN

Widely regarded as the world's greatest assassin, David Cain is affiliated with the League of Assassins and always commands a high price for his services. He fathered Cassandra Cain (formerly Batgirl) with Lady Shiva, and trained her in the art of combat. Cassandra rebelled against her father, realizing that murder was wrong. Now he is determined to recruit a squad of elite female killers to replace the daughter he feels he has lost.

CALCULATOR

Noah Kuttler began his career by attempting to steal treasures while dressed in a computerized battle suit that resembled a giant pocket calculator. He found a better outlet for his mathematical genius by becoming an information source for the super-villain community. For the right price, the Calculator will hack into security cameras or disable alarm systems. A computer expert, his untraceable activities have helped hundreds of villains escape justice.

CALENDAR MAN

Julian Day's obsession with dates caused him to refashion himself as the costumed criminal Calendar Man. His crimes are oriented around equinoxes or obscure anniversaries, but Batman is always able to deduce his theme and send him back to Arkham Asylum. The Calendar Man is imprisoned in a glass-walled cell in Arkham's basement, where he is sometimes consulted as an expert resource on the methods used by other criminals.

CATMAN

Big-game trapper Thomas Blake set his sights on a new quarry when he grew bored with hunting. Adopting a cat theme, he set himself up as the costumed criminal Catman. Though he never earned much respect in Gotham City, Catman got a fresh start as a member of the Secret Six alongside Deadshot and other lesser-known villains. Catman possesses an honorable streak and has a deep respect for endangered jungle cats.

BLACK SPIDER

The identity of Black Spider has passed from criminal to criminal over the years, with the most notable holder being mob hitman Johnny LaMonica. As the gun-toting Black Spider, LaMonica targeted crime kingpin Black Mask for assassination until Batman foiled his plans. After LaMonica was shot and killed in a confrontation with G.C.P.D. detective Crispus Allen, the Black Spider name was purchased by Derrick Coe. Coe has since earned a spot on the Injustice League.

CAVALIER

Dressed in a gray business suit, the Cavalier currently serves as a bodyguard for Dr. Leslie Thompkins — but he has a colorful past! He was once a professional thief with a swashbuckling sense of style. When Mortimer Drake first assumed the identity of the Cavalier, he wore a costume that resembled that of a 17th century musketeer. The Cavalier is one of Batman's less dangerous foes, since he holds fast to a personal code of honor that includes chivalry toward women.

LADY SHIVA

Lady Shiva, originally known as Sandra Wu-San, is one of the world's most gifted martial artists. A child prodigy in unarmed combat, she became linked to the League of Assassins when David Cain murdered her sister. This led to Sandra fully committing herself to her training, unlocking her true potential. She bore a daughter with Cain named Cassandra, who grew up to become Batgirl (and eventually Blackbat). Lady Shiva is highly sought after as a combat trainer.

DEADSHOT

The world's greatest marksman, Floyd Lawton claims that he never misses. As Deadshot, he is in demand as a mercenary and hired killer. His protective battle suit is equipped with wrist-mounted guns and a targeting eyepiece. He has fought Batman, but has been more successful as a member of villainous teams including the Suicide Squad and the Secret Six. Deadshot does not care if he lives or dies, which makes him an utterly fearless adversary.

DOLLMAKER

Barton Mathis grew up in the twisted care of his father, a cannibal who was shot by police officer James Gordon. He became the Dollmaker to gain a sense of control after his powerless upbringing, and carried out a plot to take his revenge on Commissioner Gordon. The Dollmaker uses flesh-stitching techniques to make horrifying, living patchwork dolls from the skin of his victims. His own mask is partly made from the skin of his dead father.

DR. HURT

Dr. Simon Hurt's origins are unknown, but he has assumed many false identities, including that of the late Thomas Wayne. A brilliant scientist, Hurt implanted a hypnotic trigger in Batman's mind designed to incapacitate him when a keyword was used. He also trained three "replacement Batmen" to do his bidding, but his plan was foiled. A strategic mastermind, Hurt has served as the head of both the Club of Villains and the Black Glove organization.

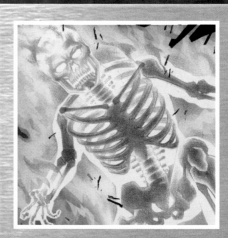

DR. PHOSPHORUS

Dr. Alex Sartorius suffered a terrible fate when a nuclear reactor accident riddled his body with tiny radioactive particles. Burning with a fire that could never be extinguished, he adopted the name Doctor Phosphorous and shared his pain with innocent victims. Doctor Phosphorous constantly leaks toxic radiation and can kill with a single touch. At Arkham Asylum, the administrators constructed a special radiation-proof cell solely for his use.

ROGUES GALLERY

FIREFLY

Garfield Lynns is a villain with a simple motivation— to make the world burn. He became the costumed Firefly to provide an outlet for his pyromaniac urges, and many of his crimes of arson are motivated by nothing more than the desire to put something to the torch. Firefly's suit gives him limited protection against extreme temperatures and also allows him to fly. His primary weapons are flamethrowers and incendiary grenades.

FLAMINGO

The mob enforcer known as the Flamingo is dangerously insane. The same gangsters who keep him on their payroll also removed parts of his brain, leaving him without a moral conscience but with all his lethal skills intact. The Flamingo relishes torturing innocents and has earned infamy as "the eater of faces." He has a taste for fast motorcycles and flashy clothes, and can easily be found by following the trail of bodies he leaves behind.

HUGO STRANGE

The gifted psychiatrist Hugo Strange earned a professorship at Gotham State University, but his obsession with Batman led him down the path of villainy. Recruited by the police department to help curb Batman's vigilante activities, Strange deduced that Bruce Wayne was his target's secret identity but chose to keep the knowledge to himself. His talents at genetic engineering have allowed him to raise an army of mindless creatures he calls "Monster Men."

KGBEAST

An elite division of the Russian KGB transformed Anatoli Knyazev into an unstoppable killing machine nicknamed the KGBeast. A crack shot, he was surgically enhanced with cybernetic implants that made him unnaturally strong. The KGBeast carried out assassinations on the orders of his Russian masters, which put him into conflict with Batman. The KGBeast lost his life during a Gotham gang war, but he was later reanimated as a zombie soldier.

JERVIS TETCH

A lifelong love of Lewis Carroll's *Alice in Wonderland* led Jervis Tetch to model himself after the book's Mad Hatter character. With a gift for microelectronics and an understanding of hypnotism, the Mad Hatter learned how to entrance others by fitting them with hats that contained tiny mind-control devices. His crimes never stray too far from classic storybook themes, and he sometimes teams up with a group called the Wonderland Gang.

MAXIE ZEUS

A one-time mild-mannered history teacher, Maxie Zeus has extreme delusions of grandeur and is convinced that he is the Greek god Zeus in human form. Insane but highly intelligent, he is active in Gotham's shipping trade and casino industry and uses his fortune to fund an active sideline of criminal activities. Like the god whose name he shares, Zeus carries weapons shaped like lightning bolts that can zap unbelievers with lethal jolts of electricity.

"TWINKLE, TWINKLE, LITTLE BAT; HOW I WONDER WHERE YOU'RE AT!"

Jervis Tetch

MAN-BAT

Scientist Kirk Langstrom's study of bats went horribly wrong when an experimental serum transformed him into a half-bat, half-human monster. His animal instincts overrode his intellect and soon he was terrorizing Gotham every night until sunrise. Like a true bat, Man-Bat can fly and can sense his surroundings through echolocation. Dr. Langstrom's wife Francine has also been altered by the serum and she has become the She-Bat.

MR. ZSASZ

The Arkham Asylum inmate with the strongest desire to kill others is probably Mr. Zsasz, who cuts a new notch in his skin to mark the death of each victim. Born into wealth, he lost it all and came to the realization that life had no meaning. To Zsasz, killing is his gift to the world as he "liberates" his victims from their futile lives while injecting some fleeting excitement into his own existence. Mr. Zsasz is an expert fighter when armed with knives or razors.

PROFESSOR PYG

An insane, mask-wearing scientist with a pig obsession, Professor Pyg started out as ringmaster of the traveling Circus of the Strange. His host of freaks captured spectators and turned them into subjects for Pyg's sick experiments. Pyg's surgery is used to create Dollotrons — lobotomized victims with blank masks permanently grafted to their faces. He is a raving lunatic whose fondest wish is to infect Gotham's citizens with an insanity-triggering virus.

SCARLET

When Professor Pyg failed to complete the lobotomization of one of his Dollotron slaves, the victim escaped and became the anti-hero Scarlet. With Pyg's Dollotron mask still attached to her face, she hooked up with Jason Todd, the Red Hood, and earned a place as his sidekick. Scarlet blamed the current Robin (Damian Wayne) for abandoning her in Pyg's lair, but they settled their scores when Robin saved her from the rampaging killer Flamingo.

SENSEI

The Sensei is the father of Rā's al Ghūl, and therefore the grandfather of Talia al Ghūl and great-grandfather of Damian Wayne. As one of the planet's best martial artists, he held a high-ranking position within the League of Assassins and often feuded with his son for control of the organization. The Sensei seemingly met his final end when Batman submerged him in the Fountain of Youth in Tibet's Nanda Parbat, where its pure waters consumed the old man's tainted spirit.

VENTRILOQUIST

Arnold Wesker was meek and soft-spoken, but he earned respect as a Gotham City crime boss when he channeled his buried rage through his puppet, Scarface. Wesker let Scarface handle the dirty work, executing mob snitches with a miniature Tommy gun cradled in Scarface's wooden arms. A second Ventriloquist, the beautiful but deadly Peyton Riley, arose in the Gotham underworld after Arnold Wesker's apparent death.

Timeline

Timeline

- Bruce Wayne is born to Martha Wayne and Dr. Thomas Wayne. He is their only child and is heir to a family fortune going back generations to the founding of Gotham City.

- Bruce grows up in Wayne Manor, attended to by Alfred Pennyworth, the family butler. His childhood friend is Thomas "Tommy" Elliot.

- At an early age, Bruce falls into a concealed pit in the grounds of Wayne Manor and lands in a huge underground cave filled with bats.

- Dr. Thomas Wayne dresses as a costumed character he calls "the Batman" for a masquerade ball, and defeats a gang of hoodlums when they crash the party.

- After taking Bruce to a movie, Thomas and Martha Wayne are shot and killed by a mugger while walking though Gotham's notorious Crime Alley. The gunman, a thug named Joe Chill, escapes and the case is never officially resolved. Leslie Thompkins is one of the first people to arrive at the murder scene and comforts a traumatized Bruce.

- Bruce grows up in the care of Alfred Pennyworth. In his early teens he leaves Gotham City to travel the world, studying criminology and forensics while training under the greatest martial arts masters.

- Years later, Bruce Wayne returns to Gotham. His body now a living weapon, he vows to battle wrongdoers and prevent crimes like the one that took his parents' lives. In his first outing he dresses in street clothes and is badly beaten. Recuperating back at Wayne Manor, he sees a gigantic bat crash through a window and takes it as an omen.

- Now determined to strike fear into the hearts of criminals as the Batman, Bruce develops his costume and weapons and begins renovating the cavern beneath Wayne Manor into his secret headquarters, the Batcave.

- In his first outings, Batman battles corrupt cops, crooked politicians, and the mobsters that control Gotham's underworld.

- James Gordon, a new face on the Gotham City police force, finds himself allying with Batman against the corruption that has taken root within the G.C.P.D. under the leadership of Commissioner Loeb.

- Selina Kyle is inspired by Batman's example and begins her career as Catwoman.

- Batman matches wits with the evil Professor Hugo Strange.

- Bruce Wayne becomes engaged to heiress Julie Madison. Meanwhile, Batman faces off against The Monk, a werewolf-vampire.

- An unknown comedian agrees to pose as a criminal kingpin called the Red Hood. While leading other crooks through a chemical factory, he is chased by Batman and falls into a bubbling vat. He emerges with his skin bleached chalk-white, and reinvents himself as the psychotic Joker.

- A horde of new "themed" villains appears in Gotham, inspired by the example that Batman himself has set. In short order the city is rocked with crimes by the Calendar Man, the Riddler, the Mad Hatter, Poison Ivy, the Scarecrow, and the slow-witted Solomon Grundy.

- The Gotham City Police Department places a Bat-Signal on the roof of its Gotham Central headquarters to alert Batman to emergencies.

- Batman teams up with James Gordon and district attorney Harvey Dent to take down the notorious Falcone crime family. In the process they find themselves on the trail of a serial killer known as Holiday.

- During courtroom proceedings, Harvey Dent is splashed with acid by a mob informant. The left side of his face suffers severe scarring, and Harvey becomes the double-sided villain Two-Face.

- The Penguin waddles into the Gotham City scene.

- Batman investigates the identity of the Hangman killer and once again crosses paths with the Falcone crime family.

- After his trapeze-artist parents are slain by gangster Boss Zucco, Dick Grayson joins the Dark Knight's crime-fighting crusade by taking on the role of Robin, the Boy Wonder.

- Thespian Basil Karlo takes on the role of serial murderer Clayface.

- Julie Madison calls off her engagement to Bruce due to his playboy lifestyle.

- Wonderland-themed, twin villains Tweedledee and Tweedledum arrive in Gotham City.

- The expert mercenary Deadshot takes aim at the Dark Knight.

- The criminal Killer Moth debuts but quickly meets defeat.

- Batman and Superman begin a semi-regular partnership to tackle large-scale threats together.

- Batman welcomes new members into his war on crime, and soon attracts an entire Batman Family. Ace the Bat-Hound is his canine partner, while former circus acrobat Kathy Kane becomes the original Batwoman.

- Batman adds the Bat-copter and the Whirly-Bat to his fleet of vehicles. These flying craft join the Batplane and give Batman dominance in the skies above Gotham.

- The brilliant scientist Victor Fries suffers a tragic accident, and soon Mr. Freeze becomes a chilling presence in Gotham's criminal underworld.

- Batman teams with Wonder Woman, Superman, the Flash, Green Lantern, Aquaman, and Cyborg to form the Justice League of America.

- Matt Hagen becomes the monstrously malleable Clayface II.

- Thomas Blake, better known as Catman, takes a swipe at the Dynamic Duo.

- Robin becomes a founding member of the Teen Titans alongside other super hero sidekicks.

- Barbara Gordon puts on the cape and cowl to become Gotham's latest hero—Batgirl!

- Dick Grayson leaves the Batcave to attend Hudson University.

- Bruce Wayne and Alfred Pennyworth relocate their main base of operations to the rooftop penthouse of the Wayne Foundation building in the heart of Gotham City. A new Batcave is established beneath the Wayne Foundation's skyscraper.

Timeline

Timeline

- Zoologist Kirk Langstrom experiences a strange genetic transmutation and becomes the monstrous Man-Bat.

- The deadly Talia al Ghūl and her father, Rā's al Ghūl, begin to take more active roles in Batman's life. With the backing of the League of Assassins, Rā's al Ghūl plots genocide in order to restore the planet's ecological balance.

- Dr. Phosphorus makes his debut as a villain after suffering the agony of a radiation accident.

- Platinum-haired Silver St. Cloud becomes Bruce Wayne's latest romantic interest, though their relationship is short-lived.

- Lucius Fox becomes Bruce Wayne's business manager and accepts responsibility for running the day-to-day business operations of Wayne Enterprises.

- Gangster Maxie Zeus surfaces in Gotham, convinced he is the living incarnation of the Greek god of lightning.

- The mutated Killer Croc begins his run of reptilian villainy.

- Batman quits the Justice League of America and assembles his own team of super heroes, the Outsiders, whose members included Katana, Metamorpho, Geo-Force, Looker, Halo, and Black Lightning.

- Jason Todd officially debuts as the second Robin.

- Dick Grayson abandons the Robin role forever, becoming Nightwing to rescue his fellow Teen Titans from Deathstroke and the HIVE.

- Roman Sionis, alias Black Mask, breaks into Gotham's organized crime ranks as a major player.

- Multiple realities are merged into one during the epic event known as the Crisis on Infinite Earths. In the aftermath, some elements from Batman's history are rewritten as a new, unified timeline takes effect.

- The Ventriloquist and his puppet Scarface carve out a piece of the Gotham underworld from rival mob bosses.

- The artificially enhanced Russian assassin known as the KGBeast ignites a cold war in Batman's territory.

- Jason Todd goes in search of his real mother, but runs into a trap set by the Joker. The Clown Prince of Crime beats the second Robin with a crowbar, then leaves him locked in a warehouse with a ticking time bomb. Batman arrives too late to save Jason from the explosion.

- The Joker shoots and paralyzes Barbara Gordon, and kidnaps Commissioner Gordon so he can subject him to psychological torture.

- No longer able to use her legs after the Joker's attack, Barbara Gordon takes on a new role as the all-seeing information broker Oracle.

- Tim Drake officially joins Batman's crusade as the third Robin.

- Deranged serial killer Mr. Zsasz becomes the latest maniac to terrorize the people of Gotham.

- Stephanie Brown, aka the Spoiler, becomes a vigilante to thwart her father, the Cluemaster.

- The villain called Bane defeats Batman in combat, breaking his back and leaving him paralyzed. Bruce Wayne is forced to relinquish the mantle of Batman to newcomer Jean-Paul Valley (Azrael) for a brief time.

• As the new Batman, Jean-Paul Valley adopts a formidable suit of Bat-armor to defeat Bane.

• Now recovered from Bane's injury, Bruce Wayne reclaims the title of Batman from Jean-Paul Valley.

• Bruce Wayne hooks up with a new flame, Gotham radio host Vesper Fairchild.

• Barbara Gordon, now Oracle, organizes a strike team called the Birds of Prey. Her partner is Dinah Lance, the Black Canary.

• A powerful earthquake rocks Gotham. Its citizens are evacuated and the city becomes a No Man's Land, ruled by criminal fiefdoms and protected by Batman and his agents.

• Martial arts prodigy Cassandra Cain inherits the mantle of Batgirl from Barbara Gordon.

• Former Arkham psychiatrist Dr. Harleen Quinzel takes the name Harley Quinn and makes a splash as the Joker's sidekick and occasional love interest.

• The Joker murders James Gordon's second wife, Sarah Essen-Gordon.

• Bruce Wayne's bodyguard, Sasha Bordeaux, learns that her employer is secretly Batman.

• Mistakenly believing he has a terminal disease, the Joker decides to go out with a bang. He infects a prison full of villains with "Jokerized" venom and wreaks havoc across the planet.

• Bruce Wayne's paramour Vesper Fairchild is found murdered. Bruce and his bodyguard Sasha Bordeaux are held as suspects but eventually cleared of all charges.

• Bruce Wayne's boyhood friend Tommy Elliot appears as the bandaged villain Hush, launching an elaborate plot against Batman that involves nearly every member of the Rogues Gallery.

• Heeding Batman's call, Stephanie Brown becomes the fourth Robin.

• Rā's al Ghūl is seemingly killed as his daughters Talia al Ghūl and Nyssa plot to usurp control of his worldwide empire.

• Stephanie Brown apparently dies after being tortured by Black Mask.

• Batman learns that his withdrawn, suspicious behaviour of recent years stems from the fact that his fellow heroes in the Justice League of America altered his memories when he discovered they were mind-wiping captured super-villains.

• Tim Drake's father is killed by Captain Boomerang, leaving Tim an orphan.

• Batman develops the Brother Eye surveillance satellite but realizes that his construction has become self-aware. Brother Eye turns thousands of innocent victims into malevolent OMAC agents.

• Jason Todd, somehow restored to life after his murder at the hands of the Joker, assumes the vigilante identity of the Red Hood. He confronts Batman about his failure to save him, and embarks on a bloody crusade to take down Black Mask.

• During the event known as the Infinite Crisis, Batman fights to stop the cosmic super-villain Alexander Luthor from restructuring reality.

• After surviving the Infinite Crisis, Batman decides to take time off to retrace the path that led to his transformation into the Dark Knight. It is a quest that spans the better part of a year.

- With Batman away from Gotham, Harvey Dent tries—and fails—to become the city's protector and put his violent past as Two-Face behind him.

- Kate Kane becomes the new Batwoman, operating in Gotham City during Batman's absence.

- Former Gotham City police detective Renee Montoya becomes the new Question, following the death of the previous hero of that name, Vic Sage.

- Bruce Wayne returns to Gotham and officially adopts Tim Drake as his legal son.

- The Riddler turns over a new leaf, refocusing his brilliant mind to the task of solving crimes rather than creating them.

- Batman joins Superman, Wonder Woman, Red Tornado, Vixen, and other heroes as a member of a newly restructured Justice League of America.

- The Joker kidnaps Robin and drives him all over town on a demented holiday spree.

- A new Ventriloquist and Scarface arrive on the scene, with the beautiful "Sugar" now animating the tough-talking puppet.

- Batman pulls together a new team of Outsiders, with members including Katana, Metamorpho, Grace, and the Martian Manhunter.

- Bruce Wayne learns he has a biological son as a result of a long-ago liaison with Talia al Ghūl. Damian Wayne is now ten years old and has little respect for authority. He is a top combatant, thanks to the tutelage of the League of Assassins.

- Bruce Wayne finds a new love interest in Jezebel Jet, though he does not detect that she has an ulterior motive for getting close to him.

- The members of the Batmen of All Nations—the Musketeer, Dark Ranger, El Gaucho, Raven Red, the Wingman, Man-of-Bats, the Legionary, and Knight and Squire—solve a mystery planted by the villainous organization the Black Glove.

- Jason Todd takes on the identity of Red Robin.

- Rā's al Ghūl returns to the land of the living.

- Stephanie Brown resurfaces as Spoiler, revealing to Tim Drake that she survived her encounter with Black Mask and had been recuperating in Africa.

- As Batgirl, Cassandra Cain searches for her father Cain and fights against Deathstroke's newest assassins.

- The villainous Hush returns to Gotham and shockingly removes Catwoman's heart from her chest.

- Doctor Hurt implements a plan to take down Batman, neutralizing his foe with a hypnotic trigger and forcing Bruce Wayne to become the "Batman of Zur-En-Arrh" to hold on to his sanity.

- Gotham City is rocked by the debut of the Club of Villains, whose members include the Hunchback, Pierrot Lunaire, King Kraken, Charlie Caligula, Scorpiana, and El Sombrero.

- At the end of the universe-shaking Final Crisis event, the New God Darkseid apparently annihilates Batman with his Omega Sanction beams.

- With Batman seemingly dead, his would-be successors—including Dick Grayson and Jason Todd—vie for the right to become the new Dark Knight.

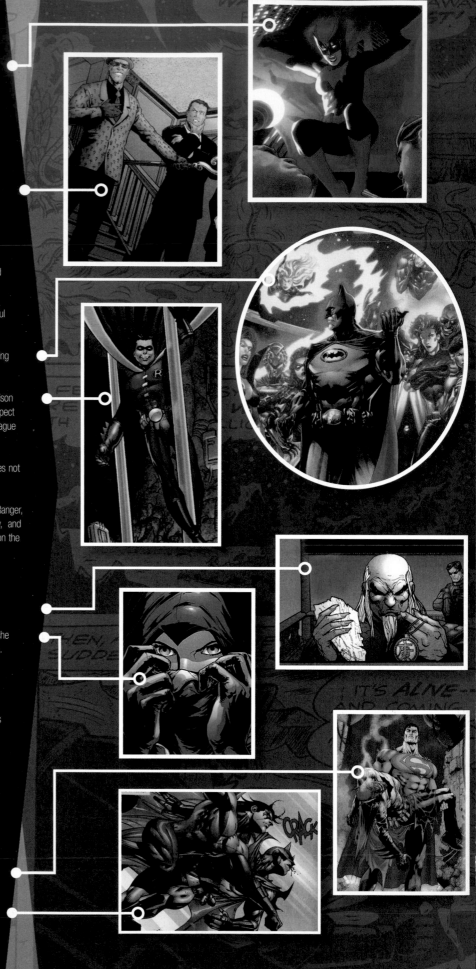

• Ex-cop Michael Washington Lane becomes the new Azrael, picking up where Jean-Paul Valley left off.

• A new Dynamic Duo emerges, with Dick Grayson as Batman and Damian Wayne as Robin. At first their partnership seems rocky, but they put aside their differences long enough to defeat the schemes of the psychotic Professor Pyg.

• Tim Drake takes up the identity of Red Robin, a role formerly filled by Jason Todd.

• Dick Grayson publicly debuts as Batman by facing off against the Scarecrow.

• Stephanie Brown becomes the latest person to wear the costume of Batgirl.

• As Black Mask and the Penguin stir up trouble, the Falcone crime family resurfaces in Gotham.

• The Green Lantern Corps faces its biggest challenge during the Blackest Night crisis. Black Lantern rings bring the corpses of dead heroes to life, including what is believed to be the body of Batman.

• Batman's dead body is revealed to be a cloned fake created by Darkseid.

• Sent back in time by Darkseid's power during the Final Crisis event, Batman embarks on a journey back to the present day. He experiences time-skips that lead him into adventures as a witch-hunter, a pirate, and a gunfighter.

• Jeremiah Arkham, administrator of the infamous madhouse, is revealed as the new Black Mask.

• A time-tossed Bruce Wayne finally returns to present-day Gotham and retakes to his role as the city's protector.

• Speaking to the news media, Bruce Wayne reveals that he has secretly funded Batman's activities for years, and announces the formation of a new global super hero team: Batman Incorporated.

• As part of his mission to recruit new heroes, Batman enlists Bilal Asselah, a French Muslim who takes the identity of Nightrunner. In the Democratic Republic of Congo, Batman recruits David Zavimbe, who assumes the costumed identity of Batwing.

• Reality is altered once again during the Flashpoint event. On a changed Earth, Dr. Thomas Wayne fights crime as Batman following the tragic murder of his son Bruce. The Flash succeeds in restoring the timeline, but some events are forever altered.

• Batman faces the threat of Gotham's oldest secret society, the Court of Owls, and the assassin called Talon.

• The hideous Dollmaker kidnaps Commissioner Gordon, spurring Batman into action.

• Father and son suit up as the Dynamic Duo, as Bruce Wayne takes the rebellious Damian Wayne under his wing.

• Barbara Gordon, now recovered from her paralysis, returns to the role of Batgirl.

• Dick Grayson takes up his Nightwing identity once more.

• Jason Todd, once again using his Red Hood identity, takes command of a new team of international operatives called the Outlaws.

Timeline

GOLDEN AGE

'30s & '40s

Amid economic depression and worldwide war, Batman emerged as a new kind of popular star: the comic book super hero.

By creating Superman and then Batman, DC inaugurated the Golden Age of Comics. Suddenly, newsstands blossomed with brightly colored covers advertising the exploits of super heroes and readers snapped them up by the millions. Under the guidance of Harry Donenfeld and Jack Liebowitz, DC built up a roster of all-stars that extended to Maxwell C. Gaines' All-American line and its own Wonder Woman, Green Lantern, and the Flash.

The collaborative efforts of writer Bill Finger and artist Bob Kane brought Batman to life in the pages of *Detective Comics* #27. After establishing himself as the lead figure in *Detective Comics*, the Dark Knight was rewarded for his staying power when he became the title's permanent cover feature and the star of a second comic book all of his own.

Batman received a sidekick, Robin, the Boy Wonder, and employed a butler named Alfred. He also attracted a Rogues Gallery that included the Joker, Catwoman, the Penguin, the Riddler, the Mad Hatter, and Hugo Strange.

Though Bob Kane received sole credit on most Batman stories of the Golden Age, Bill Finger and Kane's assistant Jerry Robinson played critical roles in spreading the Dark Knight's popularity. By the close of the 1940s, artists Dick Sprang, Lew Schwartz, and Jim Mooney were also mainstays on the Batman books.

OVERLEAF
Batman #37 (October–November 1946): The Joker was the first great comic book villain. Here, he has a Bat in his belfry, and a Robin too.

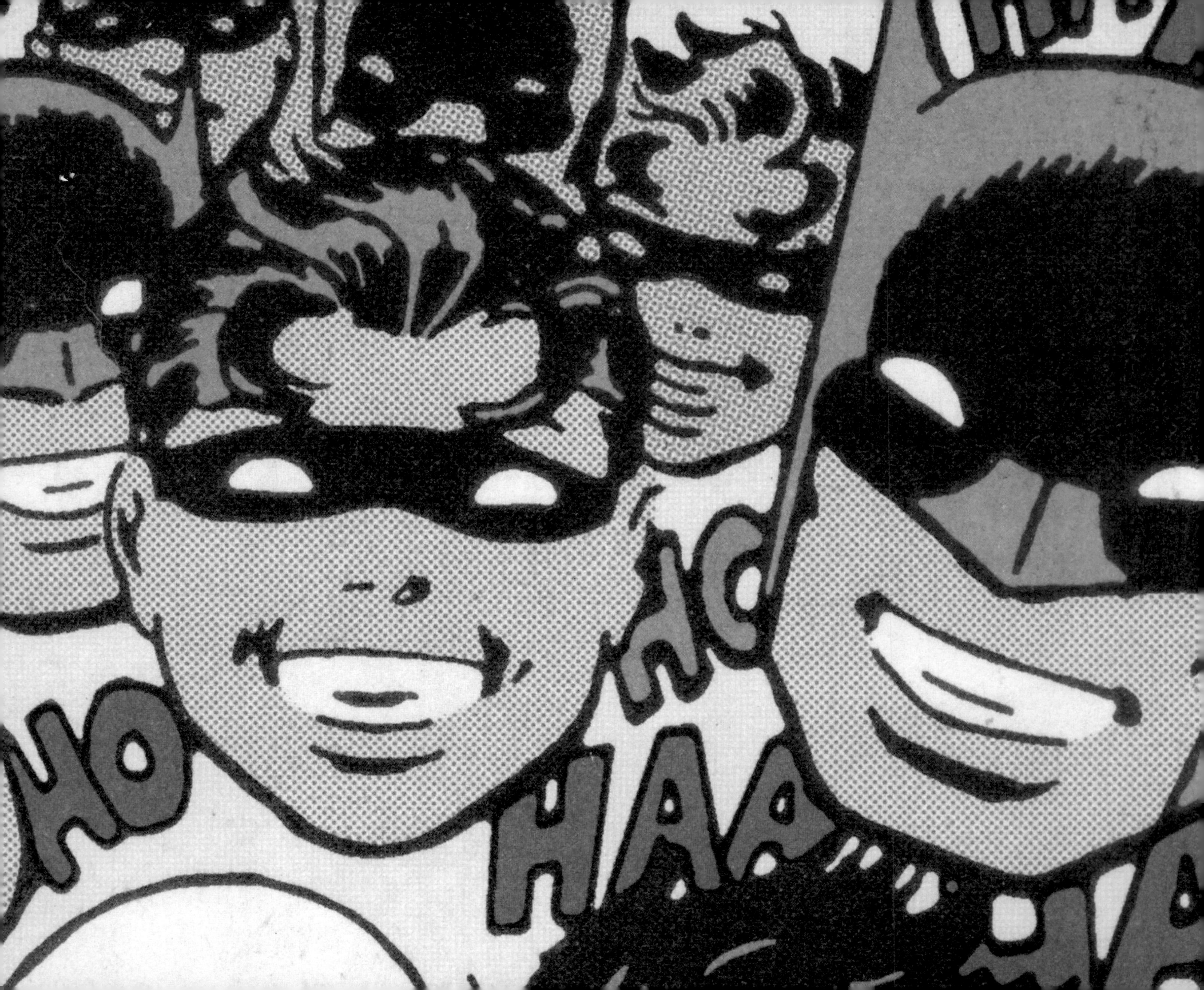
HO
HAA

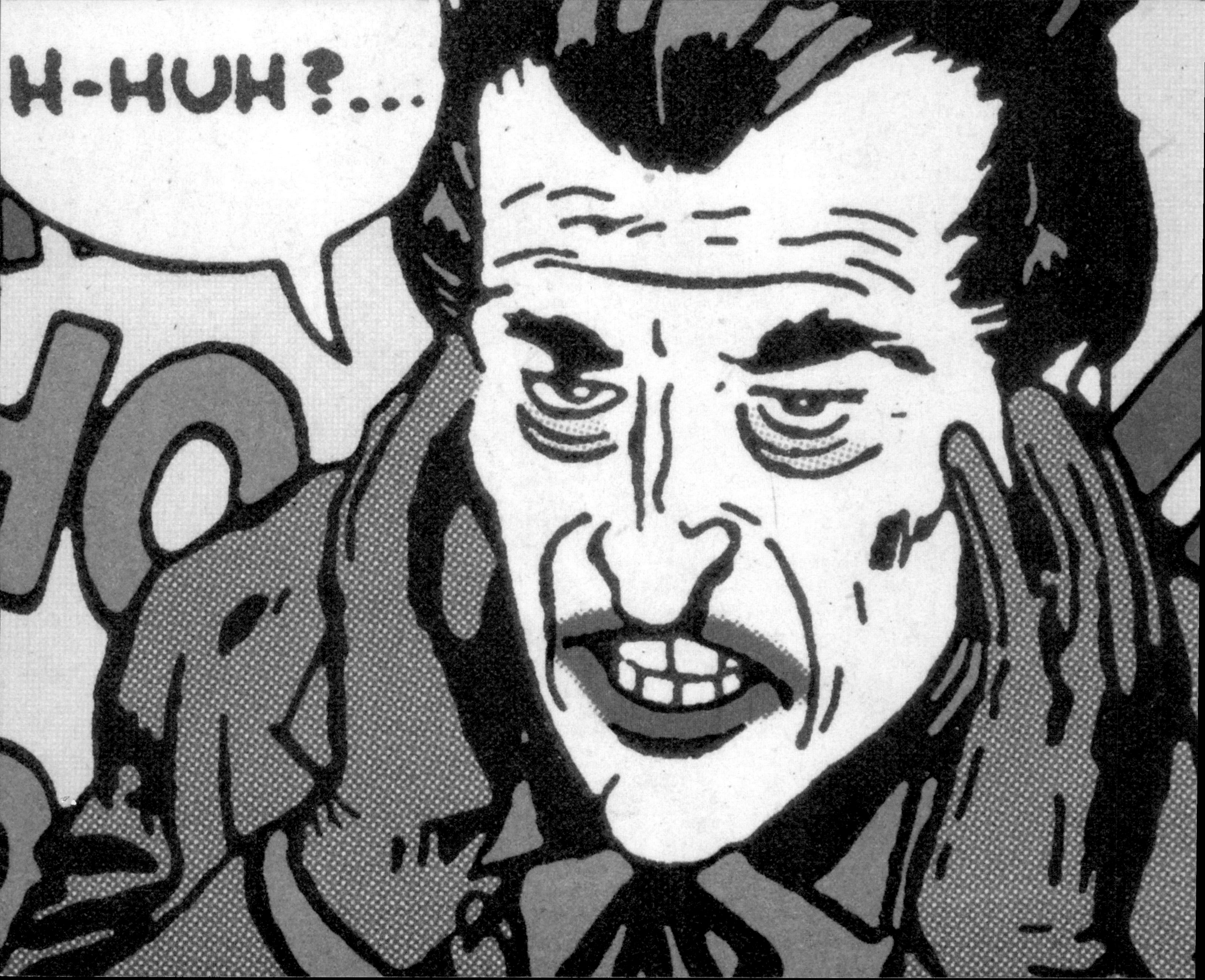
H-HUH?...

BATMAN
ISSUE #1

"You played your last hand, Joker!"

BATMAN

No.1 SPRING ISSUE

BAT MAN

10¢

ALL BRAND NEW ADVENTURES OF **THE BATMAN** AND **ROBIN,** THE BOY WONDER!

MAIN CHARACTERS: Batman, Robin, the Joker, the Cat
SUPPORTING CHARACTERS: Commissioner Gordon, Henry Claridge, Jay Wilde, Brute Nelson, Chief Chalmers, Mrs. Martha Travers
LOCATIONS: Claridge mansion, Brute Nelson's headquarters, the Joker's hideout, the Drake Museum, the Travers' yacht

BACKGROUND

With *Detective Comics'* new Batsuited hero providing a huge boost in sales during 1939, DC had few qualms about giving the Batman his own solo title the following year. *Batman #1* opened with a concise two-page origin story adapted from a similar piece in *Detective Comics #33.*

As well as recapping Batman's origins for the uninitiated, *Batman #1* also had an equally important contribution to make to the Dark Knight's comic-book canon—the development of a Rogues Gallery of colorful adversaries for Batman and Robin. The murderous Joker and the sultry "Cat"—later to be dubbed Catwoman—debuted here, expertly filling the roles of the antagonists, while leaving readers with an open-ended tease of more stories still to come.

By the conclusion of *Batman #1*, the Dark Knight's creators had established all of the essential core elements required to support a self-contained super hero mythology—one that would endure and evolve through the decades right up until the present-day.

PUBLICATION DATE
Spring 1940

EDITOR
Whitney Ellsworth

COVER ARTIST
Bob Kane

WRITER
Bill Finger

PENCILLER
Bob Kane

INKER
Jerry Robinson

LETTERER
Jerry Robinson

The Stories...

Terror gripped Gotham as a new criminal known as the Joker announced via radio broadcast that he would kill a wealthy man named Henry Claridge at the stroke of midnight and steal his heirloom diamond. The police tried to protect the target, but at 12 o'clock he fell dead with a ghastly smiile on his face **(1)**. The Joker named more victims, including Jay Wilde, owner of the Ronkers Ruby, and additional police officers were deployed as bodyguards. Their precautions proved useless as the Joker used blowguns and slow-acting poisons to turn Wilde **(2)** and later victims into grinning corpses while he stole their gems.

The gangster Brute Nelson, head of Gotham's crime scene, was irritated by the Joker's success. He vowed to get even **(3)**, but it was the Joker who arrived at Nelson's front door to kill him and claim the mantle of Gotham's crime kingpin. Batman interrupted the Joker's coup d'état, but the clown-like criminal escaped. Robin tracked the Joker to his hideout, but was captured by his grinning adversary. Batman attempted to rescue the Boy Wonder **(4)**, but the maniacal criminal unleashed a volley of bullets. This time it was the Joker's turn to be surprised, as Batman was wearing a protective bullet-proof vest beneath his costume. Soon, the Joker was behind bars **(5)**, but he escaped after he used exploding teeth to break out of his cell.

He embarked on a new killing spree—his first victim was Police Chief Chalmers, who fell dead after touching a poisoned needle in a telephone earpiece. Batman and Robin laid a trap, using a a false story about a valuable fire ruby **(6)**. The police and the Dynamic Duo ambushed the Joker when he tried to steal the gem at the Drake Museum. In a tussle with Batman, the Joker accidentally stabbed himself with his own knife **(7)**. He appeared to be dead, but as the police wagon carrying his body drove off a medic announced, "This man is alive—and he's going to live!"

Batman and Robin hit the high seas for their next adventure, in which they encountered a new adversary who would become one of their most notorious foes. When Mrs. Martha Travers, a wealthy heiress, hosted a party on her yacht **(1)**, Dick Grayson went undercover as a steward to keep an eye on her precious necklace. Dick intercepted a mysterious note signed by "the Cat," but was unable to stop the necklace from being stolen. He was then diverted from the case when a boat full of gangsters approached the yacht **(2)**. The mobsters had boarded the vessel intent on engaging in piracy. They were unable to find the necklace, but stole everything else they could lay their hands on. When they tried to shoot a man for protecting his wife, Dick stepped in to help but was knocked overboard. He used this opportunity to suit up as Robin, and before long the Boy Wonder had defeated the crooks **(3)**, with help from Batman and the new Batboat.

Meanwhile, a fire alarm interrupted a masquerade party taking place on the yacht **(4)**. An old woman was revealed to be the Cat in disguise **(5)** when her quick moves proved she wasn't as frail as she seemed **(6)**. Batman recovered the stolen necklace but was entranced by her feminine charms **(7)**. As the Dynamic Duo ferried their prisoner back to shore aboard the Batboat, the Cat tried to persuade Batman to join her in a life of crime. When Batman refused, she jumped overboard to freedom, and the Dark Knight jostled the Boy Wonder when he tried to stop her. Robin protested, but a smitten Batman was entranced by the villainess' "lovely eyes."

"I think mother and dad would like me to go on fighting crime. And as for me, well, I love adventure!"

THE DYNAMIC DUO

After losing both of his parents, Bruce Wayne found a new purpose as a crime fighter. When circus acrobat Dick Grayson suffered a similar tragedy, Bruce gave him the same chance. Gotham's crooks soon learned to fear the one-two punch of Batman and Robin!

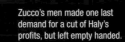
THE FLYING GRAYSONS

Zucco's men made one last demand for a cut of Haly's profits, but left empty handed.

At that evening's performance, a sabotaged rope snapped. In front of a packed crowd, John and Mary Grayson fell to their deaths.

Bruce Wayne had seen it all. Remembering his own childhood loss, he arranged for the orphaned boy to become his legal ward.

After intense training in boxing, acrobatics, jujutsu, and criminology, Dick Grayson became Robin—Batman's new partner!

TRAGEDY UNDER THE BIG TOP

Boss Zucco was one of the gangsters bleeding Gotham dry when Batman began his career. Zucco's goons tried to extort Haly's Circus for "protection" money but the owner stood firm, knowing that the Flying Graysons—husband and wife acrobats John and Mary with their young son Dick—would wow a sell-out crowd with their outstanding aerial act. But as punishment for daring to defy him, Boss Zucco chose to set an example for others by targeting the star performers.

With a bright costume that evoked both the Robin Hood legend and the red-breasted bird, Robin injected a sense of fun into Batman's grim mission.

Swinging into Action

With his small size and his costume recalling colors of the circus, Robin didn't inspire fear in thugs like Batman did. But he exploited the overconfidence of bigger and clumsier foes, outmaneuvering them with his high-wire expertise. And with Batman's training under his belt, he could punch far above his weight. After gaining experience against Catwoman, the Penguin, and other costumed crooks, Robin started taking on solo missions.

During one of their first adventures, Batman and Robin thwarted the Joker's grisly crimes.

"...And swear that we two will fight together against crime and corruption and never to swerve from the path of righteousness!"

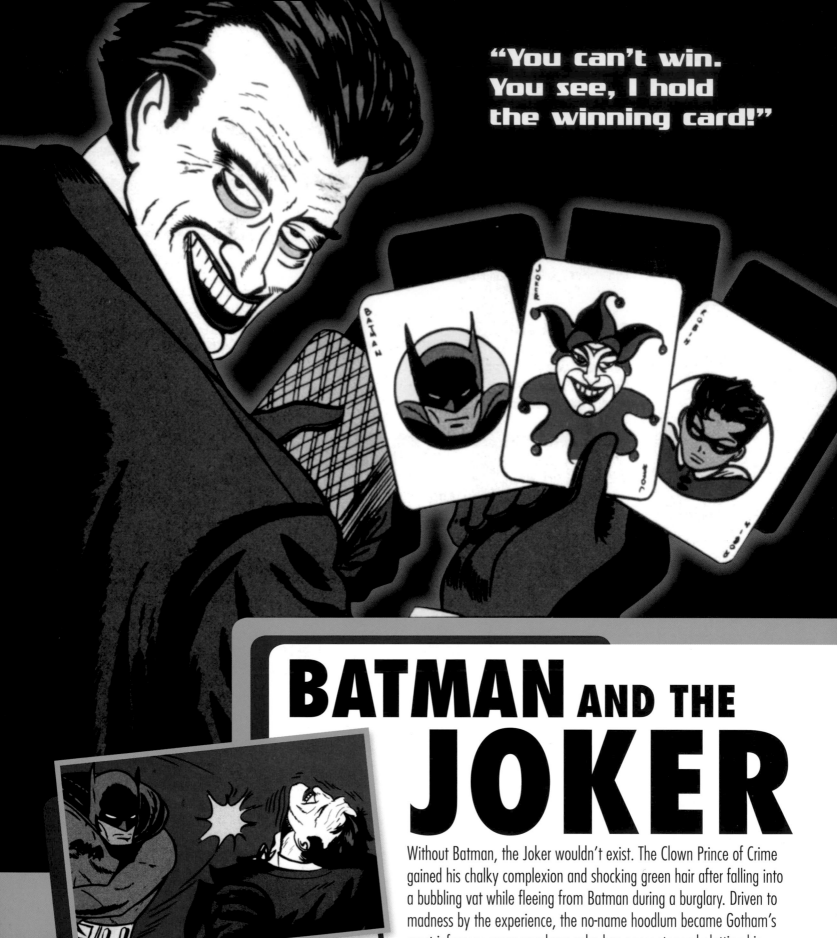

"You can't win. You see, I hold the winning card!"

BATMAN AND THE JOKER

In his first showdown with the Dark Knight, the Joker demonstrated surprising strength in one-on-one combat. But when Batman proved to be his superior, the Joker resorted to knives and guns.

Without Batman, the Joker wouldn't exist. The Clown Prince of Crime gained his chalky complexion and shocking green hair after falling into a bubbling vat while fleeing from Batman during a burglary. Driven to madness by the experience, the no-name hoodlum became Gotham's most infamous mass murderer, who has never stopped plotting his revenge. Batman and the Joker have altered their looks and methods over the years, but they still represent opposite extremes of order and chaos.

CIRCUS OF CRIME

The Joker's gruesome features have forever marked him as a clown. During one early caper, he dressed as a jester and recruited acrobats and a strongman to form a traveling circus. Giving performances at the homes of wealthy Gothamites, the Joker was in the perfect position to scope the mansions and plan after-hours robberies. Batman and Robin deduced the motive, unmasked the circus's madcap mastermind, and made short work of the Joker's carnival crew.

Demonstrating his gift for chemistry, the Joker incapacitated two guards with a gas bomb. Chemical weaponry remains one of his favorite methods.

JOKERMOBILES

Though he would deny it, the Joker has often patterned himself after the object of his obsession. In one adventure the Joker made his own utility belt, and once the Batmobile hit the streets it wasn't long before a Jokermobile followed. With his own leering face emblazoned on the vehicle's hood, the Joker cut an unmistakable path through Gotham traffic.

Not to be outdone by the Batplane, the gyro-driven Joker plane was capable of vertical ascent, taking the Joker high above Gotham City.

COMEDY OF TEARS

The Joker seemed to have become a tragedian when his thefts of autographed objects caused misery among Gotham's citizens. His goal seemed to be to make people cry, while at the same time using the stolen signatures to forge official documents and gain access to millions of dollars in valuables. In a dramatic sequence of events, Batman and Robin tracked the villain to a movie set, where they traded blows atop an artificial cliff as a studio cameraman captured their moves on film.

Continuing the chase many miles from Gotham's gray skyline, the Joker made his getaway across a sun-baked beach in a most unusual choice of vehicle—a sand sailboat, with Batman in hot pursuit.

CLAYFACE

Once, Basil Karlo was a horror-film star. But when a director passed him over in favor of a younger leading man, Karlo vowed revenge. Making himself over as the ghoulish Clayface, he wreaked havoc on the movie set until Batman and Robin brought down the curtain.

CATWOMAN

Selina Kyle's love of jewels spurred her to become a high-stakes cat burglar. Whether breaking into a penthouse apartment or raiding a luxury yacht, Catwoman was a constant headache for the G.C.P.D. She and Batman have engaged in opposites-attract flirtation ever since their first meeting.

THE PENGUIN

Batman refused to believe that oddball Oswald Cobblepot could be a master criminal until he swiped two priceless paintings from an art museum by hiding them in his umbrella. Cobblepot then shot a mobster and took over his gang, renaming himself the Penguin. He carried an impressive array of umbrellas capable of spraying stun gas or squirting acid.

ENTER THE VILLAINS

Is Batman to blame for the riot of colorful characters who commit crimes in Gotham? Maybe not, but it's hard to escape the conclusion that many of them would not be in their current roles if the Dark Knight hadn't paved the way. Catwoman was one of the first to emulate Batman and don a costume, and soon the city exploded with thieves laying claim to nicknames and crime gimmicks. Before long, Batman had an entire gallery of rogues!

JERVIS TETCH

The Mad Hatter chose to pattern himself after the *Alice in Wonderland* character. Initially he focused on nabbing treasures like the Gotham City Yacht Club's trophy, but in time he expanded his racket to include mind-control through microelectronics. This greatly increased his ranking among the most wanted criminals of Gotham City.

THE RIDDLER

Edward Nigma, also known as the Riddler, valued intellectual challenges more than monetary rewards. When the G.C.P.D. failed to solve his puzzles, the Riddler realized that only the World's Greatest Detective could be his peer. The Riddler left clues for Batman to decipher, deploying both clever wordplay and larger-than-life death traps.

TWO-FACE

After Harvey Dent suffered the physical and psychological scarring that transformed him into Two-Face, he based every decision on the flip of a coin. At first, this obsession led to equal amounts of good and bad actions—Two-Face might rob a bank one day, and donate his loot to charity the next. Some Gothamites hailed him as a hero, but in time his evil side grew to be the stronger.

SCARECROW

Professor Jonathan Crane taught a course on the psychology of fear, before realizing that terror could be used as a weapon for gaining power and riches. He dressed in a Scarecrow costume to frighten his victims, and if that didn't work he shot them with a handgun. As the legend of the Scarecrow grew, Crane began to employ his trademark hallucinatory fear gas to ensure he gave his victims nightmares.

BATMAN
ISSUE #16

"I have known since last night that you were the Batman and Robin, but I saw no reason to mention it till now."

ALFRED BEAGLE

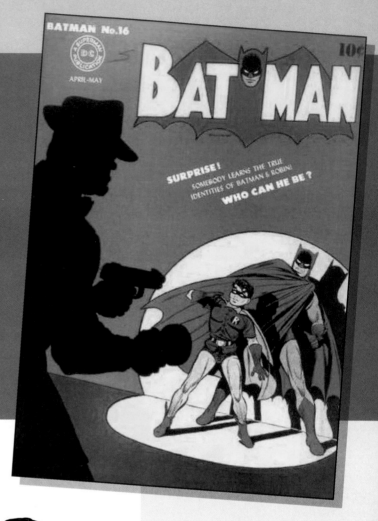

MAIN CHARACTERS: Batman, Robin, Alfred Beagle
SUPPORTING CHARACTERS: Gaston LeDuc, Manuel Stiletti, Pablo, Thomas
LOCATIONS: Gotham City pier, Wayne Manor, the Batcave, abandoned Gotham theater

BACKGROUND

Where would Batman be without Alfred? The unflappable British butler is Batman's confidante, helpmate, emergency surgeon, and father figure. However, Alfred started out in comics as a rotund comic-relief character who arrived on the boat from England to provide readers with laughs, heightening the contrast between his own well-meaning bumbling and the Caped Crusaders' derring-do. "Here Comes Alfred," one of several stories packed into *Batman* #16, not only introduced the character as a proper gentleman (the son of a butler named Jarvis, no less), it also had him discover Batman and Robin's secret identities, granting Alfred unique influence in their exploits. As the Dynamic Duo became a trio, Alfred (given the last name Beagle, later becoming Pennyworth) linked Batman's double life of nocturnal vigilantism and the public façade required of a wealthy and well-known man of leisure. Within a year of his debut, Alfred received a thinner, mustachioed makeover and later, a new backstory as a guiding presence in Batman's life since childhood.

PUBLICATION DATE
April–May 1943

EDITOR
Whitney Ellsworth

COVER ARTIST
Jerry Robinson

WRITER
Don Cameron

PENCILER
Bob Kane

INKER
Jerry Robinson

LETTERER
George Roussos

The Story...

Batman and Robin don't think they need a butler, but when Alfred discovers their secret identities, he becomes the only person who can save them from a gang of international crooks.

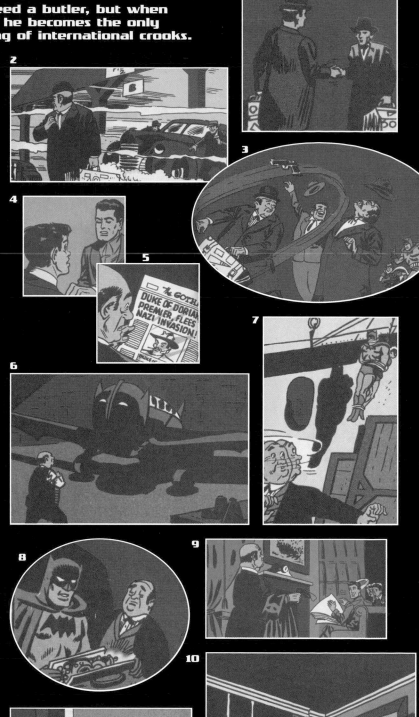

Alfred Beagle had a habit of attracting trouble wherever he went, and as he disembarked from an English freighter at Gotham City docks, things were no different. Alfred fancied himself to be an amateur detective and he was casting a suspicious eye on his fellow passenger Gaston LeDuc **[1]** when a gang of thugs led by Manuel Stiletti attempted to steal his suitcase **[2]**. Batman and Robin rushed to break up the would-be robbery **[3]** but turned down Alfred's offer to help track the crooks when they made a fast getaway.

Back at Wayne Manor, Batman and Robin were shedding their costumes to assume their civilian identities of Bruce Wayne and Dick Grayson **[4]** when they were interrupted by a knock at the door. It was Alfred again! The pair were astonished that the newcomer had somehow deduced their identities, but were reassured of his ignorance when Alfred announced his intention to serve as the Wayne household's butler, as his father had done before him. Bruce remembered Alfred's father from the past and didn't have the heart to turn Alfred away.

As night came, Alfred read a news story about the exiled Duke of Dorian, who had fled an invasion in his homeland, and recognized him as his shipmate Gaston LeDuc **[5]**. Meanwhile, the Stiletti gang tracked Alfred down to Wayne Manor. The gang tried again to nab his luggage, but Batman and Robin foiled the act once more. Concerned that his employers, Bruce and Dick, might have awoken from their slumber in all the racket, Alfred went to check on them and stumbled across a hidden tunnel that led to the Batcave. Alfred was awed to find he was working for Gotham's most famous crime fighters! **[6]**

At that moment, Batman and Robin were far from the Batcave. They had followed the Stiletti gang to an abandoned theater, where the gang swiftly captured them, tying them together with heavy ropes. The villains suspended the Caped Crusaders high above the theater's stage floor **[7]** then drove across town to find Gaston LeDuc. It turned out that Alfred's suitcase provided coded clues—sent from the crooks' overseas accomplice—which would lead them to LeDuc's location. LeDuc was indeed the exiled Duke of Dorian and he was carrying the priceless crown jewels of his homeland—something Manuel Stiletti and his gang were keen to get their hands on.

The gang took the Duke of Dorian prisoner and returned to the theater. They intended to burn it to the ground with Batman, Robin, and the Duke inside, eliminating the witnesses and destroying all evidence of their crimes in a single fiery blaze. However, Alfred had picked up on Batman and Robin's trail and soon arrived at the theater to free the crime fighters from their bonds. In short order, the crooks were collared and the crown jewels returned to their rightful guardian **[8]**.

The next evening, as Alfred attended to his duties at Wayne Manor, he spotted the Bat-Signal in the night sky. Without a word, he brought Bruce Wayne and Dick Grayson their Batman and Robin costumes, each of them impeccably cleaned and freshly pressed **[9]**. The two were flabbergasted, but with their secret in the open they realized there was little point in denying the truth **[10]**. In fact, they admitted that an accomplice to run the household and deflect attention from their curious schedules could prove a blessing. With a new respect for Alfred's sharp mind, the Dynamic Duo donned their uniforms **[11]** and took off to solve Gotham's latest crisis.

WORLD'S FINEST

Among the first super heroes to emerge onto the global stage, Batman and Superman have set the tone for all the heroes who have followed. Though their approaches couldn't be more different — Batman is a secretive Gotham vigilante, while Superman is the reassuring public face of Metropolis — the two forged a close friendship very early in their careers. This bond of trust even extends to their secret identities, allowing Bruce Wayne and Clark Kent to visit one another as professional colleagues. When World War II broke out in 1939, the world needed the two super hero friends more than ever.

The U.S.'s true heroes in the fight against the Axis were the members of its military forces. Batman, Robin, and Superman never failed to salute the Army, Navy, Marines, and Air Force for their service and sacrifices. During the war, the three super heroes usually remained stateside, where they boosted morale and busted enemy spy rings.

LIFE DURING WARTIME

As the Golden Age took hold, bank robberies in Gotham City soon took a back seat to the movements of a tyrant's armies in Europe. When Hitler's tanks rolled into Poland, Batman and Superman got ready to do their part in defending international freedom against the Axis powers of Germany and its allies. In 1940, even before the United States entered into the war, the two heroes aided their country's allies by capturing Nazi saboteurs in besieged Great Britain.

Other heroes joined their cause, and soon their numbers had swelled to the point where a super heroic strike force could arise. Batman and Superman signed on as reserve members of the Justice Society of America, serving alongside the Green Lantern, the Atom, and the Flash. Following Japan's attack on Pearl Harbor in 1941, Batman and Superman joined a second super hero team, the All-Star Squadron, and found themselves on the same side as military legends like the Blackhawks and Sergeant Rock's Easy Company.

Post-war, Batman and Superman continued their unofficial partnership. They quashed the villain team-ups of the Joker and Lex Luthor, and shut down all-new foes like the Composite Superman. The most recent timeline shakeup has placed many of Batman and Superman's adventures from this era onto the parallel world of Earth-2.

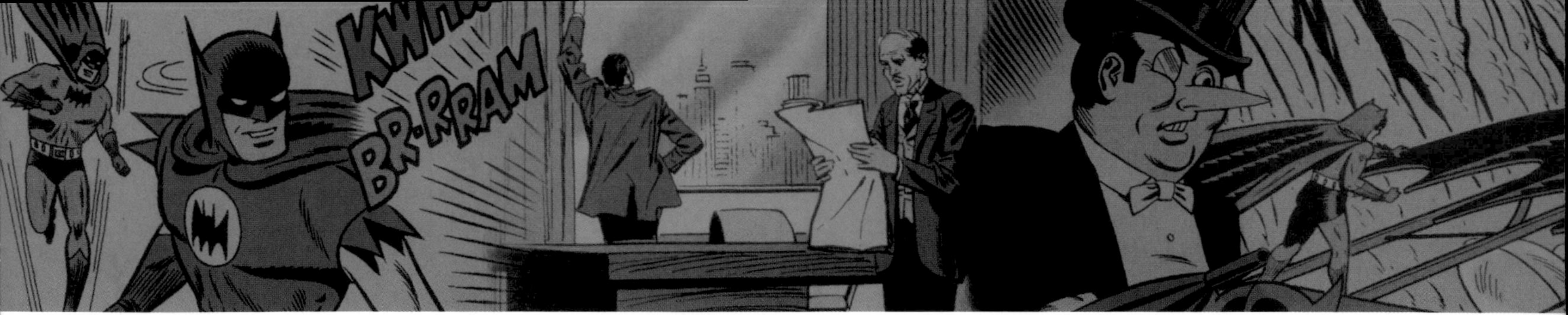
BR-RRAM

SILVER AGE

'50s & '60s

Batman found new fame in the Silver Age of Comics—but the popularity may have cost him his edge.

By the 1950s, masked vigilantes had become passé. But Batman is one of the few super heroes who never went out of style. While other super heroes' titles folded, replaced by comics starring cops, cowboys, funny animals, and lovelorn teens, Batman remained in continuous print—but he did change dramatically all the same.

Under the leadership of DC editor Jack Schiff, Batman became an unlikely sci-fi star. His adventures now came complete with aliens, robots, and radioactive freaks, and he regularly teamed up with Superman in *World's Finest Comics*.

The evolution of the Dark Knight also affected his supporting cast. Kathy Kane arrived on the scene as the first Batwoman, with her niece Betty Kane as Bat-Girl. These opposite-gender counterparts to Batman and Robin rounded out what became known as the Batman family, which also included the crime-fighting dog, Ace the Bat-Hound.

This tonal shift wasn't merely a sign of shifting public tastes. Psychologist Fredric Wertham's alarmist essays on a purported link between comic books and juvenile delinquency prompted Senate hearings and the creation of the self-regulatory Comics Code Authority. Prohibiting comic books containing "gore, sexual innuendo, or excessive violence," the CCA effectively quashed anything that might be considered envelope-pushing.

When *Batman* sales declined, editor Julius Schwartz was brought in to give the series a more modern, realistic new look spearheaded by artist Carmine Infantino. Stripped of the science-fiction elements and extended Batman family, the revamped series was a critical success, and Schwartz prepared to take the character back to his dark roots as the 1960s abated.

OVERLEAF
Detective Comics #252
(February 1958):
Dinosaurs? No problem!
Batman dispatches a toothy
foe in another colorful
Silver Age adventure.

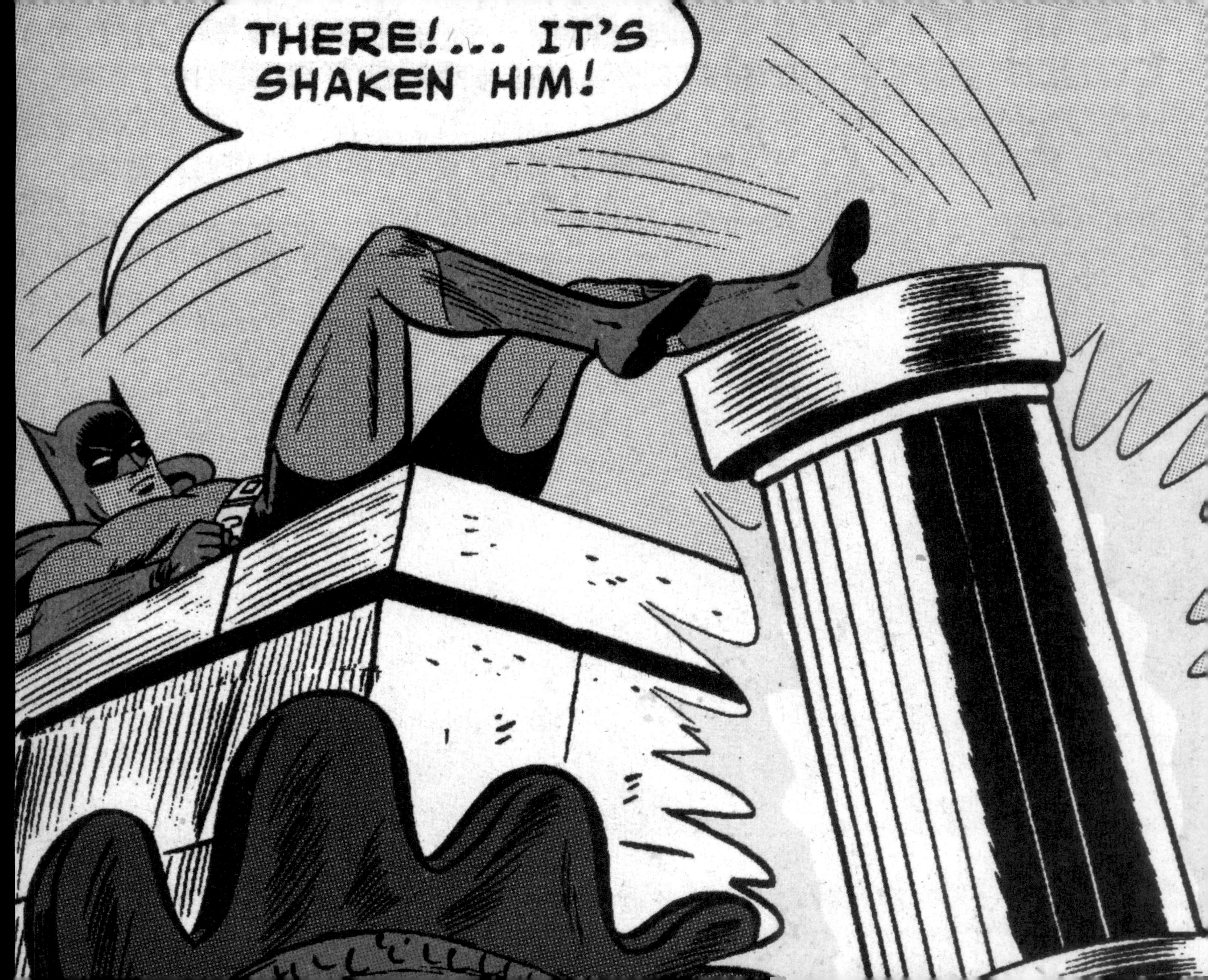
THERE!... IT'S SHAKEN HIM!

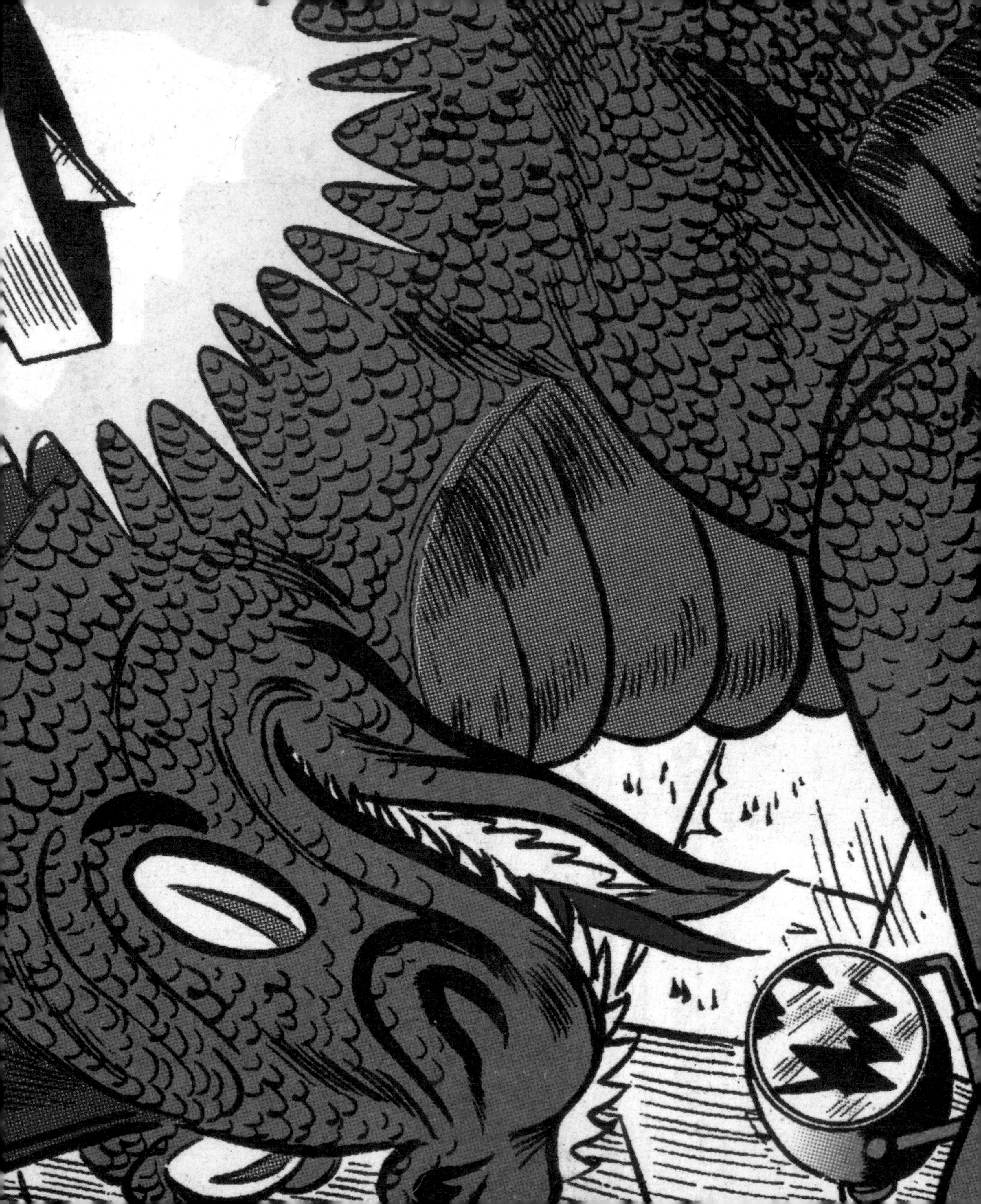

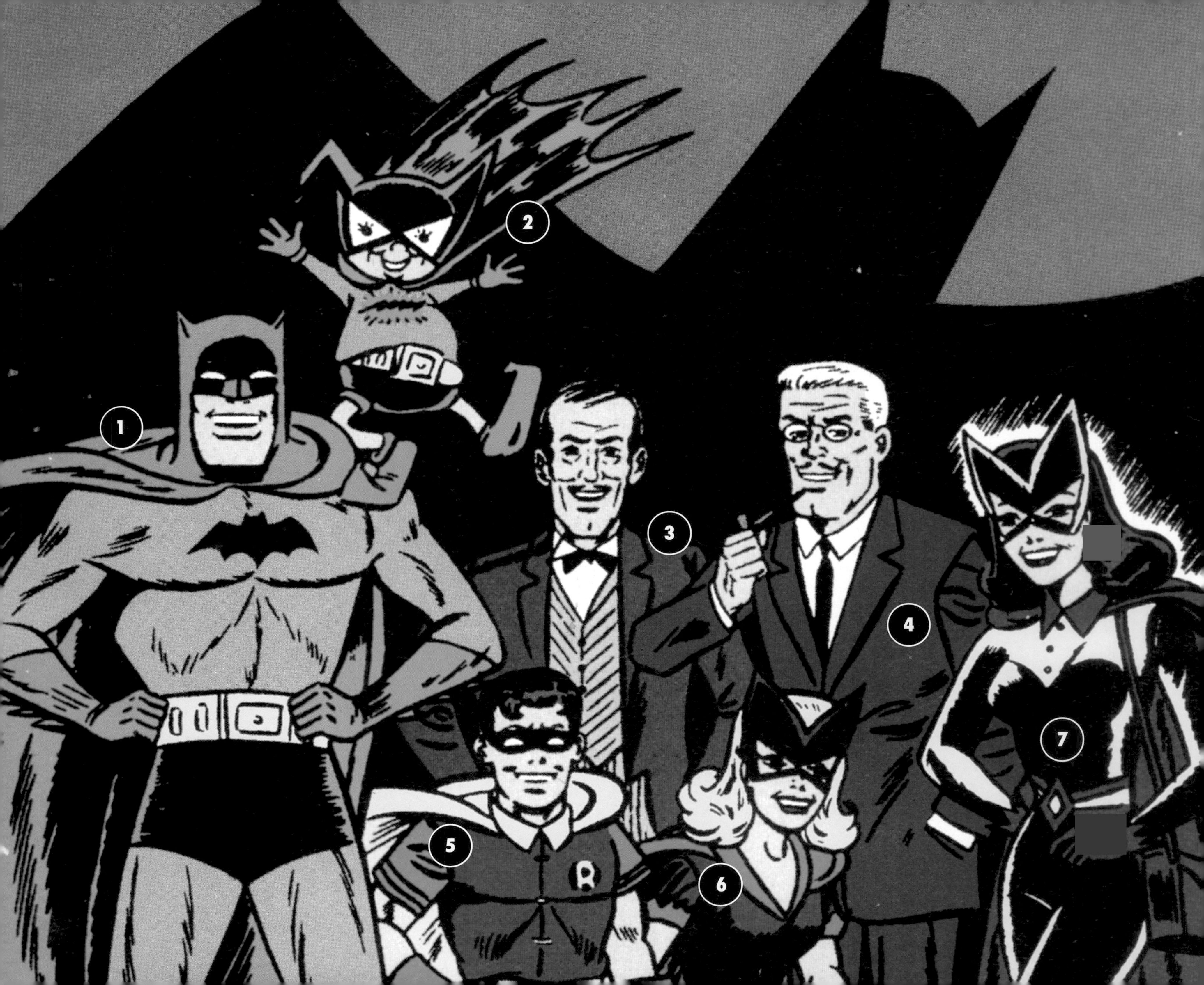
1
2
3
4
5
6
7
R

THE BATMAN FAMILY

After emerging as Gotham's champion, Batman rapidly became an inspiration to many others. Before long he had gathered around him a group of allies so fiercely loyal that they became known as the Batman Family. Robin was the first, but before long circus performer Kathy Kane and her niece Betty followed his example to become the original Batwoman and Bat-Girl. Commissioner Gordon of the Gotham City Police Department had already been welcomed into the fold, as had Alfred Pennyworth—perhaps the Dark Knight's most trusted ally of all. More unusual members of the Batman Family included the German Shepherd Ace the Bat-Hound and a strange being from another Dimension who called himself Bat-Mite.

1 BATMAN
2 BAT-MITE
3 ALFRED
4 COMMISSIONER GORDON
5 ROBIN
6 BAT-GIRL (BETTY KANE)
7 BATWOMAN (KATHY KANE)
8 ACE THE BAT-HOUND

BATMAN
ISSUE #113

"That's because I'm the Batman of Zur-En-Arrh! Through a powerful telescope I've observed your every action!"

BATMAN OF ZUR-EN-ARRH

MAIN CHARACTERS: Batman, Batman of Zur-En-Arrh (Tlano)
SUPPORTING CHARACTERS: None
LOCATIONS: Wayne Manor, replica Batcave of Zur-En-Arrh, capital city of Zur-En-Arrh

BACKGROUND

By the late 1950s, DC had a host of comics on the shelves that spanned every genre from the Wild West to romance. Nonetheless, the company's only ironclad superstars were Batman and Superman. The Man of Steel had arrived first, and now, as the Silver Age of Comics took hold, he was leading the way into a new era of sci-fi strangeness.

Superman and Batman had teamed up in every issue of *World's Finest Comics* since 1954. For the first few years, their adventures were mostly earthbound, but they were soon influenced by the increasing popularity of science fiction and monster movies. Green-skinned aliens, killer androids, and many other oddities that fit in on Superman's beat began showing up more often in Batman's series.

In "Batman—The Superman of Planet X" the similarities between the two heroes are made plain. Brought to an alien world where he possesses abilities far beyond those of mortal men, Batman experiences space fantasy wish-fulfillment far removed from the back alleys of Gotham City. Although firmly a product of its time, this story was remembered fondly by writer Grant Morrison, who layered many elements into his 2008 saga "Batman R.I.P." In this story, Batman's memories of Zur-En-Arrh were reimagined as delusions created by Bruce's strained psyche.

PUBLICATION DATE
February 1958

EDITOR
Jack Schiff

COVER ARTIST
Sheldon Moldoff

WRITER
Ed Herron

PENCILLER
Dick Sprang

INKER
Charles Paris

LETTERER
Milton Snapinn

The Story...

On the alien world of Zur-En-Arrh, Batman becomes a superpowered defender and an inspiration to millions of extraterrestrials.

Seized by an inexplicable need to suit up and take the Batplane out for a spin **[1]**, Batman suspected he might be the victim of hypnosis. But the appearance of a blinding light **[2]** heralded something even stranger—a trip halfway across the galaxy! This world was one that Batman had never seen, but a man in a modified Batsuit was there to greet him **[3]**. The man informed Batman that he had been teleported to the planet Zur-En-Arrh, where the population was kept safe thanks to the example that Batman himself had set. I lis host was a scientist named Tlano, who explained that he had long watched the Dark Knight's escapades through a telescope. In time he had chosen to model himself after his idol, becoming the Batman of Zur-En-Arrh.

The extraterrestrial hero gave Batman a tour of his replica Batcave, which housed an atomic-powered Batmobile, a rocket-shaped Batplane, and a remarkable piece of equipment called the Bat-radia **[4]**. Using Tlano's futuristic science, the Bat-radia interacted with atmospheric molecules. Its energies could stall the getaway vehicles of fleeing crooks and create many other amazing effects.

Batman was shown a tele-view screen which brought grim news—invaders from a neighboring planet were advancing on Zur-En-Arrh's capital city. Tlano chose this moment to spring another surprise, drawing a ray-gun and firing it at Batman's chest. The shots bounced away harmlessly **[5]**. Just as Superman gained amazing abilities when exposed to Earth's yellow sun and lower gravity, so Batman found that he possessed similar powers on Zur-En-Arrh. An astonished Dark Knight verified that he could bend girders with his bare hands **[6]** and even fly like a bird **[7]**. On Zur-En-Arrh, he had become like the Man of Steel.

The tele-view screen warned them that the enemy had deployed ray-cannons, which were spewing jets of flame to dry up Zur-En-Arrh's reservoirs and force its people to surrender or face a catastrophic drought. Batman leapt into action, using a chunk of metal to swat aside deadly nuclear orbs **[8]**. The invaders retaliated with their best soldiers, but they crumpled beneath Batman's mighty fists. Switching tactics, the warriors suddenly vanished! Batman retreated to the duplicate Batcave where he learned that the invaders had deployed giant robots to wreak havoc in the capital city **[9]**.

The Dark Knight discovered that the robots also had invisibility fields, but Tlano used the Bat-radia to turn the robots visible once more. Rushing to the scene in his Batplane, Tlano issued a molecular shower from the Bat-radia that overloaded the robots' stealth screens. The enemy's secret weapons were exposed for Batman's counterattack **[10]**. Batman located a ray-beam tower and pulled it into a mile-long strand of wire. He fashioned a gigantic lasso and ensnared the robots, tossing them to the ground as the invaders fled to their ships.

With the planet of Zur-En-Arrh safe from its foes, Tlano prepared to reverse the teleport beam and send his hero home. "It has been fun playing Superman on your planet," admitted Batman, confident that Zur-En-Arrh would stay secure under the watch of its own native super hero. Before he was beamed back to Gotham, Batman accepted a souvenir— the Bat-radia of Zur-En-Arrh would make a fine addition to the Batcave's trophy room.

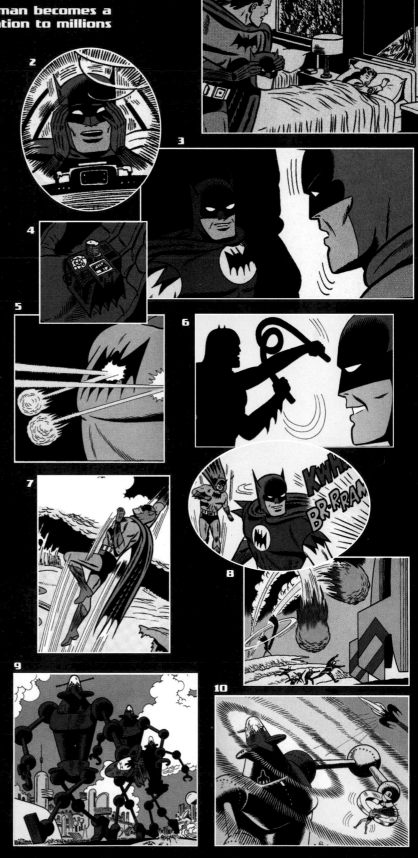

BATTLING BACK

During the years she spent without the use of her legs, Barbara had no reason to believe she would ever walk again. Yet she kept her upper body in top shape and put her brilliant mind to work as Oracle, ensuring her fighting spirit never left her.

The cape is a vital part of Batgirl's costume, creating a billowing silhouette that confuses crooks.

Batgirl is at home taking to the night skies of Gotham City and loves the life of a costumed vigilante.

Batgirl's mask lacks the white eyepieces of Batman's cowl but contains advanced audio sensors.

It took nothing short of a miracle and intense physical therapy for Barbara Gordon to regain the use of her legs after her injury.

INJURED PARTY

Barbara Gordon had been relaxing at home with a mug of cocoa on the fateful evening when she answered the door to the Joker. The Joker gave her no time to react before shooting her.

KEY DATA

REAL NAME *Barbara Gordon*

OCCUPATION *Crime fighter, computer expert, forensic psychologist*

WEAPONS/ POWERS/ ABILITIES *Batarangs, Utility Belt gadgets, martial artist, photographic memory, unrivaled skill in hacking and controlling computer networks*

AFFILIATIONS *Suicide Squad, Birds of Prey*

RELATIVES *Barbara Kean Gordon (mother), James Gordon (father), James Gordon Jr. (brother)*

FIRST APPEARANCE DETECTIVE COMICS #359 (January 1967)

> "Feeling a creep crumble beneath my feet? I didn't even know how much I missed it."
>
> BATGIRL

BATGIRL

Batgirl's back! Barbara Gordon was always the exuberant high-flyer of the Batman family, until the Joker brought her down to earth with a bullet to the spine. After a long rehabilitation, Barbara has proudly retaken the identity she first made famous.

Commissioner Gordon worries for his daughter's safety but he is proud of her rehabilitation and her inner strength.

NEVER GIVE IN

The adopted daughter of Gotham City Police Commissioner James Gordon, Barbara Gordon followed her father into crime fighting in a way he never expected! Inspired by the Dynamic Duo, Barbara invented the identity of Batgirl in her teenage years and snuck out every night to battle villains like Killer Moth. Her father never knew the truth, and Barbara always made it home in time to pursue her studies in forensic psychology.

Barbara's costumed capers came to a sudden end when the Joker shot her during a raid to kidnap Commissioner Gordon. Left without the use of her legs, Barbara tapped her near-photographic memory into a new career as the mysterious Oracle. With her ability to hack into surveillance cameras and unlock classified military databases, Oracle became an indispensible asset to super heroes around the globe. As Oracle, Barbara briefly served with the covert government strike team Suicide Squad and later built a state-of-the-art headquarters inside a Gotham clock tower. She also recruited Black Canary as her primary field operative, eventually teaming her with the Huntress as the three of them informally became known as the crime-fighting team Birds of Prey.

During Barbara's time as Oracle, three others filled the Batgirl role. The Huntress briefly wore a stealthy version of the Batgirl costume before it was passed to Cassandra Cain. Raised by one of the world's deadliest assassins, Cassandra is now the heroic Black Bat. Stephanie Brown, who was also Robin for a time, tried her hand as Batgirl but now fights crime under her original identity, the Spoiler.

When Barbara regained her mobility, it wasn't long before Gotham City welcomed Batgirl's return. Though still haunted by the memory of the Joker's violence, Batgirl is one of the few heroes with an intellect that surpasses her amazing physical skills.

Years of unarmed combat training have allowed Batgirl to take on enemies many times her size and weight.

Stephanie Brown became Batgirl for a time following a brief turn as Robin.

Cassandra Cain used her martial-arts upbringing to become a silent, terrifying Batgirl.

Batgirl has a close—but competitive—relationship with Nightwing, who she has known since she was a teenager.

As Oracle, Barbara learned to fight from a sitting position. She is a trained martial artist and an excellent hand-to-hand combatant.

DETECTIVE COMICS
ISSUE #275

"Since he smashed my machine, he'll never be free! Batman's a prisoner of the force-lines now!"

ZEBRA-MAN

**MAIN CHARACTERS: Batman, Robin, Zebra-Man
SUPPORTING CHARACTERS: Commissioner Gordon,
Jo-Jo Forbes, Tommy (a child)
LOCATIONS: Gotham Art Museum, the Batcave,
the Gotham waterfront, Zebra-Man's hideout,
Gotham Storage Company**

BACKGROUND

Who says Batman can't have fun? In the Silver Age of comics, even the Dark Knight got light-hearted once in a while. "The Zebra Batman" was typical of the outlandish fare increasingly found in American super hero comics after the introduction of the Comics Code Authority (CCA), which stamped out horror, gore, and sexual innuendo in comics. It all began in 1954, when psychologist Dr. Fredric Wertham's testimony before Congress on the evils of comic books made the industry's self-regulation a foregone conclusion. After that, writers like Bill Finger could no longer present Batman as a noirish vigilante. Instead, he slowly became a Gotham celebrity who did most of his work during daylight hours and operated as a deputized member of the police department. This Batman was equally at home starring in ticker-tape parades or sending giant gorillas packing. Brightly lit and quirkily imaginative, the comics of this era were like no Batman stories seen before or since.

PUBLICATION DATE
January 1960

EDITOR
Jack Schiff

COVER ARTIST
Sheldon Moldoff

WRITER
Bill Finger

PENCILER
Sheldon Moldoff

INKER
Charles Paris

The Story...

What happens when Batman becomes Zebra-Batman? The Caped Crusader deals with some truly weird science during one of his strangest cases.

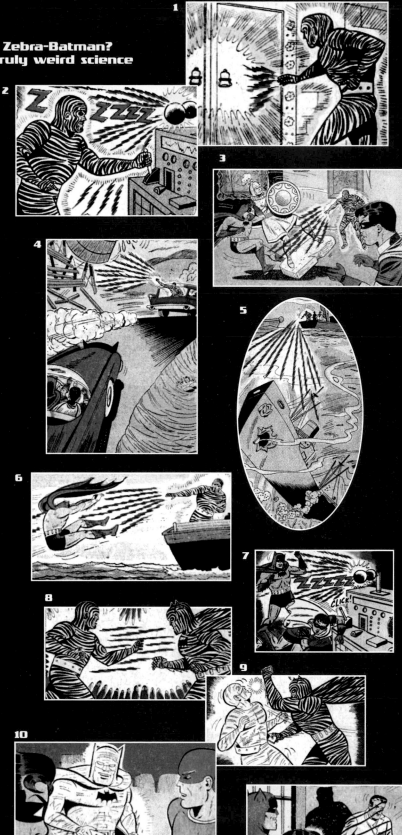

During a heist on the Gotham Art Museum, a new Gotham villain appeared on the scene. He called himself Zebra-Man, but the black-and-white stripes of his costume didn't indicate his love of African safaris. Instead, Zebra-Man was marked with "lines of force," similar to those emanating invisibly from the tips of a magnet **[1]**.

With his body infused with energy from a machine of his own design **[2]** and a device on his belt capable of modulating that energy, Zebra-Man could repel or attract any object, no matter how heavy. During the heist, he used his magnetic powers to make off with the art museum's masterpieces. When Batman and Robin tried to stop him, Zebra-Man humiliated them, nudging a huge statue into their path **[3]** and toppling a water tower to prevent them from pursuing him in the Batmobile **[4]**.

The next day, Batman tracked Zebra-Man and his gang to the Gotham waterfront. Zebra-Man had purchased a boat and, using his strange abilities, was beginning to raise a sunken freighter loaded with a cargo of gold bullion from the bottom of the bay **[5]**. When Batman tried to interfere by boarding Zebra-Man's boat, he was thrown overboard for his trouble **[6]**. Batman staged a flyover in the Batplane but it proved disastrous when Zebra-Man tossed the raised freighter in the air, clipping the Batplane's wings and forcing him to make an emergency water landing.

Things started to look up for the Dynamic Duo when they discovered the muddy footprint of one of Zebra-Man's henchmen. A quick analysis of the soil identified the location of Zebra-Man's remote hideout. Batman and Robin rushed to apprehend their foe in his lair, but in the scuffle that ensued Batman accidentally irradiated himself with Zebra-Man's machine **[7]**, turning him into a Zebra Batman!

Zebra-Man left the scene, confident that Batman would never undo his curse and catch him, while Batman began to come to terms with the reality of his condition as a living anti-charge. Without the modulating device that Zebra-Man wore on his belt to suppress the uncontrollable lines of magnetic force, Batman repelled every object he reached for. He was trapped by his own energy! A troubled Batman wandered away alone trying to collect his thoughts, but at an industrial junkyard, the sight of a heavy-duty electromagnet gave him an idea.

Batman made fresh preparations to draw out Zebra-Man. As the villain robbed a cargo of rare furs at the Gotham Storage Company, Batman and Robin leaped from hiding. The overconfident villain dismissed the monochromatic Dark Knight as a mere annoyance, but then suddenly found himself hurtling toward Batman at great speed **[8]**. As the two figures came together, Batman greeted his enemy with a fist to the jaw **[9]**.

After retrieving Zebra-Man's belt device and restoring his natural pigmentation, Batman pointed out that science provided the key to victory **[10]**. Inspired by the scrapyard's electromagnet, he had deduced that if similar charges repelled each other, he needed only to invert Zebra-Man's own lines of force to make them attract each other. "Knowing you were coming here," he explains, "I charged that manhole cover so that it would reverse your force field, making it opposite to mine!" Thanks to the "opposites attract" principle, Batman and Robin won the day. They left Zebra-Man to contemplate the basic laws of science from behind prison bars **[11]**.

THE SILVER AGE

Rays of daylight seemed to illuminate Batman's shadowy world during this era, as new friends joined his quest and Gotham City welcomed him with open arms. The villains of the Rogues Gallery gave him a break too: even the Joker abandoned mass murder and embraced harmless theatrical crimes. At the same time, Gotham became a magnet for otherworldly weirdness, with aliens touching down nearly every day and giant robots striding through town. This period wouldn't last, but it was a lighthearted and unexpected diversion.

THE BATPLANE

THE WHIRLY-BAT

BAT-GADGETS AND GIZMOS

Batman increased his daytime visibility as he took to patrolling Gotham in vehicles of all shapes and sizes. New, sleek designs for the Batplane took wing as Batman implemented Wayne Enterprises' latest technological advances. The Whirly-Bat, another product of aerial experimentation, gave Batman a whole new vantage point on crime fighting, and the bulletproof Batmobile evolved into a near-tank with a steel-reinforced bat-symbol that doubled as a battering ram.

BATMOBILE

A crash in the old Batmobile broke Batman's leg but gave him a great excuse to bring in a sleek new vehicle.

FAMILY LIFE

Kathy Kane and Betty Kane didn't remain in the roles of Batwoman and Bat-Girl for long, but they showed Batman that he could accept help from people besides Robin. With Ace the Bat-Hound rounding out his odd family unit, Batman received newfound public praise and earned law-enforcement legitimacy as a deputized officer of the G.C.P.D. The Batman Family welcomed its final member when a tiny extra-dimensional being with reality-shaping powers adopted the name of Bat-Mite.

Bat-Mite always meant well, but he usually underestimated his own strength. After blessing Bat-Girl with temporary superpowers to help her to win Robin's heart, Bat-Mite discovered that his meddling only placed her in jeopardy.

As Robin matured and grew in strength and experience, he started flying solo without Batman on hand to back him up. While routing the criminals who sought to exploit a teachers' strike, the Boy Wonder succeeded in disarming one thug with a flying kick.

FREAKY FOES

As their city experienced an outbreak of science fiction-tinged weirdness, the citizens of Gotham grew accustomed to the sight of 35-foot mechanical men. The "all hands on deck" emergencies created by such unfamiliar threats required the contributions of every member of Batman's family of crime fighters. But when the strangeness subsided and Gotham returned to its former levels of menace, the Bat Family shed most of its members.

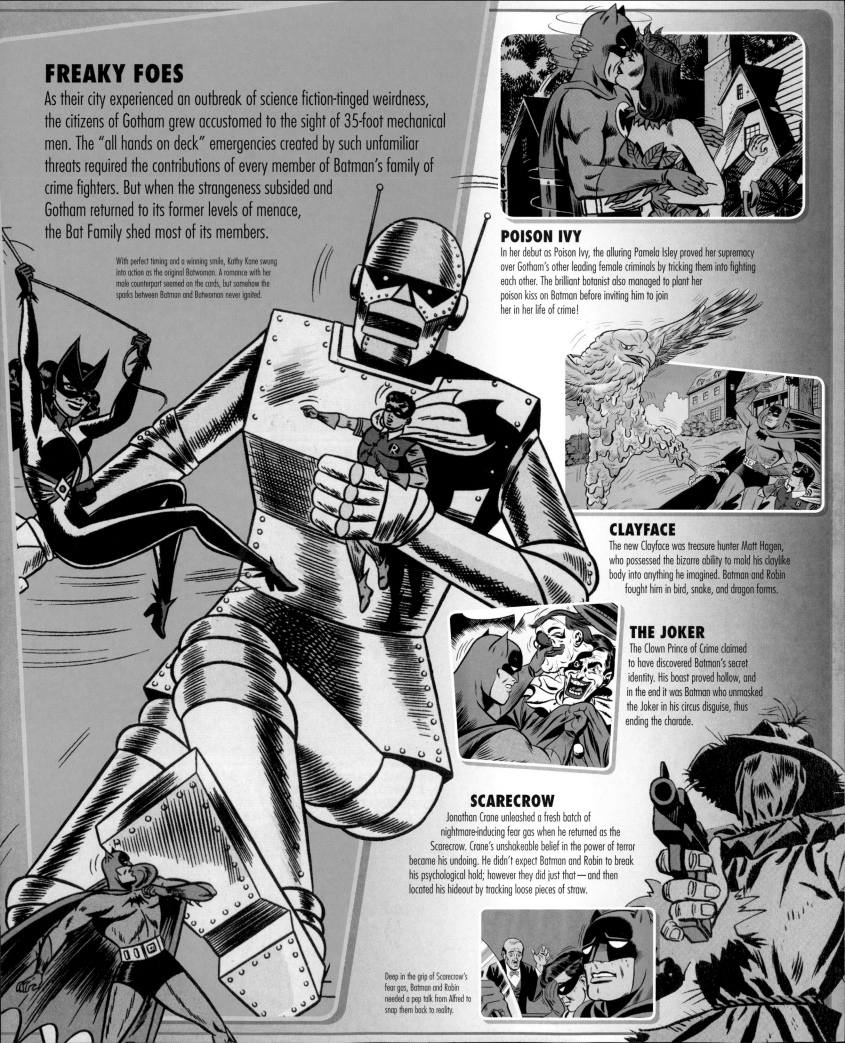

With perfect timing and a winning smile, Kathy Kane swung into action as the original Batwoman. A romance with her male counterpart seemed on the cards, but somehow the sparks between Batman and Batwoman never ignited.

POISON IVY

In her debut as Poison Ivy, the alluring Pamela Isley proved her supremacy over Gotham's other leading female criminals by tricking them into fighting each other. The brilliant botanist also managed to plant her poison kiss on Batman before inviting him to join her in her life of crime!

CLAYFACE

The new Clayface was treasure hunter Matt Hagen, who possessed the bizarre ability to mold his claylike body into anything he imagined. Batman and Robin fought him in bird, snake, and dragon forms.

THE JOKER

The Clown Prince of Crime claimed to have discovered Batman's secret identity. His boast proved hollow, and in the end it was Batman who unmasked the Joker in his circus disguise, thus ending the charade.

SCARECROW

Jonathan Crane unleashed a fresh batch of nightmare-inducing fear gas when he returned as the Scarecrow. Crane's unshakeable belief in the power of terror became his undoing. He didn't expect Batman and Robin to break his psychological hold; however they did just that — and then located his hideout by tracking loose pieces of straw.

Deep in the grip of Scarecrow's fear gas, Batman and Robin needed a pep talk from Alfred to snap them back to reality.

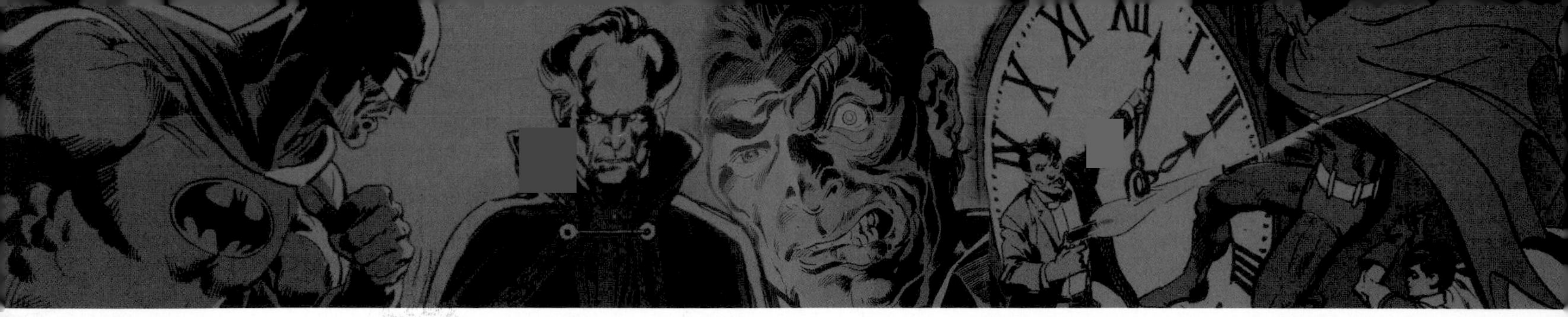

BRONZE AGE

'70s–MID '80s

Times were changing, and so was Batman. The hero reclaimed his relevance during an artistic explosion.

The end of the 1960s brought seismic cultural changes. With anti-war protests on the evening news and psychedelic rock on the radio dial, the comics of the Silver Age seemed hopelessly square. The solution, argued a new wave of comics writers and artists, was to restore relevance to the medium.

The results were mixed. At DC, writer Denny O'Neil and artist Neal Adams collaborated on titles like Green Lantern. The stories looked gorgeous, with an unprecedented realism in capturing the human form, while the writing acknowledged the hero's fallibility and wove in contemporary problems like pollution and drug abuse. But readers didn't respond with the sales figures that the comics arguably deserved.

Things were better on Batman. There, O'Neil and Adams restored an edge of menace to the Dark Knight's Rogues Gallery, letting classic villains like the Joker and Two-Face show their murderous sides once more. Editor Julius Schwartz even sent Robin away to college—a clear sign that comics were growing up.

Creators such as Steve Englehart, Marshall Rogers, Dick Giordano, Len Wein, Frank robbins, Irv Novick, Jim Aparo, and Mike W. Barr took Batman through the era, as DC head Jenette Kahn brought the company into an age of experimentation. Among the new titles released at the time were *Batman Family* (which ran for 20 issues), *Batman and the Outsiders* (32 issues), and *The Joker* (which only lasted nine).

OVERLEAF
Detective Comics #410
(April 1971):
*The realism of artists like
Neal Adams gave the
Bronze Age of Comics a
distinctive look.*

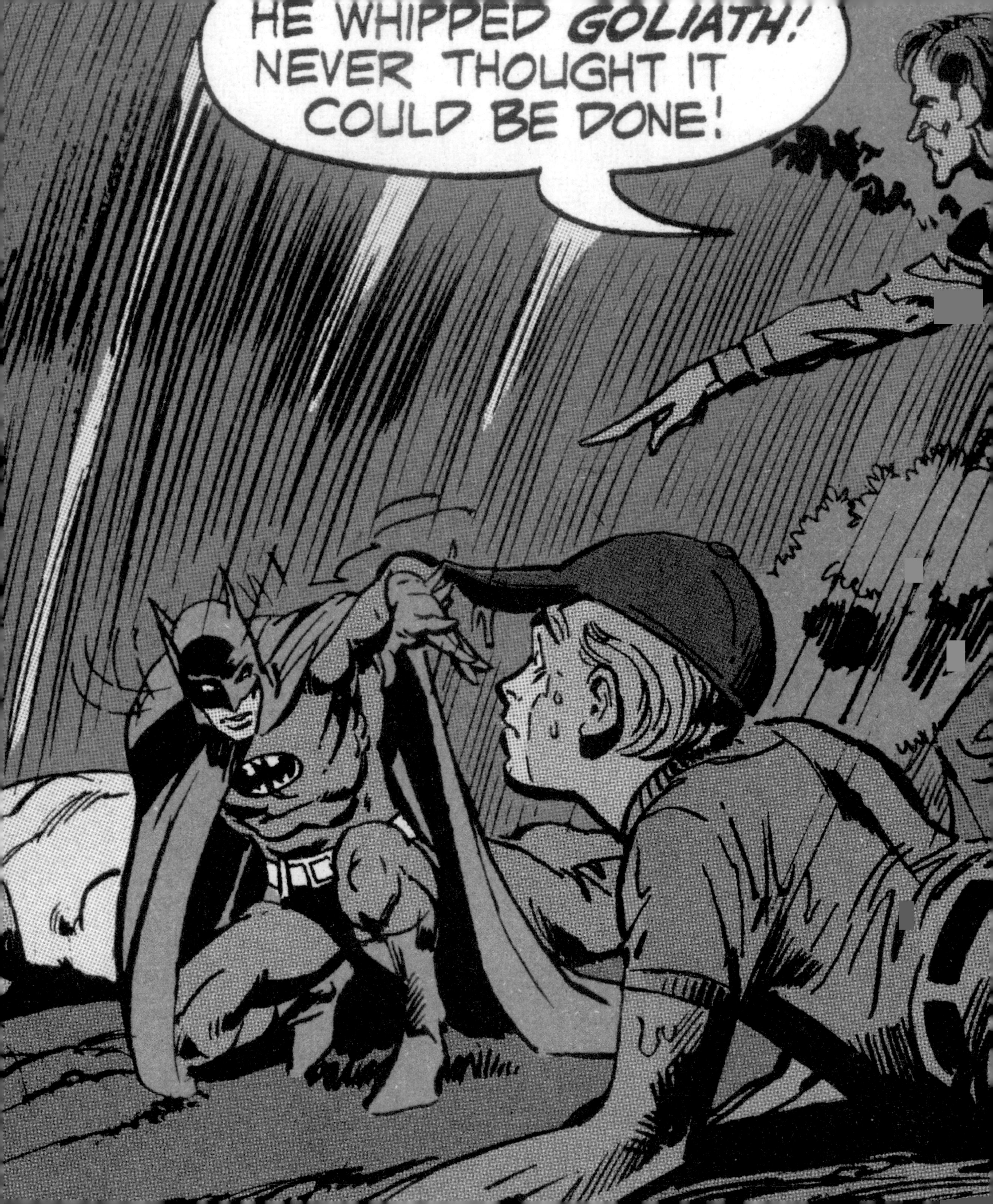
HE WHIPPED GOLIATH! NEVER THOUGHT IT COULD BE DONE!

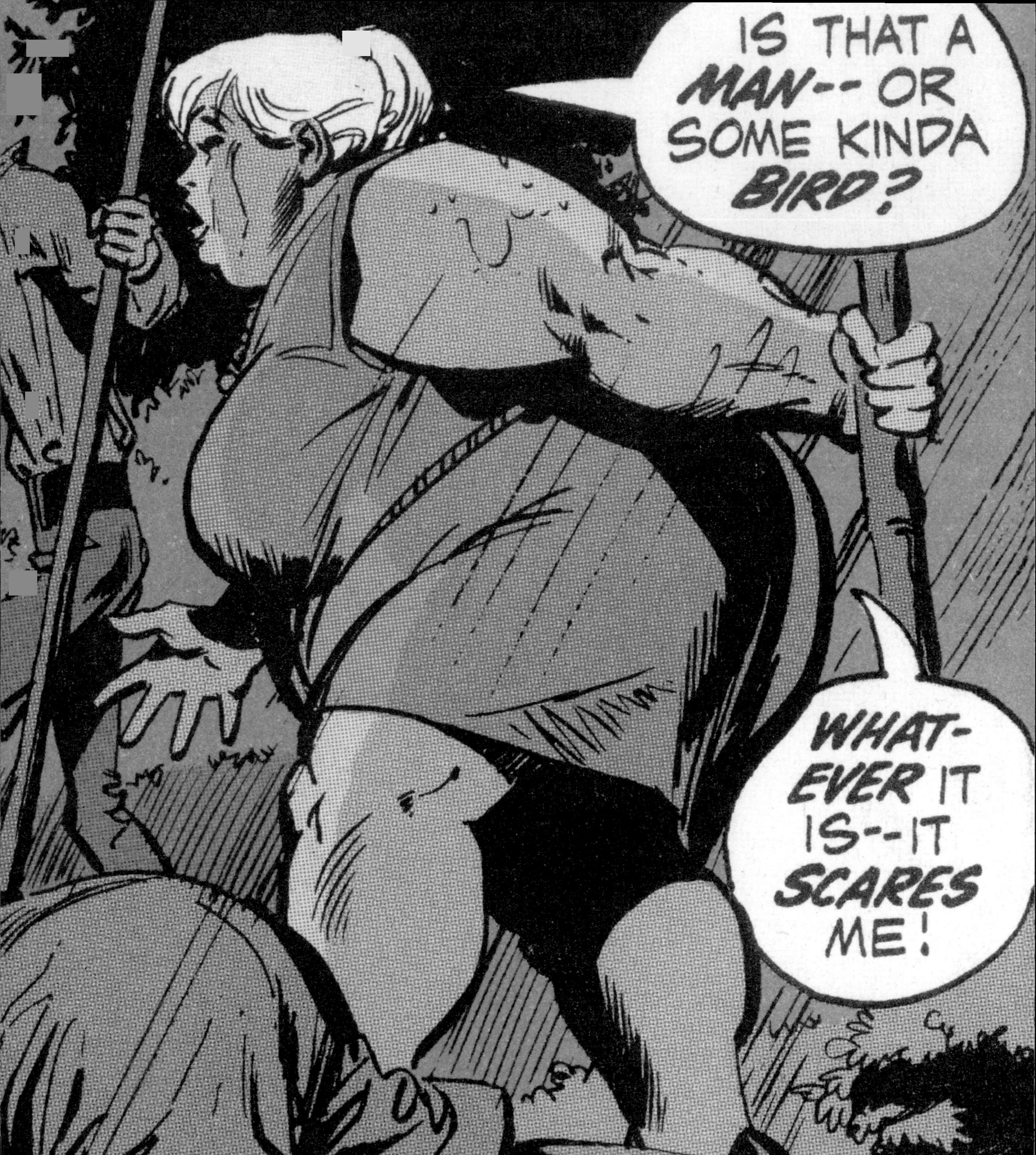
IS THAT A *MAN*-- OR SOME KINDA *BIRD*?
WHAT-EVER IT IS--IT *SCARES* ME!

BATMAN'S EVOLUTION

Not even Batman can halt the passage of time, and this was a time when great changes were afoot for the Dark Knight.

"Didn't think I'd take it this hard."

His bags packed, Dick Grayson took one last look at Wayne Manor— his home ever since the circus accident that left him an orphan.

LEAVING THE NEST

Dick Grayson had grown out of his Boy Wonder role, and needed to choose a future that wasn't defined by Batman. He elected to attend Hudson University to pursue a degree. A gloomy Bruce Wayne and Alfred Pennyworth took in their now-quiet surroundings, then resolved to make their own break from the past. They abandoned Wayne Manor in favor of a downtown skyscraper where Batman could operate closer to the action.

Bruce Wayne could see no reason to remain at his family's ancestral home. He and Alfred piled into a coupe and left for central Gotham.

Dick tried to keep his emotions in check during his farewells, but he did allow a single tear to fall as he rode away toward a new life.

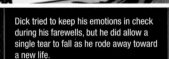

THE PENTHOUSE

"Take a last look Alfred...
...Then seal up the Batcave...FOREVER!"

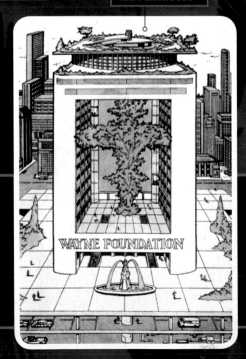

WAYNE FOUNDATION

BATMAN'S PENTHOUSE

After Robin went off to college, Batman and Alfred relocated to a penthouse apartment in the heart of Gotham City. Perched atop the Wayne Foundation Building, headquarters of the charitable arm of Wayne Enterprises, the penthouse served as a luxurious home for Bruce Wayne, while the building's sub-basements concealed the Batmobile, Batplane, and other tools needed to carry out the Dark Knight's war on crime. Its location also put Batman within easy reach of the areas of the city he patrolled by night. Alfred had doubts about the move, but they vanished when he saw how energized Bruce had become.

Bruce Wayne found a new way to do good through Victims, Inc., but some problems could only be solved by Batman.

ONE BULLET TOO MANY

Recognizing that the police and the courts were often incapable of delivering fair outcomes, Bruce Wayne announced the creation of VIP, the Victims Incorporated Program. Victims, Inc. would aid those who had fallen through the cracks of the justice system, like Dr. Fielding, a woman whose husband's killer had gone unpunished due to sloppy investigative work. Bruce gave the woman an interest-free loan to help keep her practice afloat, while Batman tried to identify the killer.

Bruce took a tough-love approach with Dr. Fielding, urging her to stop mourning her husband and take steps to avenge him. It didn't go smoothly.

Batman spread word that Dr. Fielding was ready to testify against her husband's killer. The crook got to her first and tried to silence her forever.

During a scuffle with the intruder, a shot went off, and Batman fell to the floor in a pool of blood.

The bullet, lodged in Batman's shoulder, proved to be the key to cracking the case —it could be used to identify the gunman.

After removing the bullet, Batman was able to run it through a ballistics database and find the culprit.

ARKHAM

WELCOME TO THE MADHOUSE

The Arkham Asylum for the Criminally Insane sits on the outskirts of Gotham like an unwelcome guest. It is home to the worst villains the city has to offer. Criminals who have been ruled insane by Gotham's courts aren't sent to prison, they're sent to Arkham—ostensibly to receive treatment for their mental disorders and become productive citizens. But the asylum has been a poorly run hellhole and a breeding ground for psychosis ever since it was built generations ago by Amadeus Arkham. Most members of Batman's gallery of rogues, including the Joker, Poison Ivy, Mr. Freeze, Two-Face, and the Mad Hatter, are caged in Arkham's squalid cells, but the inmates frequently walk out of the asylum's doors to commit even worse crimes on the citizens of Gotham.

REHABILITATION OR LOCKDOWN?

Unlike the maximum-security Blackgate Penitentiary, which houses criminals who have not been deemed insane, Arkham Asylum has relatively few safeguards to prevent escape. That's because its doctors argue that they look after house patients, err... and their goal is to rehabilitate their charges through treatment and therapy. This attitude, however, has proven ... er ... while inmates sometimes embrace treatment ... observe them that they have been cured ... of them soon fall back into crime upon their release. Other patients simply break out of Arkham by ... escape tunnels, bribing guards, or enlisting the help of ... the outside.

DR. JEREMIAH ARKHAM

A direct descendent of asylum founder Amadeus Arkham, Dr. Jeremiah Arkham has succumbed to the madness of the place he oversees. His psychotic break is so severe that he can no longer distinguish reality from his own hallucinations, and he regularly "treats" patients who are nothing more than projections of his own insecurities. After Catwoman shot and killed the original Black Mask, Dr. Arkham assumed control of the crime lord's empire. It is unclear whether he even realizes the extent of his double life as Gotham's new Black Mask.

ASYLUM

Equipment room

Perimeter catwalk to central tower connecting bridge

Security risk cases

Minimum confinement rooms

Main security-controlled elevator

Violent ward

Line of rear wall

Air-conditioning plant

Orderly catwalk

Engineer offices

Stores

Stores

Heating plant

Offices

Offices

Main security

Internal high-security doors

INFERNAL ARCHITECTURE

Amadeus Arkham built his namesake asylum following the brutal murders of his wife and daughter. With his sanity in tatters, Dr. Arkham designed a floorplan that evoked occult runes. He believed that the pattern would drive away the mysterious bat that haunted his dreams. To this day, inmates and administrators report that the asylum seems to breed madness. Patients are often made worse, and some staff members—including Dr. Jeremiah Arkham and Dr. Harleen Quinzel—have become villains themselves.

UP FROM THE ASHES

Arkham Asylum has been destroyed more than once, most recently at the hands of the new Black Mask. It has been reconstructed each time, occasionally incorporating elements of the bizarre architecture laid out by Amadeus Arkham. This cycle of death and rebirth ensures that insanity is always renewed and that Arkham remains a place of bleak hopelessness. Despite the facility's terrible track record, the courts continue to send Gotham's most dangerous maniacs to Arkham—in part because no one else will take them.

BATMAN
ISSUE #251

"Without the game that the Batman and I have played for so many years, winning is nothing!"

THE JOKER

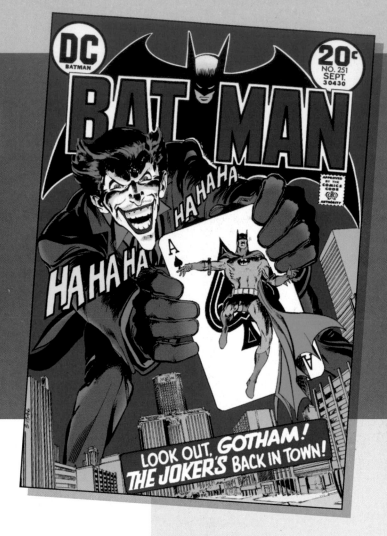

MAIN CHARACTERS: Batman, the Joker
SUPPORTING CHARACTERS: Commissioner Gordon, Packy White, Alby, Bigger Melvin, Bing Hooley
LOCATIONS: Boxing gym, Alby's hotel, Gotham City Aquarium, Gotham Harbor

BACKGROUND

The Silver Age of Comics may have been imaginative and fun, but it was seldom serious. After years of embarking on sci-fi quests and adventuring with a costumed Bat-hound, Batman reached the pinnacle of parody with 1966–1968's tongue-in-cheek *Batman* TV show. It was time for someone to put the dark back into the Dark Knight.

Enter writer Denny O'Neil and artist Neal Adams, shaking Batman up by returning him to his gritty roots. "The Joker's Five-Way Revenge" starred a truly murderous Joker instead of a harmless prankster, and the Boy Wonder was nowhere to be seen. Batman was shown to be vulnerable, failing to save most of the Joker's victims. However, this Batman possessed an unquenchable, heroic fighting spirit, setting the tone for future Batman stories as DC entered the period of creativity known as the Bronze Age of Comics.

PUBLICATION DATE
September 1973

EDITOR
Julius Schwartz

COVER ARTIST
Neal Adams

WRITER
Denny O'Neil

PENCILLER
Neal Adams

INKER
Neal Adams

LETTERER
Unknown

The Story...

When the Joker decides to settle some old scores, Batman is drawn into a race against time to save the hardened criminals on his archenemy's hit list.

Giggling with unhinged glee, the Joker sped away from his latest felony **[1]**. The Bat-Signal summoned the Dark Knight to the crime scene on the city outskirts, where Commissioner Gordon's officers had cordoned off a body sporting a telltale death rictus **[2]**. Any hope that the murder might be the handiwork of someone other than the Clown Prince of Crime was dashed when Batman presented his own evidence—a playing card left at the scene. It was, of course, a joker.

Upon learning that the dead man had been one of five members of the Joker's former gang, Batman concluded that the remaining four were in mortal danger from a clown out for revenge. Boxing trainer Packy White looked like the next on the Joker's hit list. Batman engaged in an impromptu sparring session with the hard-headed pugilist. After enough punches had been thrown, Packy agreed to Batman's suggestion that he go into hiding until the danger has passed. But after taking a sip from a ringside bucket of water **[3]**, his face contorted into a gruesome grin and he fell dead to the canvas.

Confident that the poisoned water did its work on Packy, the Joker took a more direct approach with his third target. Reassuring the terrified Alby that he had nothing to fear, the Joker offered a peace offering by way of a cigar **[4]**, not mentioning that it was packed with nitroglycerin. The Joker exited Alby's sleazy hotel room just as it erupted in flames **[5]**.

Batman received word of the death, and realized he needed to act fast to prevent the Joker from scoring his fourth and fifth hits. He tracked down one of them—Bigger Melvin—near the docks, but underestimated the common crook's treachery. When Batman's back was turned, Bigger Melvin knocked him flat. But the Joker appeared in the doorway and notched up another kill. When Batman returned to groggy wakefulness, he saw Bigger Melvin swinging from a noose **[6]**.

Batman sensed danger, but the Joker had been waiting for this opening. The Joker battered and kicked his weakened opponent to the edge of death **[7]**, but suddenly hesitated. He recognized that victory over the Batman should be an epic clash worthy of two mortal enemies, not an ugly little execution. He departed, giving Batman the opportunity to find him again under more theatrical circumstances.

Just as the Joker had hoped, Batman payed him a visit at the abandoned Gotham City aquarium **[8]**. Bing Hooley, the fifth and final target of the Joker's vengeance, sat in a wheelchair high above a glass tank **[9]**. Within it swam a hungry great white shark. The deal was simple: if Batman took Hooley's place, the Joker would set his captive free. Batman agreed. The Joker shackled his enemy's wrists, and then dumped both his hostages into shark-filled waters **[10]**. "I'm a notorious liar!" he reminded the floundering hero.

Less than a minute remained until the air in Hooley's lungs expired. Batman rode the shark like a bronco buster, snapping his manacles on its serrated teeth. He followed this up by using Hooley's sunken wheelchair as a battering ram, smashing the glass and taking off in pursuit of their grinning tormentor.

On the oil-slicked sands of Gotham Harbor, Batman caught up with the fleeing Joker, flooring him with an uppercut before he could reach his getaway car **[11]**. Though he had to settle for a partial victory, Batman could at least be reassured that the Joker's killing streak had been stopped at four.

With his muscular manservant, Ubu, at his side, Rā's al Ghūl led Batman on a trail of carefully laid clues, all of which Batman solved.

As he freed Robin, Ba[...] long ago. Impressed, Rā's [...]

Talia al Ghūl was no damsel in distress, but a willing participant in her father's plan.

LESLIE THOMPKINS

Every year on the anniversary of his parents' deaths, Batman visited Crime Alley to honor their memories. Leslie Thompkins, who had comforted young Bruce after the tragedy, had remained in the Crime Alley neighborhood as a charitable force for good. When Batman saw thugs harassing her, he swung into action.

Enraged by the callousness of the would-be muggers, Batman lost his usual restraint. He was about to beat them senseless, but Leslie stayed his hand.

Despite the dangers, Leslie Thompkins remained in Crime Alley to care for the needy. She is still motivated by the memory of the orphaned boy she helped long ago.

NIGHT OF THE REAPER

Even after Dick Grayson abandoned the Batcave to pursue higher education, danger seemed to follow him wherever he went. As Rutland, Vermont celebrated a super hero masquerade party, the deadly Reaper burst onto the scene and began a string of vicious killings. Dick donned his Robin costume and teamed up with Batman to halt the Reaper's rampage.

After saying goodbye to the woman he loved, Batman hung up his costume.

WHO IS THE HUNTRESS?

On the parallel world of Earth-2, Batman and Catwoman married and raised a daughter, Helena. The family was struck by tragedy when a criminal from Catwoman's past blackmailed her into committing one last crime. She died after falling from a great height — partly because of events resulting from Batman's efforts to stop the heist. With her father too heartbroken to carry on his work, Helena vowed to do so in his absence, and picked up a crossbow to fight evil as the Huntress.

At her mother's graveside, Helena swore to continue the Wayne family's war on crime.

In the woods, Robin found a lifeless Batman, impaled through the heart. A second look told him that the body was that of a costumed partygoer.

MARRIAGE IMPOSSIBLE

It was too late for Batman to save Dr. Kirk Langstrom, who had become the mutated Man-Bat after taking an experimental serum, but he hoped to save Kirk's fiancée Francine from a similar fate. However, Francine spurned Batman's help and seemed strangely determined to follow through on her marriage to the Man-Bat. Batman's worst suspicions were confirmed when he realized that Francine's pretty features were just a latex mask. He pulled the mask away and was shocked at what he saw beneath. Francine had already swallowed her own dose of the serum and become a She-Bat!

CIRCUS LIFE

Having grown up in the rough-and-tumble world of Haly's Circus, Dick Grayson is accustomed to a nomadic lifestyle and has an easygoing nature that is the complete opposite to that of his brooding mentor, Bruce Wayne.

Nightwing's glove gauntlets contain his "wing-ding" mini-Batarangs and other gadgets.

Nightwing's costume is insulated against extreme temperatures and electrical shocks, and protects against projectile weapons.

KEY DATA

REAL NAME *Richard John Grayson*

OCCUPATION *Crime fighter, acrobat, detective, circus owner*

WEAPONS/ POWERS/ ABILITIES *Wing-ding Batarangs and collapsible eskrima sticks, unparalleled acrobatic skills, master martial artist, natural leader*

AFFILIATIONS *Haly's Circus, Teen Titans, Outsiders*

RELATIVES *Jonathan and Mary Grayson (parents, deceased), Bruce Wayne (legal guardian)*

FIRST APPEARANCE DETECTIVE COMICS #38 (April 1940)

LEGACY OF THE BAT

Nightwing is grateful for the upbringing he received in Batman's care, but never wanted to succeed his mentor as the next Batman. He changed his mind during a period when Batman was believed dead.

Nightwing's costume is streamlined for maximum mobility. Unlike many other costumed heroes, Nightwing doesn't wear a cape.

> "I haven't been the 'circus kid' in years, but that doesn't mean I don't still love it." NIGHTWING

NIGHTWING

The Boy Wonder grew up! After wowing Gotham City as the original Robin, Dick Grayson used what he'd learned to launch a solo career away from home as Nightwing. Now Nightwing is back in Gotham and he is always available to assist Batman on a case.

Batman has absolute trust in Nightwing. He is Batman's first choice as a partner on sensitive missions.

MAKING HIS MARK

From the big top to the rooftops, Dick Grayson has never backed down from a challenge. Having learned acrobat skills as part of a traveling circus when he was child, Dick first put his talent to work as Robin, absorbing Batman's teachings but often investigating crimes on his own. Eventually, Robin flew the nest and Dick assumed a new costumed identity as Nightwing, leading the Teen Titans and briefly finding love with his teammate, Starfire.

Nightwing operated out of Gotham's neighboring municipality of Blüdhaven for a time, and even joined the Blüdhaven police force. He later relocated to New York City. His adventuring as Nightwing frequently put him into contact with Barbara Gordon, who he had known as Batgirl before an injury caused her to start a new life as the computer-hacking expert Oracle. The two crime fighters shared a romantic bond until Barbara returned to her former costumed identity of Batgirl.

Nightwing is an astonishing athlete whose dexterity and grace outshines the gifts of his teacher. Batman's grueling training regimen gave Nightwing lightning-fast reflexes, and his lifetime of swinging on ropes has made him a superb navigator of the big city's urban canyons. Like Batman, Nightwing fights crooks from a distance with weighted throwing devices similar to Batarangs—which he calls "wing-dings"— but he also uses collapsible eskrima sticks for close-quarters combat. Nightwing has proved he is a natural leader and he is widely respected in the super hero community.

The biggest challenge of Dick Grayson's life came in the aftermath of Bruce Wayne's supposed death at the hands of Darkseid. He reluctantly accepted the cape and cowl of Batman, becoming the symbol that Gotham City needed during a dark time. Now that the real Batman has returned, Nightwing can continue to build a legend of his own.

As the youngest member of the Flying Graysons, Dick learned to perform the quadruple somersault.

Dick wore the first version of the Nightwing costume when he was part of the Teen Titans.

Nightwing had strong romantic feelings for Barbara Gordon. When Barbara reciprocated them, he hoped to find true love.

As a cop on the Blüdhaven police force, Dick got a street-level view of the city.

Nightwing carries a light arsenal of weapons, but his enemies should never underestimate him—they are often surprised when he outsmarts them.

BATMAN AND THE OUTSIDERS

"I'VE HAD ENOUGH OF YOUR JUSTICE LEAGUE... FROM NOW ON, THESE ARE MY NEW PARTNERS."

ORIGIN

Batman doesn't take orders, he gives them! This was never clearer than in the aftermath of the Justice League of America's refusal to stop a violent revolution in the eastern European nation of Markovia. Superman had already promised the United Nations that the JLA would not interfere, so Batman had no choice but to resign his membership and build a strike team of his own. Batman and Black Lightning infiltrated Markovia, where they met the amnesiac Halo, the vengeful Katana, and the malleable hero Metamorpho. Joined by Geo-Force, heir to the Markovian aristocracy, the fledgling team defeated Baron Bedlam and restored peace to the land. The telepathic Looker later became the Outsiders' final core member.

GEO-FORCE

HALO

KATANA

LOOKER

BLACK LIGHTNING

METAMORPHO

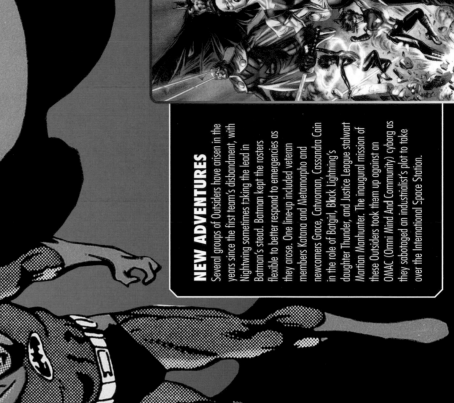

NEW ADVENTURES

Several groups of Outsiders have arisen in the years since the first team's disbandment, with Nightwing sometimes taking the lead in Batman's stead. Batman kept the rosters flexible to better respond to emergencies as they arose. One line-up included veteran members Katana and Metamorpho and newcomers Grace, Catwoman, Cassandra Cain in the role of Batgirl, Black Lightning's daughter Thunder, and Justice League stalwart Martian Manhunter. The inaugural mission of these Outsiders took them up against an OMAC (Omni Mind And Community) cyborg as they sabotaged an industrialist's plot to take over the International Space Station.

THE MASTERS OF DISASTER

FEARSOME FOES

The Outsiders lived up to their name by tackling the missions that the big groups either couldn't or wouldn't take on. They didn't hesitate to break international laws if they needed to, and they made plenty of enemies along the way. The Masters of Disaster became regular foes, with members Shakedown, Coldsnap, Heatstroke, New Wave, and Windfall each possessing control over a specific element of nature. Shakedown could create powerful vibrations with his mighty strength, Coldsnap and Heatstroke could generate extreme cold and heat respectively, while New Wave could transform into living water, and her younger sister Windfall possessed the ability to manipulate the air itself. The group once nearly killed Black Lightning, but were left fraught with tensions after Windfall had a change of heart and left to join the Outsiders.

However, new threats to Batman and the Outsiders soon emerged, including the ultra-patriotic metahumans of the Force of July. Baron Bedlam even returned to the land of the living — information which Batman withheld from The Outsiders for a while, angering them and prompting him to quit as team leader. The gang soldiered on without him until drifting apart into new super hero careers of their own.

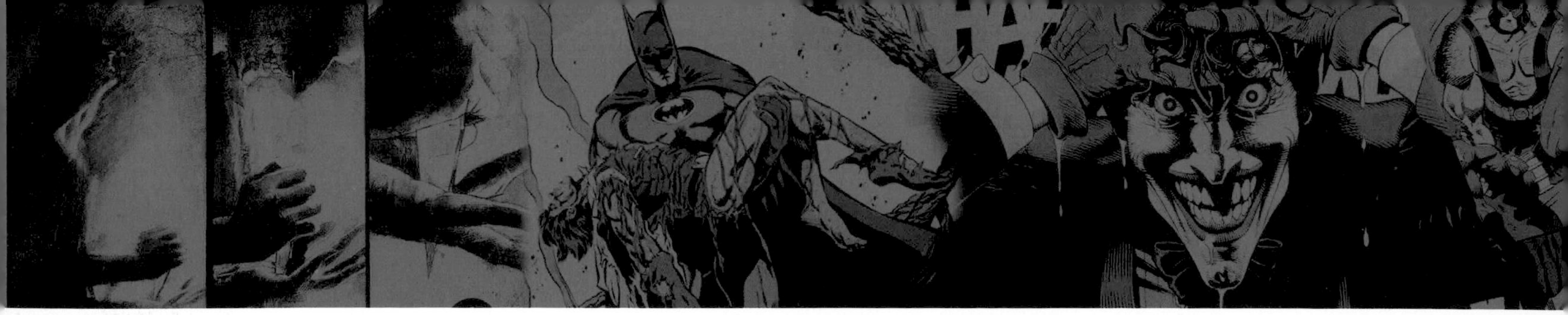

DARK AGE

MID '80s–MID '00s

Super hero comics earned new respect by appealing to an adult audience. Batman, who had reclaimed his dangerous edge, stood at the forefront of the movement.

The yearlong miniseries *Crisis on Infinite Earths* gave DC the chance to clear away generations of tangled backstory. Armed with the in-story explanation of a time-altering catastrophe, several of DC's super heroes received streamlined, updated origins that would be more accessible to new readers.

For Batman, it meant a gritty reboot from writer Frank Miller and a shocking farewell to the last vestiges of the Batman family. Jason Todd, the second Robin, died after fans gave him a thumbs-down in a telephone promotion. Barbara Gordon, the former Batgirl, was left paralyzed after the Joker shot her in the spine. These storylines—plus Miller's dystopian tale *Batman: The Dark Knight Returns*—demonstrated the maturation of comic book storytelling. Adult themes were no longer taboo.

This "Dark Age" coincided with a shift in the distribution market. Comic book specialty stores were now the preferred retail outlet, not the newsstands and grocery stores of years past. With an older fanbase willing to follow the Dark Knight into increasingly terrifying territory, writers and artists put the hero through his biggest challenges ever. In the "Knightfall" storyline, the muscular Bane broke Batman's back, leaving him incapacitated and opening the door for the fanatical Azrael to briefly take his place.

OVERLEAF
Batman: The Dark Knight
Returns #3 (May 1986):
In Frank Miller's Batman: The
Dark Knight Returns, *the
aging hero took a new Robin
under his wing.*

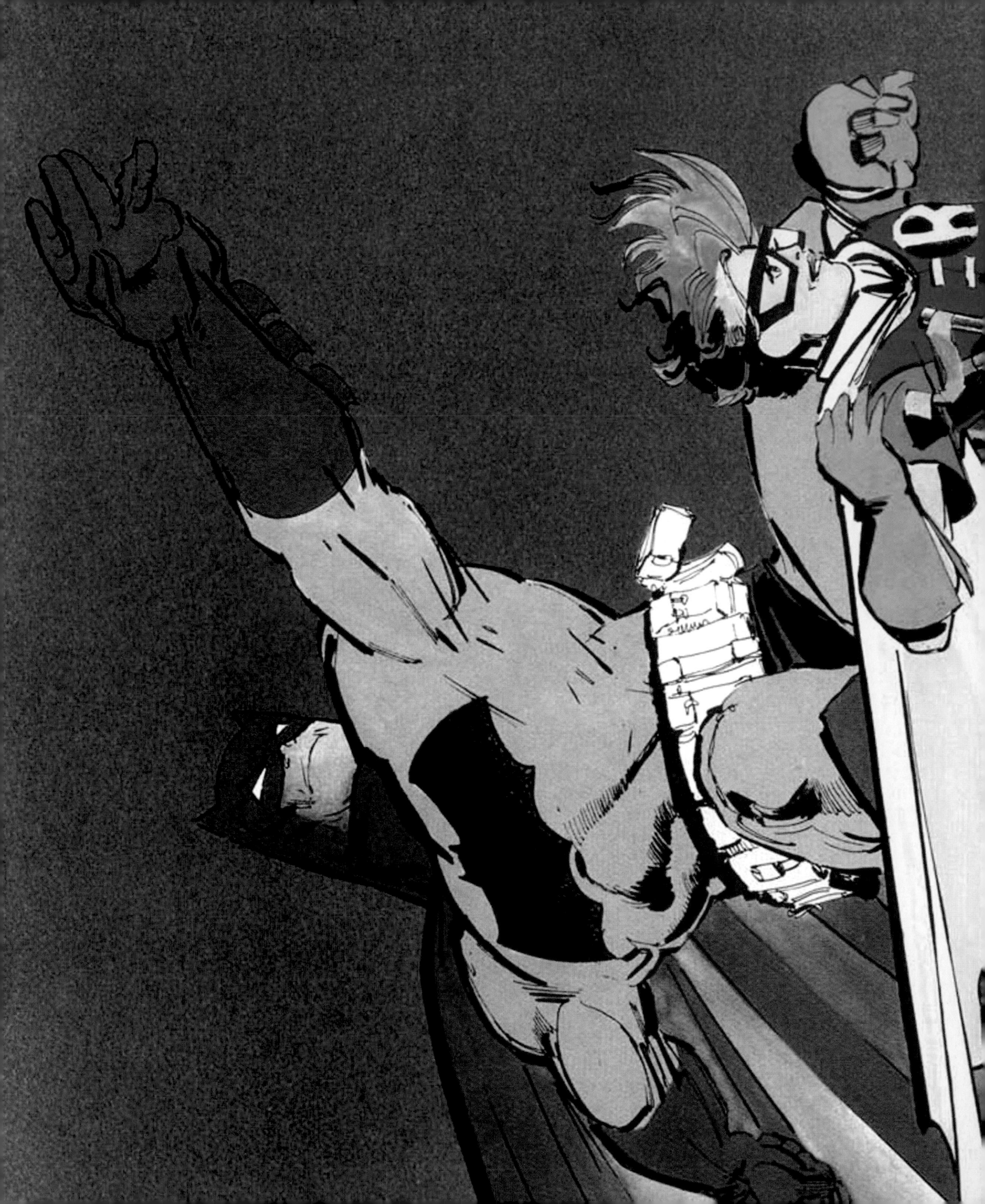

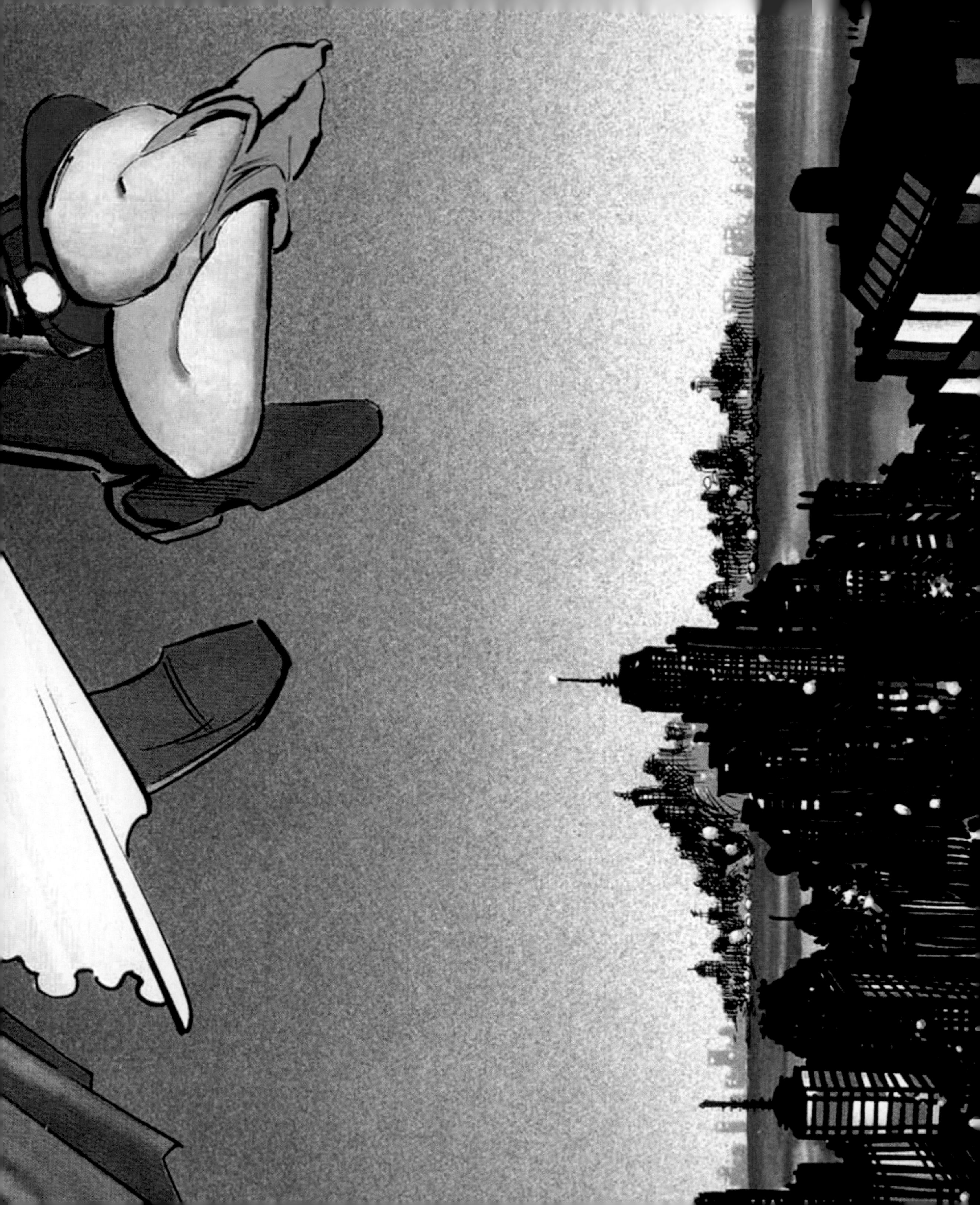

THE DARK KNIGHT RETURNS

When Harvey Dent relapsed into Two-Face to terrorize Gotham, Batman knew he had to stop him.

A DARK FUTURE

In a shifted timeline, all super heroes had been hounded out of existence. Only Superman, a lackey of the U.S. government, remained. Batman had been gone for a decade, but the reemergence of old foes prompted Bruce Wayne—now in his fifties—to don the costume one last time. Opposed by a hostile mass media and a new Gotham police commissioner, the Dark Knight recruited an army and set an example of self-determination among a populace that had grown complacent.

James Gordon left the Gotham police force after a lifetime of service. His replacement, Commissioner Ellen Yindel, took a harsh view of Batman's vigilantism and only made things worse for the people of the city.

A NEW ROBIN

Carrie Kelly was only thirteen years old, but she saw in Batman's reappearance an opportunity to reverse her directionless upbringing. Dressed in a homemade Robin costume, she shadowed Batman as he faced off with the leader of a Gotham gang called the Mutants and saved him from certain death. Under Batman's guidance, Carrie gained discipline and direction, becoming his first soldier in a war against corruption.

Since Batman's retirement, Gotham City had fallen to the Mutants. The leader of the youth gang was a monument of muscle who had no conscience and left no law. He hoped and lived ahead of Gotham's majority with his team to show the weakness of those who were simply living in the city. Batman knew he had to defeat the mutant leader using his own language, beating him and hurt in a bone bloody beatdown, proving that he was Gotham's one true leader.

CELEBRITY JOKER

The Joker emerged from a catatonic state the instant he heard the name "Batman" on the evening news. He charmed his psychiatrist into believing he was sane and captured the attention of a superficial public. On live TV, the Joker killed hundreds and then lured Batman into a violent showdown. When his nemesis refused to deliver a killing blow, the Joker snapped his own neck—ensuring that Batman would face a murder charge.

Flanked by his duped psychiatrist and a popular sex therapist, the supposedly cured Joker enjoyed a chat with the host of the David Endocrine talk show. Moments later, poison gas filled the TV studio giving every person inside a fatal, Jokerized grimace.

The Joker beat up Selina Kyle, the former Catwoman, then dressed her in a Wonder Woman costume. He left Selina bound and gagged for Batman to find.

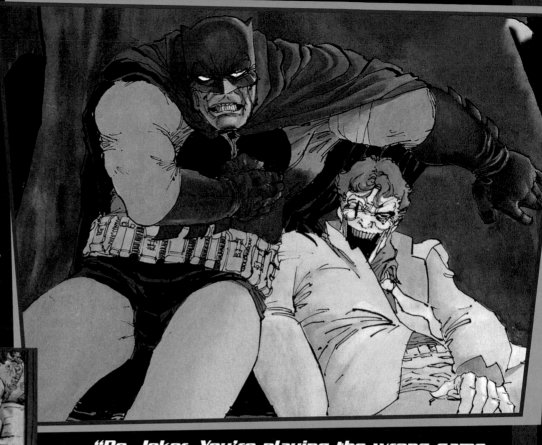

"No, Joker. You're playing the wrong game. The old game." – Batman

DARK KNIGHT VS. MAN OF STEEL

Batman's high profile had become an embarrassment to the U.S. president, who ordered Superman to eliminate his old friend. Superman anticipated a quick fight, but Batman was well prepared for their confrontation. With synthetic Kryptonite giving him the edge, Batman closed his fingers around Superman's throat—and then fell dead, the apparent victim of a heart attack.

The distant detonation of a nuclear warhead triggered an electromagnetic pulse, which plunged Gotham into darkness. With the city in chaos, Batman led the former Mutants gang members—now calling themselves the Sons of Batman—to end the looting.

After Bruce Wayne's funeral, Bruce walked away from his grave. His death was a ruse! In a new headquarters, Batman formed an army, with Robin and the Sons of Batman as his first draftees.

BATMAN YEAR ONE

"You've eaten Gotham's wealth. Its spirit. Your feast is nearly over. From this moment on, none of you are safe."

BATMAN

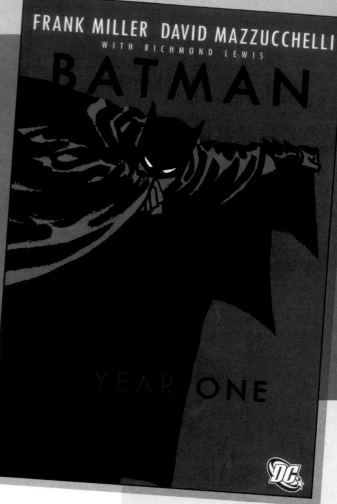

FRANK MILLER DAVID MAZZUCCHELLI
WITH RICHMOND LEWIS

BATMAN

YEAR ONE

MAIN CHARACTERS: Batman, James Gordon
SUPPORTING CHARACTERS: Barbara Gordon, Detective Flass, Commissioner Loeb, Sarah Essen, "The Roman"
LOCATIONS: Police headquarters, Wayne Manor, Gotham slums, Falcone's mansion, Gotham River

BACKGROUND

Frank Miller's *The Dark Knight Returns* set a new standard for ambitious graphical storytelling, but it was an "imaginary story" with little impact on DC's overall continuity. Inspired by Miller's success, DC commissioned the writer to update the mainstream Batman's origins in the wake of the companywide revisions brought about by the *Crisis on Infinite Earths* crossover. Miller's gritty Gotham—as yet untouched by super-villainy—is plagued by common street crime, an epidemic desperately in need of eradication.

The four-part *Batman: Year One* didn't appear as a standalone miniseries, but rather as issues #404–407 of the main Batman title. Miller and artist David Mazzucchelli told parallel tales, contrasting Jim Gordon's first months at the Gotham City Police Department with Bruce Wayne's experimental efforts to become a crime-fighting vigilante. The two men demonstrate why they are the heroic champions needed by a corrupt city, even if their paths don't intersect until the finale.

PUBLICATION DATE
February–May 1987

EDITOR
Denny O'Neil

COVER ARTIST
David Mazzucchelli

WRITER
Frank Miller

PENCILLER
David Mazzucchelli

INKER
Richmond Lewis

LETTERER
Todd Klein

The Story...

James Gordon and Batman show their mettle as the future champions of Gotham, fighting crime and corruption in their own ways in this updated origin story.

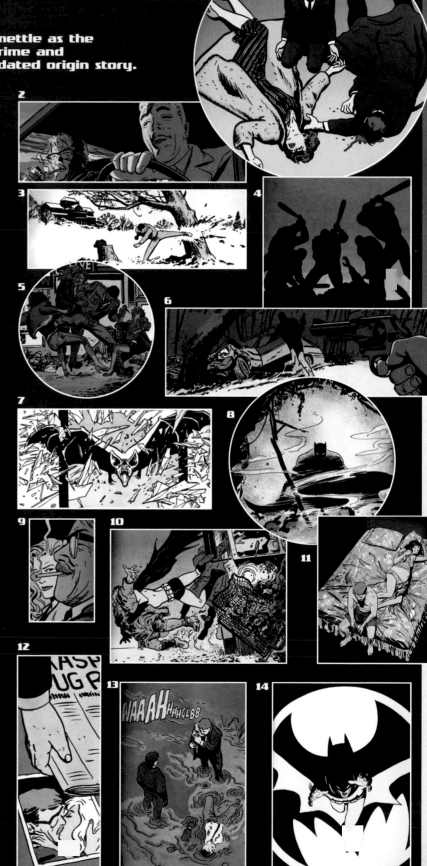

Lieutenant Gordon, recently transferred from the Chicago police force, had arrived in Gotham City just as Bruce Wayne had come home from years spent abroad following his parents' murders **[1]**. Setting up house in Gotham with his pregnant wife Barbara, Gordon was shown the ropes of the Gotham City Police Department by his new partner Detective Flass **[2]**. Men like Flass ignored the weak, protected the powerful, and took bribes at every turn.

Flass encouraged Gordon to embrace the perks offered by a broken system. Gordon refused to bend, even when pressured by the corrupt Commissioner Loeb. As Bruce Wayne honed his skills at Wayne Manor **[3]**, a cocky Flass and gang of officers decided to beat up Gordon to teach him a lesson **[4]**.

Dressed in street clothes, Bruce Wayne ventured into the most dangerous section of Gotham to protect the innocent. However, a gang of street criminals made aggressive, confident moves that Bruce couldn't counter **[5]**. His first patrol ended with multiple stab wounds and a run-in with the police.

Jim Gordon refused to back down from his partner's bullying, running Flass's car off the road **[6]** and forcing him into a one-on-one fistfight. Back at Wayne Manor, as Bruce contemplated his future, a bat soared through the window of his study **[7]**. Inspired, he decided to don a bat-like costume that would strike fear into the hearts of criminals. Dressed as the mysterious Batman, Bruce began to turn the tide against the muggers, murderers, and Mafiosos dominating Gotham. The G.C.P.D. was ordered to arrest him, but Jim Gordon was one officer who was grateful for the help.

At a private banquet for the city's biggest criminal power brokers, Batman emerged from a cloud of smoke **[8]** and announced that "none of you are safe." The next day, Police Commissioner Loeb made Batman's capture the force's top priority. Lieutenant Gordon had been growing closer to fellow officer Sarah Essen, despite the risk if Loeb discovered his affair **[9]**. Gordon and Essen accidentally ran into Batman while he was saving a pedestrian from an out-of-control truck **[10]**. Before they could speak to him, Batman disappeared into an abandoned tenement. The G.C.P.D. leveled the building with an incendiary device and sent in a riot squad. Batman knocked the officers out one by one, then used an ultrasonic signal to summon a cloud of bats to cover his escape.

Gordon was tormented by the reality of his crumbling marriage **[11]**. After Commissioner Loeb tried to force his loyalty through blackmail **[12]**, Gordon confessed to his wife about his affair. With this bargaining chip removed, Loeb—operating on orders from crime boss "The Roman"—arranged for the kidnapping of Gordon's wife and newborn son. Bruce Wayne rushed to the scene, out of costume but determined to help. In a confrontation on a bridge, Gordon fought the thug carrying his son but the baby fell over the side. Bruce dived into the Gotham river to save Gordon's child. Although Gordon suspected he was in the presence of the unmasked Batman, he couldn't be sure, claiming to be "blind without my glasses," which were lost in the struggle on the bridge. **[13]**

Later, as the G.C.P.D. buzzed with news about a villain called the Joker, Gordon headed for the rooftop. Turning on the newly installed Bat-Signal, he waited for the imminent arrival of his new, costumed ally in the fight against crime **[14]**.

The Joker kidnapped Commissioner Gordon and paralyzed Barbara Gordon in a tale that shed light on the Joker's mysterious origin.

THE KILLING JOKE

Double Trouble
Escaping from Arkham Asylum was easy for the Joker. The hard part was tricking people into thinking he never left! The Joker left a duplicate in his place, but when Batman questioned him and noticed his pale skin was merely white makeup, the game was up.

A MAD PLAN
The Joker was convinced of one simple truth: all it takes is one bad day for a normal person to slip into insanity. But it wasn't enough to just believe this theory; he had to test it too, and his subject was Police Commissioner James Gordon. After breaking into Gordon's home, taking him captive, and leaving his daughter Barbara bleeding from a gunshot wound, the Joker forced his captive into a nightmarish ride through an abandoned amusement park. Batman rushed to stop it, but the Joker had planned for that too. Through it all, new facts came to light about the kind of man the Joker used to be before his own "bad day."

It was a quiet evening at the Gordon household when Barbara Gordon answered a knock at the door to find the Joker aiming at her with a gun. She had no time to react before he fired.

Unspeakable Crimes
The Joker invaded the Gordon home with ruthless force. Barbara Gordon fell to the floor after taking a bullet, her legs paralyzed from the injury, while the Joker's henchmen beat and kidnapped Commissioner Gordon. The Joker took

photos of Barbara lying among the carnage, later projecting them on giant screens for Commissioner Gordon to watch at his horror-show funhouse.

The Joker's macabre circus assistants used cattle prods to keep Gordon in line.

By leading Batman into a Hall of Mirrors, the Joker tried to show him that the two of them had more in common than he realized. Batman didn't agree.

Order vs Chaos
Batman tracked down the Joker. He freed Commissioner Gordon, then went deeper into the theme park to find the madman behind the crimes. As Batman worked his way past the Joker's death traps, he was taunted by the Joker's proclamations that both hero and villain shared the same degree of insanity. But Batman would not crack, and he swiftly ended the Joker's rampage.

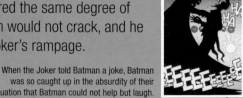

When the Joker told Batman a joke, Batman was so caught up in the absurdity of their situation that Batman could not help but laugh.

Birth of the Joker

He had a wife who loved him, a baby on the way, and ambitions to earn a living as a stand-up comedian—but the man who would become the Joker just couldn't scare up any laughs. To help pay the bills he agreed to assist in a one-time criminal caper, hoping that for once the cards would come up in his favor.

Troubled and insecure about his failure to provide for his wife and unborn child, the Joker agreed to lead the notorious Red Hood mob through a chemical plant on their way to a robbery.

The crooks ordered the Joker to wear the costume of the Red Hood, explaining that it would boost their gang's hoodlum reputation.

Just before the robbery, the Joker was devastated by the news that his wife and their unborn baby had died in an electrical accident at their home.

Despite his terrible news, the gang forced the Joker to go ahead with the robbery. Chased by Batman and unable to see anything in his Red Hood getup, the Joker fell into a chemical stew that bleached his skin white and dyed his hair bright green.

After the day's events, the sight of his changed appearance pushed the Joker to breaking point. His only comfort was madness—and a new villain was born.

Bruce was worried that Jason Todd had become too brutal in his approach to fighting crime. When Bruce decided to relieve the second Robin of his duties temporarily, Jason stormed away. Disillusioned, he began a solo mission to locate his biological mother.

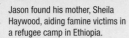

Jason found his mother, Sheila Haywood, aiding famine victims in a refugee camp in Ethiopia.

His oldest enemy crossed the ultimate line, forcing Batman to live with Robin's death on his conscience.

DEATH IN THE FAMILY

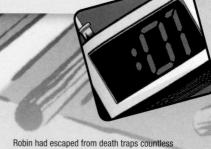

Robin had escaped from death traps countless times, but on this day his number was up.

THE FINAL HOUR

The Joker's scheme to steal medical supplies in Ethiopia brought the Joker—with Batman on his trail—into a collision with Robin's family reunion. Seizing an opportunity when Batman wasn't around, the Joker beat Robin with a crowbar, then left him and his mother inside a locked warehouse containing a ticking time bomb.

Jason Todd's biological mother looked on as her son was beaten unconscious by the Joker.

FALLEN SOLDIER

Batman arrived at the scene too late to stop the Joker's time bomb from exploding and taking his partner's life. Batman recovered Jason Todd's body from the wreckage and mourned the first Robin to die in the line of duty. The Joker had to be punished, but first Batman returned to Gotham to bury Jason.

Batman carried overwhelming guilt over Jason Todd's death and resolved to work alone. But Batman wasn't the same without his partner, and soon Tim Drake became the third Robin.

ARKHAM ASYLUM

A SERIOUS HOUSE ON SERIOUS EARTH

"You're in the real world now, and the lunatics have taken over the asylum."

THE JOKER

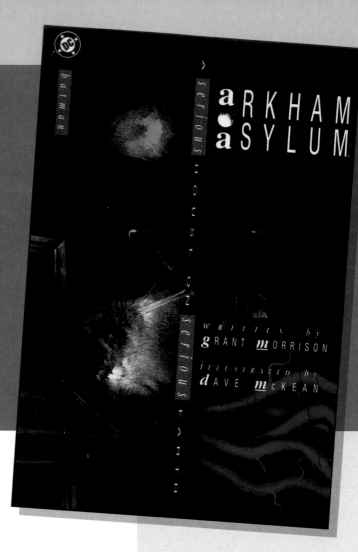

MAIN CHARACTERS: Batman, the Joker
SUPPORTING CHARACTERS: Amadeus Arkham,
Commissioner Gordon, Dr. Ruth Adams, Two-Face,
"Mad Dog" Hawkins, Clayface, Doctor Destiny,
Mad Hatter, Killer Croc, Dr. Charles Cavendish
LOCATIONS: Arkham Asylum

BACKGROUND

When a man dresses up like a bat to avenge his dead parents, where does one draw the line between sanity and madness? Writer Grant Morrison explored this theme in the dreamlike graphic novel *Arkham Asylum: A Serious House on Serious Earth.* During a wave of late '80s stories that brought mature themes and psychological complexity to Batman's world (including *The Dark Knight Returns* and *The Killing Joke*), Arkham Asylum took its action inside—within the walls of Arkham and the recesses of Batman's brain.

The impressionistic art of Dave McKean illuminated a journey through the Asylum that doubled as an exhumation of long-buried secrets. In the process, the Dark Knight was revealed as a tightly wound stoic who still blamed himself for the death of his mother. By contrast, the Joker and his fellow inmates demonstrated chaos, self-hate, duality, and more, with each character's dialogue printed in a unique style of text.

Morrison's narrative weaved between the creation of the asylum in the 1920s and the present day, and referenced everything from the occult to the I-Ching. The story also cemented Arkham Asylum as a place of primal nightmares.

PUBLICATION DATE
October 1989

EDITOR
Karen Berger

COVER ARTIST
Dave McKean

WRITER
Grant Morrison

PENCILLER
Dave McKean

INKER
Dave McKean

LETTERER
Gaspar Saladino

The Story...

The inmates are running free at Arkham Asylum, and Batman goes in alone despite worries for his own mental state.

In an introductory prologue set in 1901, the young Amadeus Arkham had been left alone to care for his mentally ill mother **(1)**. Horrified by her suffering, Arkham pledged himself to the study of psychiatry to help those with similar afflictions.

In modern-day Gotham, the Bat-Signal warned the Caped Crusader of a breakout at Arkham Asylum. With the Joker as their ringleader, the inmates had taken the staff members hostage. In response, Batman agreed to enter the facility alone to prevent further violence **(2)**. Before departing, Batman confessed to Gordon that he feared the Joker might be right about him—that his legendary calm might conceal a depth of insanity to rival any inmate. Batman feared that walking through the asylum's doors might feel like returning home.

Batman's arrival was met with great amusement from the Joker **(3)**. The Caped Crusader soon discovered that some of the Arkham staffers were not hostages, having voluntarily remained behind to continue their own treatment programs. Among them was Dr. Ruth Adams, who theorized that the Joker was gifted with "super sanity." She had also weaned Two-Face off his coin and onto a tarot deck, to provide him with more choice options than a simple yes or no **(4)**.

Having lured his prey into the asylum, the Joker announced the rules of a new game to the inmates—to hunt Batman! After shooting a hostage in the head, he forced Batman to start running, pursued by the citizens of the madhouse.

In a flashback to the 1920s, Amadeus Arkham had now become a noted psychologist. Agreeing to treat the mass murderer "Mad Dog" Hawkins, he returned from a trip to find the bodies of his wife and daughter—Mad Dog's newest victims. Despite this, Arkham opened his namesake asylum, accepting Hawkins as his first patient. After enough time had passed to allay suspicions, he took his revenge by frying the unrepentant killer on an electroshock couch.

In the present-day institution, Batman stumbled through the winding corridors. He was beset by the self-loathing sickness of Clayface **(5)**, the impotent rage of Doctor Destiny **(6)**, and the Mad Hatter's reality-bending riddles **(7)**. He also relived his mother's murder, experiencing unimaginable mental pain.

In the flashback, Amadeus Arkham **(8)** had gradually become obsessed with the vision of a giant bat **(9)**. Descending into madness, he reached the end of his life as an inmate in a windowless cell in his own asylum, surrounded by occult runes scratched into the walls and floor with his fingernails **(10)**.

On his way to the heart of the madhouse, Batman withstood the raw fury of Killer Croc, who evoked imagery of the dragon that fought St. George in the ancient legend **(11)**. Eventually the Dark Knight came face to face with the asylum's current administrator, Dr. Cavendish. Gripped by the same madness that consumed Amadeus, Cavendish revealed that he triggered the breakout. He was prepared to do even worse, but then Dr. Adams slashed the administrator's throat with a knife.

The Joker, however, remained king of the Arkham Asylum, leaving it to Two-Face to determine Batman's fate. Two-Face flipped his coin, stating that if the scarred side came up, Batman would die **(12)**. If the unblemished side showed its face, he would go free. The result was freedom for Batman. Unseen by the other inmates, Two-Face studied the coin as Batman left the asylum. It sat in his palm, scarred side face up.

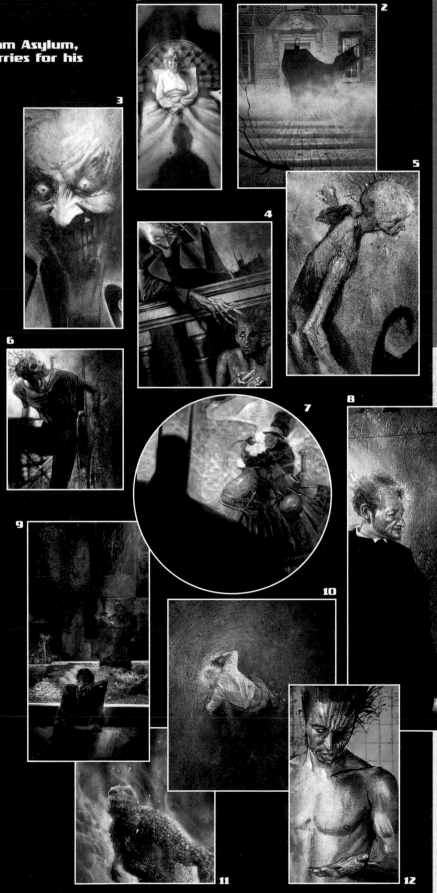

Though he had faced a thousand foes, the Dark Knight finally met his match when Bane broke the Bat.

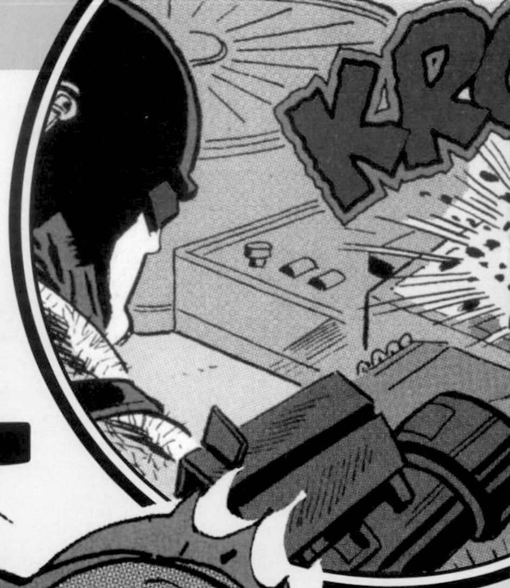

Packing high-tech weaponry, Bane freed the inmates of Arkham Asylum.

KNIGHTFALL

A HERO MEETS HIS END

Juiced up with the superpowered steroid Venom, Bane is a towering grappler who seems to be made of solid muscle. But he also possesses a keen strategic mind, and his plan for wearing down Batman succeeded where other schemes had failed. After freeing Gotham's villains from Arkham Asylum, he steered Batman into dozens of fights, studying his enemy's techniques at a distance. Then, when Batman's stamina was spent, Bane delivered the final blow.

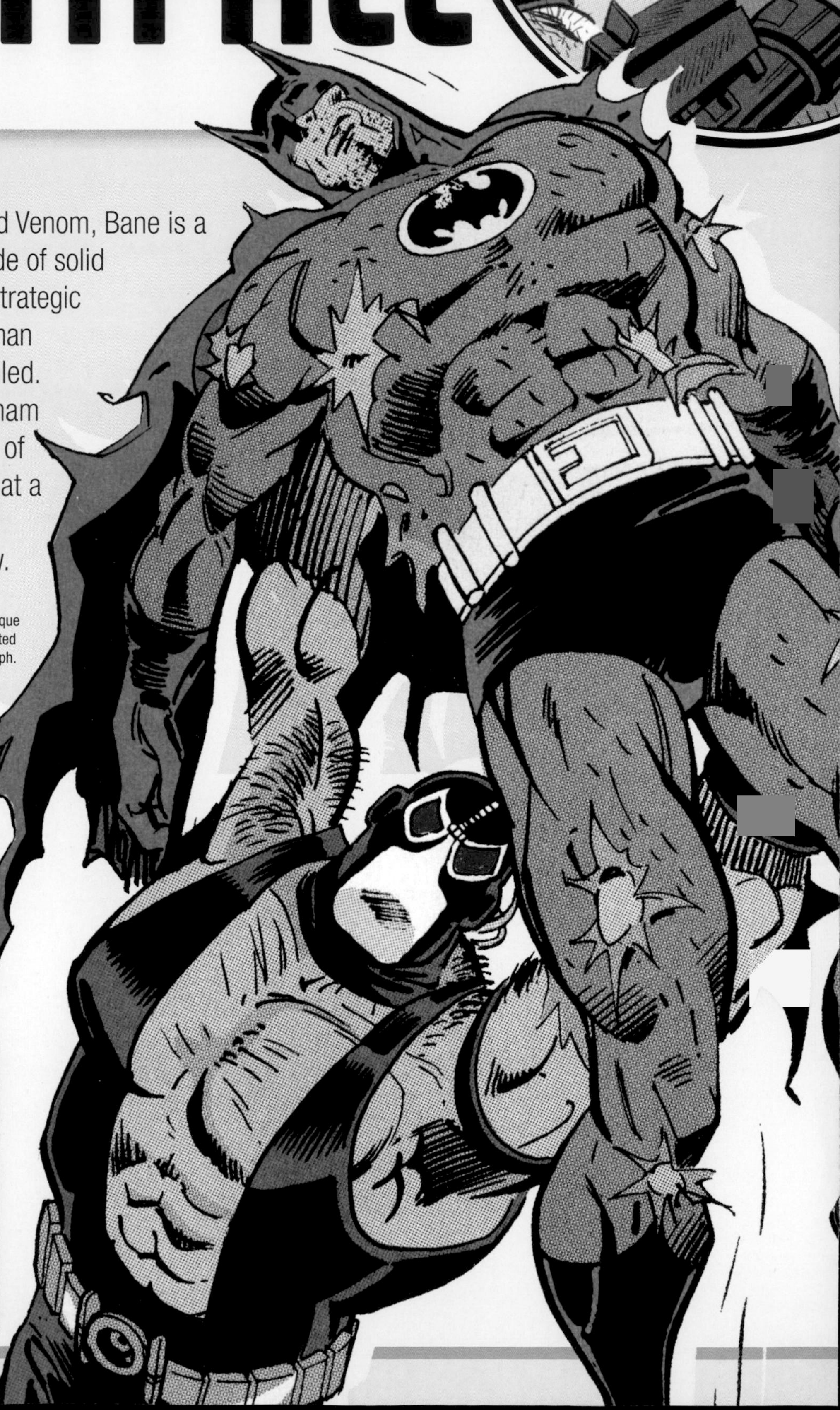

With Venom chemicals invigorating his hulking physique and boosting his rage, Bane hoisted the defeated Batman over his head in triumph.

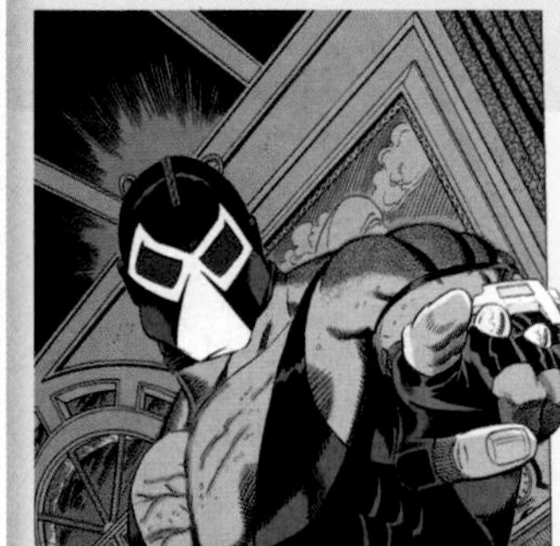

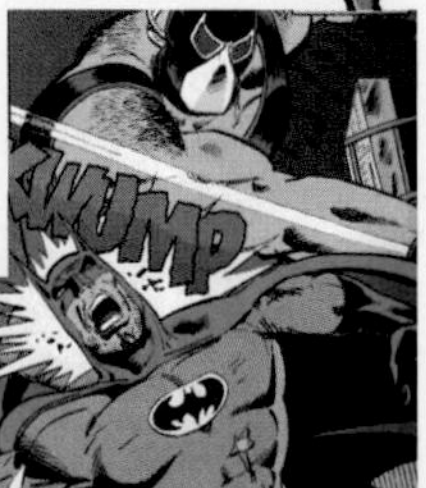

After battling his Rogues Gallery for days on end, Batman returned to the peace of Wayne Manor to rest. But it was no safe harbor. Alfred lay unconscious on the floor, and Bane was spoiling for a fight.

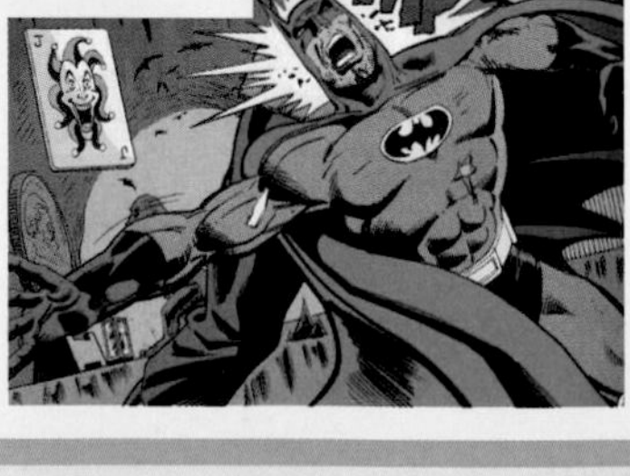

Batman and Bane's battle took them down into the Batcave. Among the trophies of Batman's triumphs, Bane beat down his exhausted opponent.

The Mad Hatter sent his mind-controlled monkey henchmen to battle Batman.

Amygdala unleashed shocking violence on anyone who was a threat—even Batman.

Poison Ivy infected innocents with plant pollen, turning them into an army of zombie slaves.

The tally marks on Mr. Zsasz's skin number his kills—and he wanted to add one more victim.

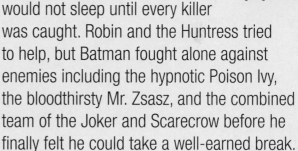

Saving the people of Gotham was always Batman's first priority when his enemies triggered city-wide disasters.

Batman tackled the flames of pyromaniac Firefly and gave the Joker a kicking.

WEARING DOWN BATMAN

Freeing Arkham's patients to run riot across the city was Bane's masterstroke. He knew Batman could not ignore citizens in danger, and that he would not sleep until every killer was caught. Robin and the Huntress tried to help, but Batman fought alone against enemies including the hypnotic Poison Ivy, the bloodthirsty Mr. Zsasz, and the combined team of the Joker and Scarecrow before he finally felt he could take a well-earned break.

Batman knew he could only go on fighting for so long.

BREAKING A BAT

After cornering Batman in Wayne Manor, Bane had his enemy at his mercy. Batman fought back, but his blows were weak and his moves easily countered. Though he could have killed his enemy without a thought, Bane chose another fate— to let Batman live as a broken man. "Death would only end your agony and silence your shame," he said.

With a brutal slam across his knee, Bane crushed Batman's vertebrae.

AZRAEL

Azrael took up the mantle of the bat while Bruce Wayne rehabilitated from his injuries, with Wayne acting as his mentor. Wayne was later forced to fight his protégé to reclaim his identity.

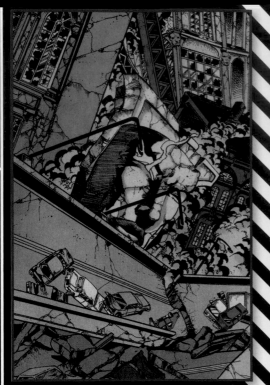

The Quake

An earthquake killed thousands and left Gotham's infrastructure in ruins. With no money in the city's budget and no outside parties willing to finance the necessary repairs, Gotham faced a grim future.

THE GANGS MOVE IN

The magnitude 7.6 earthquake had freed inmates from Arkham Asylum and Blackgate Penitentiary. With the near-empty city at their mercy, criminals carved out their own fiefdoms. Between them, Two-Face and the Penguin controlled the most territory.

Bruce Wayne left Gotham City believing he could do more good in Washington, D.C. to advocate for federal intervention. His pleas fell on deaf ears. Gotham would receive no disaster relief.

Helena Bertinelli, otherwise known as the Huntress, remained in Gotham to protect the helpless and assumed the identity of Batgirl. Batman approved of Helena's new identity, recognizing that Gotham's survivors needed a Bat-like symbol of hope in his absence. But soon things turned sour. Two-Face's gang went on the offensive, reclaiming territory that Batgirl had thought secure.

THE STREET DEMONZ

KILLER CROC

TWO-FACE

THE PENGUIN

NO MAN'S LAND

SCARFACE

POISON IVY

BLACK MASK

Power Shift

Not every criminal had evil intentions. Batman ceded Robinson Park to Poison Ivy provided she harmed no Gotham citizens who had retreated there—mostly children who had been orphaned in the quake. But re-establishing law and order meant winning Gotham back from the gangs headed up by the likes of Two-Face, the Penguin, and the Joker. James Gordon and his law-enforcing Blue Boys formed an alliance with Two-Face and his gang to put an end to the worst of the fighting, but Gordon's former friend betrayed him. First, Two-Face tried to kill Gordon, then he subjected him to a mock trial for breaking their alliance. G.C.P.D. detective Renee Montoya appealed to Harvey Dent's sense of justice, deeply buried within Two-Face's psyche, and convinced him to aquit Gordon.

Two-Face hired top assassin David Cain to eliminate James Gordon. Cain's daughter Cassandra stopped her father and joined Batman's team, taking over from the Huntress as the newest Batgirl.

As the No Man's Land period reached its end, the Joker shot and killed Sarah Essen, James Gordon's wife. Commissioner Gordon took revenge by putting a bullet in the Joker's knee.

GOTHAM STANDS ALONE

The earthquake left utter devastation in its wake. Gotham's citizens waited for disaster relief, but soon learned that the U.S. government had written off Gotham as a lost cause. Not only would the quake damage go unrepaired, but city services—including the police—would be discontinued. All residents were ordered to leave, with Gotham's bridges dynamited to prevent anyone from returning. But some Gothamites remained. The stubbornly loyal and the desperately poor became prey for the gangs—the new leaders of No Man's Land Gotham. Criminals battled for control of each city block. Opposing them stood the "Blue Boys," Commissioner Gordon's volunteer police officers. At first Batman seemed to have abandoned the city, but once Bruce Wayne returned from a failed mission to Washington, D.C., Gotham once again fell under the protection of the Bat.

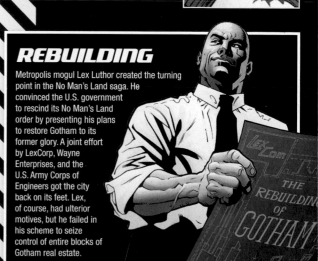

REBUILDING

Metropolis mogul Lex Luthor created the turning point in the No Man's Land saga. He convinced the U.S. government to rescind its No Man's Land order by presenting his plans to restore Gotham to its former glory. A joint effort by LexCorp, Wayne Enterprises, and the U.S. Army Corps of Engineers got the city back on its feet. Lex, of course, had ulterior motives, but he failed in his scheme to seize control of entire blocks of Gotham real estate.

BIRDS OF PREY

POISON IVY
A notorious eco-terrorist and longtime member of Batman's Rogues Gallery, Poison Ivy has recently made efforts to reform and leave her criminal past behind her. Ivy's mental control of plant life and mind-altering pheromones certainly make her a powerful asset to the team, but she hasn't yet earned her colleagues' complete trust.

STARLING
A friend of Black Canary's since their college days, Starling is a reckless and somewhat fiesty operative with talents in unarmed combat and marksmanship. She has been labelled an outlaw by the United States government but has found a measure of protection as a member of Black Canary's new team.

KATANA
Tatsu Yamashiro wields the Soultaker, a Japanese blade which contains spirits, including that of her murdered husband. As the costumed Katana, Tatsu took revenge on the Yakuza gang responsible for taking her husband's life and later served with Batman's Outsiders. Her all-business approach makes her the most serious member of the Birds of Prey.

BLACK CANARY
One of the two founding members of the original Birds of Prey, Black Canary now heads up the team. She is an expert martial artist who possesses the metahuman ability to shatter eardrums with her ultrasonic Canary Cry. As team leader, she has the challenging task of corralling several strong personalities while pulling off impossible missions.

BATGIRL
Back in her original Batgirl costume after finally regaining the use of her legs, Barbara Gordon has ceded control of the team to her friend Black Canary. Though she is more accustomed to acting as the Birds of Prey's operations chief, Barbara is gradually getting used to following orders instead of giving them.

THE FEARLESS FLOCK

This covert strike force populated by a diverse range of crime fighters came into existence under the direction of Barbara Gordon during her time as the information broker Oracle. While Barbara monitored trouble spots from the Birds of Prey's headquarters, Black Canary, Huntress, and other operatives executed global field missions. The team began operations in a Gotham City clock tower but often shifted headquarters. After Barbara departed to resume the role of Batgirl, Black Canary decided to remodel the Birds of Prey by handpicking her own team.

Judomaster and Huntress lend Big Barda a hand. The operatives of the Birds of Prey learn to work together or risk mission failure—not to mention death.

ORACLE
After an injury left her paralyzed from the waist down, Police Commissioner James Gordon's daughter, Barbara, was forced to abandon her role as Batgirl. Instead, she became the computer virtuoso known only as Oracle. By tapping surveillance cameras and hacking into computer feeds, she acted as the the eyes and ears of the Birds of Prey, calling the shots from thousands of miles away.

OTHER MEMBERS
The Birds of Prey have a rotating roster that changes based on mission and member availability. Previous members have included:

BIG BARDA
An alien New God from the world of New Genesis, this statuesque warrior was unstoppable in combat.

MISFIT
An orphaned girl with the power of teleportation, Misfit was seen as an unwanted annoyance until she proved her value to Oracle.

HAWK AND DOVE
The living embodiments of chaos and order, these two crusaders were late additions to the team.

JUDOMASTER
Sonia Sato was the latest hero to claim the mantle of Judomaster. She possessed an "aversion field" that prevented anyone from hitting her with a targeted attack.

BLACK ALICE
A powerful teenaged magician, Black Alice could siphon off the abilities of other supernatural beings for a limited time.

MANHUNTER
Kate Spencer was part of a long line of heroes to carry the Manhunter name. A former prosecutor, she became a costumed vigilante to correct flaws in the justice system.

SPY SMASHER
Katarina Armstrong was an elite anti-terrorism agent employed by governmental bodies. She schemed to take over the Birds.

HUNTRESS
Prior to the Flashpoint timeline shift, the Huntress was Helena Bertinelli, the only survivor of a mob family wiped out by a rival Mafia clan. She became a member of the team after saving Black Canary, but walked a fine line between justice and vengeance. The Huntress often clashed with Oracle over her overbearing attitude, and ended up leaving the team.

LADY BLACKHAWK
Trained by the international team of aviators known as the Blackhawks, Zinda Blake was an expert pilot qualified in flying everything from helicopters and jet fighters to massive cargo carriers. Transported decades into the future, she became a pilot for the Birds of Prey, and was loved for her big heart and her ability to drink anyone under the table.

BRUCE WAYNE : MURDERER?

A WANTED MAN

Batman's crime-fighting crusade was brought to a halt when Bruce Wayne became a suspect in the shocking murder of radio host and ex-girlfriend Vesper Fairchild. Unable to account for his whereabouts without revealing his double life, Bruce was held without bail in Blackgate Penitentiary. With his bodyguard Sasha Bordeaux also under arrest for the crime, it was left to Bruce's trusted inner circle to prove his innocence.

The real killer framed Bruce by dumping Vesper's bullet-riddled body in a Wayne Manor hallway. Moments after Bruce discovered it, the G.C.P.D. burst in with weapons drawn, and found him holding the dead Vesper in his arms.

"Given Mr. Wayne's wealth and resources, I feel it is in the best interest of the city that he be held without bail."

The hardened criminals of Blackgate thought a frightened billionaire would be an easy target, but Bruce Wayne easily took down the gang of inmates who rushed his cell.

Fugitive

Bruce escaped from custody during a prison transfer. It made him look even guiltier, but it meant he could now launch his own investigation as Batman. Although he insisted on going it alone, it was the efforts of Batman's team that identified assassin David Cain as the murderer and Lex Luthor as the author of the smear campaign.

Every member of Batman's inner circle pitched in to exonerate him. Robin, Nightwing, Batgirl, Spoiler, Oracle, and Alfred uncovered new details on Vesper's death and determined how the killer had got past the manor's security systems.

Doubts as to whether her boss fully trusted her led Sasha Bordeaux to resign her bodyguard position at the end of her ordeal.

Spoiler Becomes Robin

Having proven her crime-fighting skills as the Spoiler, Stephanie Brown was thrilled when Batman agreed to train her as Robin. But he fired her for disobeying orders, and in a bid to regain his trust she implemented one of his plans for subduing the Gotham underworld. Unfortunately, Stephanie had only half understood the plan, and when it all went wrong Gotham fell into chaos.

In Batman's plan, his agent Matches Malone would bring all Gotham's rival gangs under his own control. Stephanie didn't know that Batman was Malone, and when he failed to show at the meeting she set up, the gangsters opened fire on each other. A city-wide bloodbath was to follow.

WAR GAMES

A full-scale gang war proved disastrous for Gotham—and for Stephanie Brown's position within Batman's organization.

ALL-OUT WAR

As the gang war raged in Gotham, Batman struggled to get things under control. He worked to draw every gang member to a pre-arranged location where his ally Orpheus would leave them open to mass arrest by the G.C.P.D. But the criminal Black Mask killed Orpheus and spurred the mob to even greater acts of violence.

After torturing Stephanie Brown for information about Batman, Black Mask shot her and left her for dead. She would be secretly nursed back to health by Dr. Leslie Thompkins. Continuing his rampage, Black Mask destroyed the clock tower headquarters of Oracle and the Birds of Prey.

Black Mask Rules

The massacre wiped out a substantial portion of Gotham's underworld hierarchy, including costumed gangs and old-world crime families. By the time the last shots had been fired, Black Mask stood unopposed at the top of Gotham's new criminal order. He wasted no time in flaunting his power.

FALCONE
CRIME FAMILY

Vincent Falcone (father)

Carla Viti (sister)

Lucia Viti (niece)

Johnny Viti (nephew)

Sophia Gigante (daughter)

Mario Falcone (son)

Alberto Falcone (son)

CARMINE FALCONE
The kingpin of the Falcone family, Carmine "The Roman" Falcone had both Gotham's mayor and its police commissioner on his payroll and ran the entire city from behind the scenes. His headaches began with the raids conducted by Batman and district attorney Harvey Dent, but his son Alberto turned against his own family by becoming the Holiday killer. Carmine enlisted help from Gotham's costumed freaks, but he lost his life after Harvey Dent became the crazed Two-Face.

GOTHAM'S ORIGINAL GANGSTERS

When Batman arrived on the scene, old-world crime families like the Falcones had Gotham City in their pocket. The vigilante smashed their operations and ate away at their profits, and inspired a new breed of costumed lunatics who had no respect for tradition. The Falcone family was the first to feel the effects of the new order.

The Falcones enjoyed an exuberant lifestyle in Gotham City, and the wedding of Carmine Falcone's nephew, Johnny Viti, was a typically lavish affair, with all members of the criminal empire in attendance.

Catwoman was no friend to the Falcones. Carmine Falcone got his facial scars after a swipe from her claws, while Carmine's daughter, Sophia Gigante, targeted the Cat for elimination.

SELINA KYLE

The mysterious Selina Kyle had the charm to win an invitation to the wedding of Carmine Falcone's nephew, and the guts to return after dark as Catwoman so she could break into Falcone's safe. Her connection to the Falcone family remained a mystery to Batman, though rumors swirled that Selina might be Carmine Falcone's daughter.

Though she fought the Falcones, Catwoman wasn't on Batman's side either.

BATMAN AND THE FALCONES

Years ago, Bruce Wayne's father Thomas saved Carmine Falcone from a gunshot wound, and the Mafia don felt that he owed a debt to the Wayne family. He never knew that Bruce had taken up the identity of Batman, thwarting and humiliating Carmine at every turn. When Batman torched the Falcones' warehouse containing millions of dollars in cash, Carmine called for his head.

Batman's ability to come and go as he pleased in Gotham City enraged Carmine Falcone.

"THE ROMAN" EMPIRE

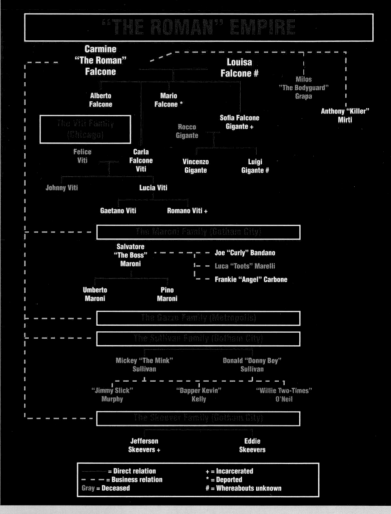

- Carmine "The Roman" Falcone
- Louisa Falcone #
- Milos "The Bodyguard" Grapa
- Alberto Falcone
- Mario Falcone *
- Anthony "Killer" Mirti
- The Viti Family (Chicago)
- Rocco Gigante
- Sofia Falcone Gigante +
- Felice Viti
- Carla Falcone Viti
- Vincenzo Gigante
- Luigi Gigante #
- Johnny Viti
- Lucia Viti
- Gaetano Viti
- Romano Viti +
- The Maroni Family (Gotham City)
- Salvatore "The Boss" Maroni
- Joe "Curly" Bandano
- Luca "Toots" Marelli
- Frankie "Angel" Carbone
- Umberto Maroni
- Pino Maroni
- The Gazzo Family (Metropolis)
- The Sullivan Family (Gotham City)
- Mickey "The Mink" Sullivan
- Donald "Donny Boy" Sullivan
- "Jimmy Slick" Murphy
- "Dapper Kevin" Kelly
- "Willie Two-Times" O'Neil
- The Skeever Family (Gotham City)
- Jefferson Skeevers +
- Eddie Skeevers

———— = Direct relation	+ = Incarcerated
- - - - = Business relation	* = Deported
Gray = Deceased	# = Whereabouts unknown

THE MARONI FAMILY

The Maroni family was the chief rival to the Falcone family in Gotham's underworld. Sal Maroni infamously threw acid into district attorney Harvey Dent's face during a courtroom trial, inadvertently creating Two-Face. The Maronis and the Falcones both found themselves under fire from the Holiday Killer, and accused each other of orchestrating the mysterious assassinations.

- Umberto Maroni (son)
- Pino Maroni (son)
- Salvatore "The Boss" Maroni
- Luigi "Big Lou" Maroni (father)

THE LONG HALLOWEEN
ISSUE #1

"We can all talk around it, but we know what needs to be done."

BATMAN

MAIN CHARACTERS: Batman, Commissioner Gordon, Harvey Dent, Carmine "the Roman" Falcone, Catwoman
SUPPORTING CHARACTERS: Alberto Falcone, Richard Daniel, Johnny Viti, Barbara Gordon, Gilda Dent
LOCATIONS: Carmine Falcone's mansion, Gotham Bank boardroom, Gotham police headquarters, Gotham warehouse, Harvey Dent's home

BACKGROUND

This issue marked the start of writer Jeph Loeb and artist Tim Sale's stylish, 13-part *The Long Halloween*. Its storyline took Batman back to the early years of his crime-fighting career, serving as a sequel of sorts to Frank Miller and David Mazzucchelli's *Batman: Year One* (February–May 1987) and inspiring further collaborations between the award-winning team of Loeb and Sale.

A murder mystery formed *The Long Halloween*'s backbone, as Batman, Police Captain James Gordon, and District Attorney Harvey Dent raced to apprehend the mysterious Holiday Killer, who struck once a month on days of public celebration. But the story's real heart was its exploration of the professional partnership between the three men, and the heartbreaking manner in which it splintered after Dent was scarred by acid and transformed into the horrifying villain Two-Face.

The Long Halloween also provided an exploration of Batman's Rogues Gallery. Catwoman, the Joker, the Riddler, the Scarecrow, the Mad Hatter, and even Solomon Grundy played key roles. The true villains, however, didn't wear costumes. The Falcone mobsters, introduced in *Batman: Year One*, got an updated family tree as readers learned how organized crime operated in Gotham City.

PUBLICATION DATE
December 1996

EDITOR
Archie Goodwin

COVER ARTIST
Tim Sale

WRITER
Jeph Loeb

PENCILLER
Tim Sale

INKER
Tim Sale

LETTERER
Richard Starkings

The Story...

Batman teams up with Police Commissioner James Gordon and District Attorney Harvey Dent to take on Gotham's godfather, Carmine "The Roman" Falcone.

A new hero called the Batman was beginning to make his mark in Gotham, but the city remained under the thumb of Carmine "The Roman" Falcone, head of the notorious Falcone crime family. When Bruce Wayne received his invitation to the wedding of Falcone's nephew, Johnny Viti, he knew it came with strings attached [1]. As a member of the board at the Gotham Bank and one of the most powerful men in the city, Bruce knew that Falcone hoped to persuade him to help convince the bank to launder money for the mob. But Bruce wasn't afraid to reject Carmine Falcone to his face [2]. After an intense discussion, he walked out of Falcone's office and rejoined the wedding festivities, where he was cheered by the presence of his friend, the alluring Selina Kyle.

District Attorney Harvey Dent hadn't been invited to the gala, but he went anyway. In the parking lot of Falcone's mansion apartment, he jotted down license plate numbers in his ongoing effort to collect evidence and bring down Carmine Falcone [3]. Later, that evening, Bruce Wayne donned the guise of Batman to go outside the law and achieve what Harvey could not. He broke into Carmine Falcone's safe and took his private ledger, but Batman first had to fight off Catwoman, who had her own designs on Falcone's secrets [4].

Batman brought his prize to a rooftop meeting with Harvey Dent and police captain James Gordon [5]. Silhouetted by the light of the Bat-Signal, the three men reconfirmed their mutual desire to dismantle organized crime in Gotham City [6]. Batman demonstrated why he had to remain a silent partner in the operation by producing the Falcone ledger [7]. The book contained enough evidence on illegal activities to help the district attorney's office immeasurably.

Carmine Falcone, meanwhile, made a successful end-run around Bruce Wayne. He had enough members of the bank board in his pocket to render Bruce's objection to laundering his money irrelevant. But when Batman paid a visit to bank president Richard Daniel—who had voted in favor of doing business with the Falcones—he scared the executive into voting against the deal. Daniel's act of defiance against the Falcones earned him a death sentence, and the mob carried out the hit with cold precision.

The Falcones were soon beset with trouble of a different sort when the Holiday Killer struck for the first time. On Halloween night, Carmine Falcone's newly wed nephew, Johnny Viti, was shot dead in his bathtub, with a Jack-o'-lantern left as a calling card [8]. For the next year, the Falcones would experience a string of murders targeted at their family, an ordeal they would call the "Long Halloween."

Harvey Dent and Batman were about to make the Halloween holiday even worse for the Falcones. Since the banks were refusing to launder the mob's money, Carmine Falcone had been stockpiling it in a Gotham warehouse instead [9]. With a single match [10], Harvey ignited a blaze that consumed the warehouse and the ill-gotten gains within [11].

Harvey returned home to his wife Gilda [12], finally satisfied that he had struck a blow against Falcone that would have lasting repercussions. But the mob had already drawn a target on the Dents. As trick-or-treaters passed by on the sidewalk, Harvey discovered a strange package. Moments later, it exploded, and the Dent home was consumed in a fireball [13].

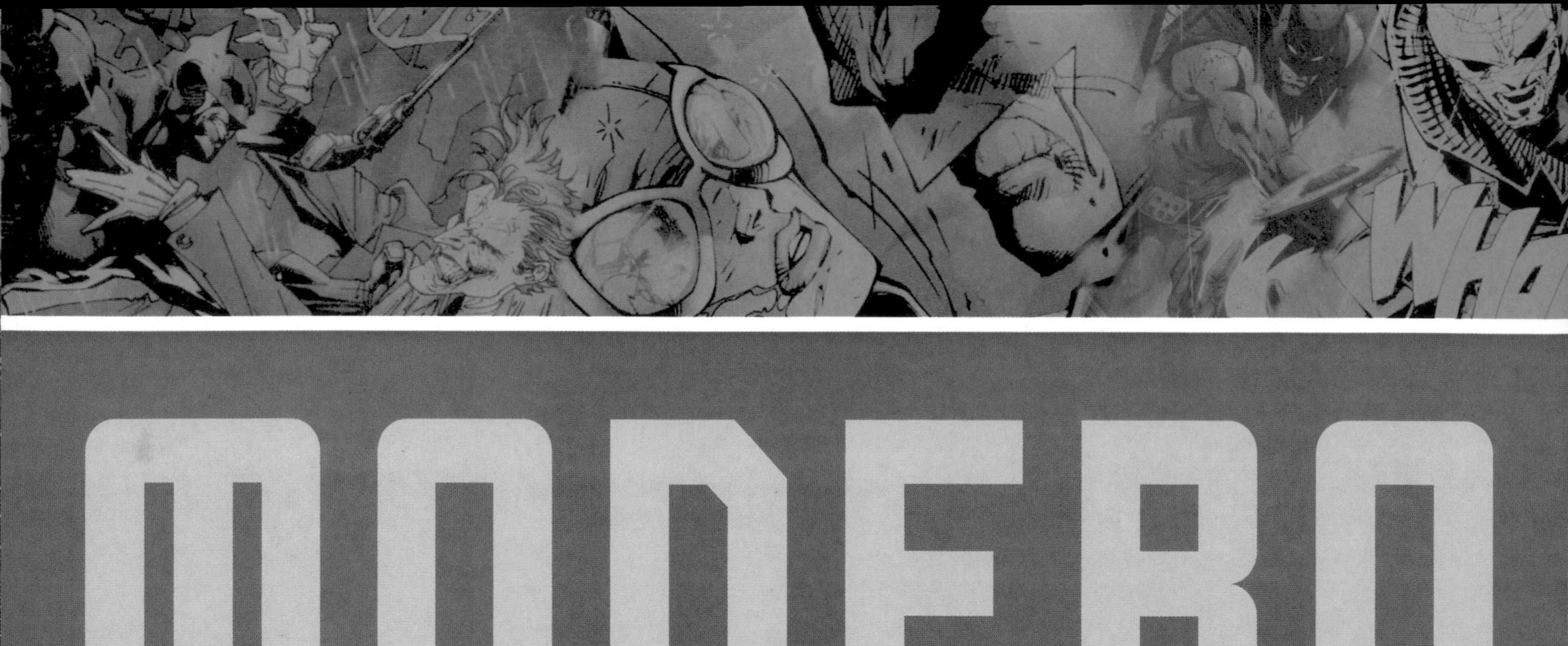

MODERN AGE

MID '00s AND ON

At the dawn of a new millennium, Batman became a bigger star than ever and led the relaunch of the new DC Universe.

From 2005, Batman was entering a new era of cultural fame, with his magic touch extending into other media including gaming and television animation—but comics were a cornerstone of the Dark Knight's resurgence. The yearlong "Hush" saga united writer Jeph Loeb with hot artist Jim Lee, and starred a greatest-hits lineup of Batman's villains. It also contributed a new member to the Rogues Gallery: the titular, mummy-wrapped Hush. And as DC published more crossover events to bring its interconnected titles closer together, Batman became a starring player in the events of *Identity Crisis*, *Infinite Crisis*, *Final Crisis*, and more.

Batman's supporting cast expanded, too, as Stephanie Brown briefly became Robin and Kate Kane debuted as the all-new Batwoman. Even Jason Todd came back from the dead thanks to a reality-warping loophole, becoming the bloodthirsty Red Hood.

Writer Grant Morrison took the reins on Batman in 2006 and led off by revealing the existence of Batman's ten-year-old son, Damian Wayne. Over the course of Morrison's storyarcs, Batman suffered a mental breakdown at the hands of Dr. Simon Hurt and seemingly perished while fighting the omnipotent god Darkseid.

In late 2011, to attract new readers and mark a bold move into digital distribution, DC rebooted its entire universe. *Batman* and *Detective Comics* started fresh with #1 issues, and many more titles in the new DC line starred Batman and his Gotham crew.

OVERLEAF
Detective Comics #4
(February 2012):
New villain the Dollmaker is
pulling all the strings when
he—or is it his doll-like
decoy?—comes to blows
with Batman.

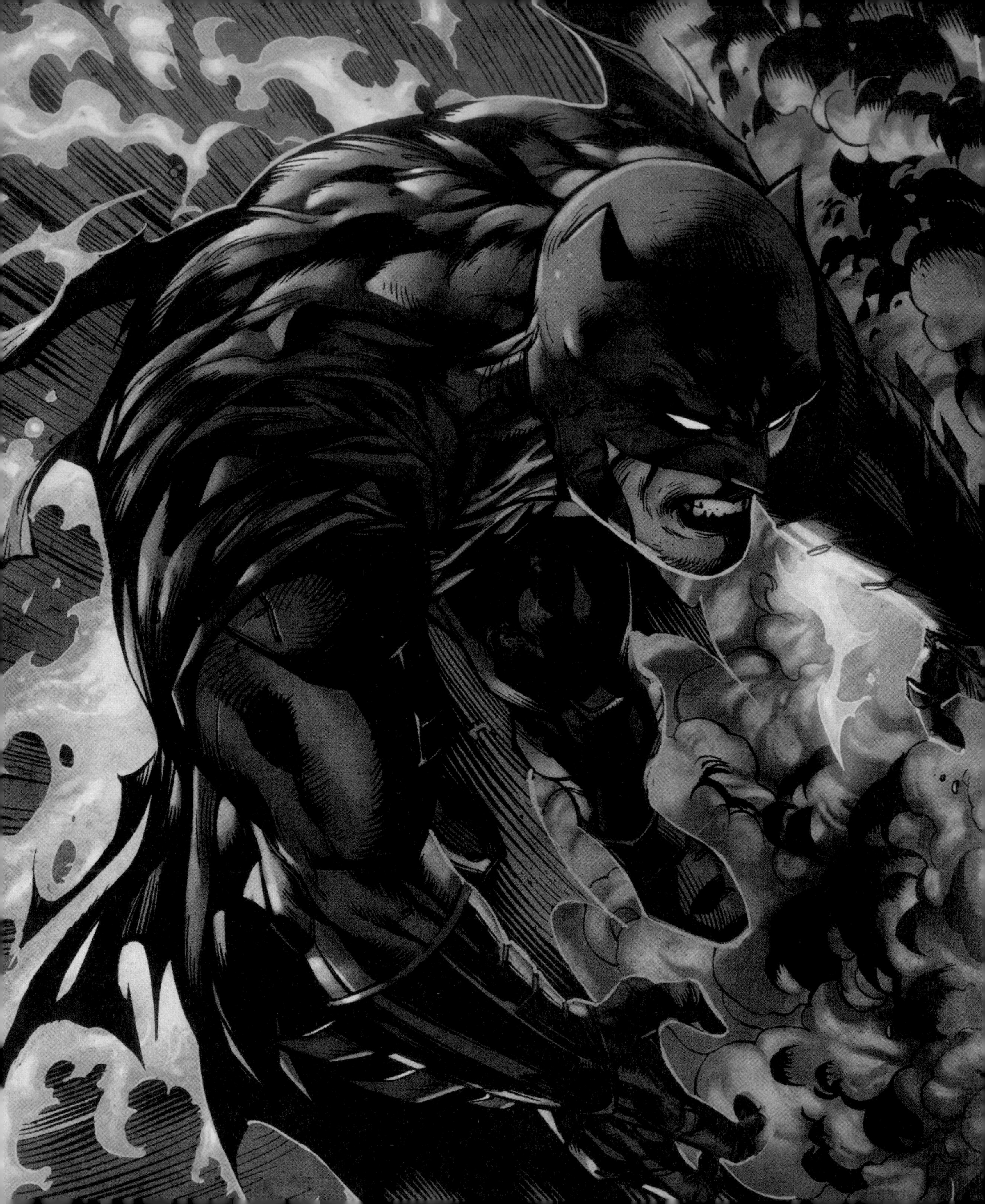

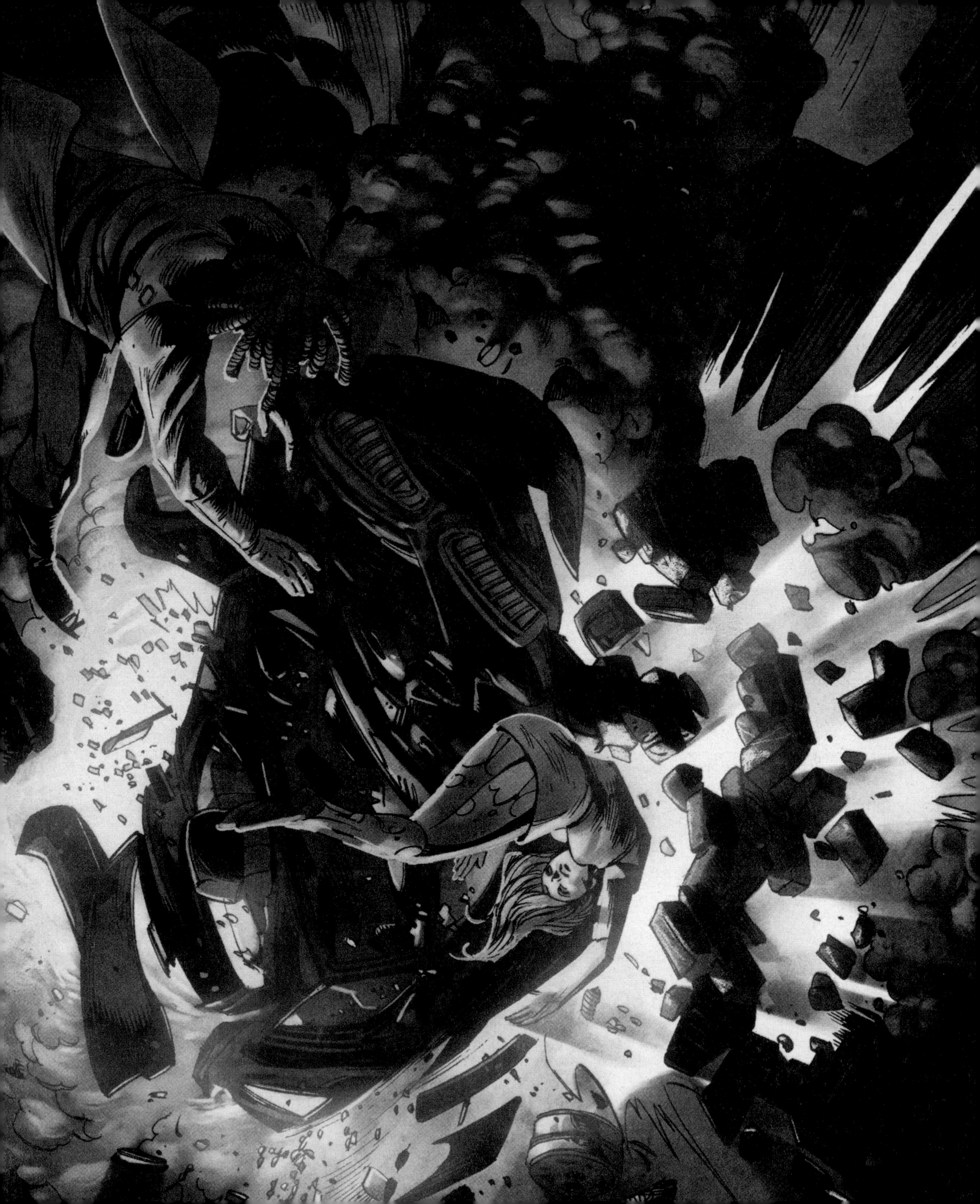

A SHARED PAST

A prestigious Gotham surgeon, Dr. Thomas Elliot is also one of Bruce Wayne's oldest friends. When the two were children, Bruce's father had saved the life of Tommy's mother. But Tommy knew the act had robbed him of the chance to inherit his family's large fortune, and he vowed to take revenge. Many years later—and now somehow armed with the secret of Bruce's double identity—Tommy Elliot became the mysterious bandaged villain named Hush.

A new foe sets a grand plan in motion. But his mask of bandages conceals a face that Bruce Wayne knows well.

HUSH

The First Contender

Investigating a kidnapping, Batman entered the lair of Killer Croc, one of his most bestial opponents. Batman couldn't imagine the drumbeat of clashes with his enemies that would follow, all of them orchestrated by a strange new villain known only as Hush.

Rogues Gallery

Poison Ivy and Harley Quinn took their own shots at Batman as Hush's vengeful scheme unfolded. Ivy enslaved Superman using plant pheromones and ordered him into battle against an outmatched Dark Knight, while Harley Quinn interrupted Bruce Wayne's night at the theater when she tried to rob the packed house.

Flipping the Script

Just as Tommy Elliot began to surface as a potential suspect for Hush's crimes, he took a fatal bullet. The Joker appeared to have fired the shot and Batman nearly beat him to death with his fists—not realizing he had been fooled by Hush. The shapeshifting Clayface had played the role of Elliot's corpse as Hush looked on approvingly from the shadows.

The "Hush" Plot

Hush might have gotten things moving, but it was the Riddler who ultimately profited from them. The Riddler had joined forces with Elliot, and it was the Riddler who was running what he called the "Hush" plot behind the scenes. It was also the Riddler who had deduced Batman's secret identity of Bruce Wayne.

KEY ISSUE

IDENTITY CRISIS
ISSUE #6

"This is Batman we're talking about! You can't do that to Batman!"

THE FLASH

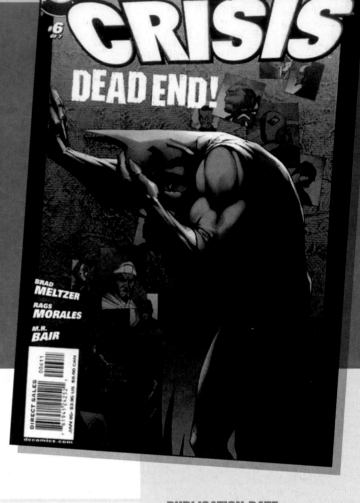

MAIN CHARACTERS: Batman, Robin, Green Arrow, Flash, Captain Boomerang
SUPPORTING CHARACTERS: Doctor Light, Calculator, Deadshot, Merlyn, Monocle, Zatanna, Dr. Mid-Nite, Mister Terrific, the Atom
LOCATIONS: Gotham City, JLA satellite, New York City, Ivy Town

BACKGROUND

Though it bore the same "crisis" keyword as *Crisis on Infinite Earths*, 2004's *Identity Crisis* spent more time on personal revelations than cosmic crusades. Writer Brad Meltzer cast a cynical eye on the adventures of the Silver Age, suggesting no era is truly innocent. The seven-part saga centered on the murder of Sue Dibny, the wife of the good-natured Elongated Man. By issue #6, the whodunit had cast a harsh light on cases from the archives of the Justice League of America, revealing that some Justice League members had been mind-wiping their foes. This act seemed justified to keep their secret identities safe, but issue #6 revealed that Batman's objection to the process caused his teammates to brainwash him, too. The Dark Knight's memories later returned, but his trust in his teammates was forever shattered. Batman even began to stockpile countermeasures to deploy against his allies if they ever turned on him. In another development, the third Robin (Tim Drake) became an orphan in issue #6, prompting Bruce Wayne to adopt him in a 2006 storyline.

PUBLICATION DATE
January 2005

EDITOR
Mike Carlin

COVER ARTIST
Michael Turner

WRITER
Brad Meltzer

PENCILLER
Rags Morales

INKER
Michael Blair

LETTERER
Kenny Lopez

The Story...

Batman is too late to prevent the death of Robin's father, but he is about to witness a shocking act that breaks his trust in his teammates.

Tim Drake—the third Boy Wonder—rushed to his father's home only to discover two bodies lying on the floor. Jack Drake and the assassin Captain Boomerang had killed one another in a showdown. Even though Tim Drake knew his father's condition was fatal, he desperately made frantic efforts at resuscitation. With the words, "I've got you," Batman gently pulled him away. Tim, like Bruce, was now an orphan **[1]**.

Jack Drake wasn't the only man who had left behind a son. Owen Mercer, the new Captain Boomerang, arrived at the scene and demanded to see his father's body. The authorities had locked down the area and refused to give him access, denying that Batman was anywhere on the premises with the same "see no evil" attitude that the G.C.P.D. routinely deployed whenever the Dark Knight's behind-the-scenes assistance was questioned **[2]**. The younger Captain Boomerang stalked off, determined to live up to his father's legacy.

His setback was offset by victories for costumed criminals throughout the legal system. Deadshot, Merlyn, and the Monocle all escaped prosecution for their crimes due to their participation in dangerous missions for the U.S. government's Suicide Squad program **[3]**. Doctor Light—responsible for an earlier brutal assault on Sue Dibny aboard the Justice League of America's satellite—was also unpunished **[4]**.

The Justice League of America had always been a force for good, but now even its integrity came into question. The Flash confronted Green Arrow about an incident from the history of the Justice League, admitting that he doubted the "official story" after experiencing a memory jolt **[5]**. Green Arrow then confessed what the League had tried to keep under wraps for years—in the aftermath of Doctor Light's attack on Sue, he and several other League members voted to use Zatanna's magical powers to erase the villain's memories. They were interrupted in the middle of the act by a shocked Batman **[6]**. The Dark Knight, one of the most strong-willed people on Earth, was incredulous that his teammates—his friends—would willingly eliminate anyone's ability to make their own decisions **[7]**. The other Leaguers were left to decide what to do next, and the majority agreed to work Zatanna's magic on Batman, too. "You took Bruce's memories?" asked the Flash, stunned. Green Arrow made no apologies, reminding the Flash about the death of Robin's father, and pointing out the difficulty of keeping loved ones safe from super-villains. "When it comes to family," he said, "we can't always be there to protect them."

Batman hadn't yet discovered the truth about his teammates' questionable decisions. He continued his investigation into Sue Dibny's murder and returned to the Batcave to analyze the forensic data from Sue's autopsy. At the same time, at the Justice Society of America's headquarters, Dr. Mid-Nite and Mister Terrific were pursuing the same line of investigation **[8]**. Both teams came to an identical, startling conclusion: Sue Dibny had died when a brain obstruction cut off her blood supply. High-resolution imaging of the damaged area of her mid-medulla revealed a tiny pair of footprints **[9]**. Batman rushed into action **[10]** to find the only person who it seemed could have left behind such microscopic evidence—Ray Palmer, the size-changing hero known as the Atom. By the end of the case, Batman had learned the true identity of the murderer (Palmer was innocent of the crime) and that the trust shared by comrades-in-arms could easily be broken.

INFINITE CRISIS

During the Crisis on Infinite Earths, a hero named Alexander Luthor helped to save the universe by combining many realities into one. When he next appeared, he was a corrupted madman intent on remaking the universe to his own design.

ON THE DEFENSIVE

Batman met with Superman and Wonder Woman aboard the Justice League's orbital headquarters following Alexander Luthor's preliminary assault. The three didn't yet know their enemy's true goals, and tensions between them stood in the way of cooperation on a counterattack. When the alien warlord Mongul arrived to mop up any survivors of Alexander's attack, the heroes were barely able to fight him off. An angry Batman concluded that this was one crisis he would face alone.

Batman felt his colleagues had betrayed his trust. He brushed aside offers of help, even from Alfred.

"You know, there was one thing your father never wanted to be. Alone." – Alfred

A Second Superman

Somebody else remembered the way things were before the Crisis on Infinite Earths. A pre-Crisis version of Superman urged Batman to join Alexander's cause, showing him visions of friends and family members who had existed on alternate Earths erased during the first Crisis. They could all live again, if multiple realities were restored.

Brother Eye

The Brother Eye surveillance satellite, built by Batman, became self-aware and turned living beings into OMAC cyborgs. Alexander used it to spread chaos.

A New Plan

The stakes had now become far too great for Batman to handle everything on his own. Booster Gold and a new, teenaged Blue Beetle became his first recruits in a mission to strike at Brother Eye. As Batman's squad rocketed into space, Superman and Wonder Woman took aim at Alexander Luthor's other agents.

Taking Down the Eye

Batman and his team penetrated Brother Eye's defenses and stormed the corridors leading to the AI core. Brother Eye fought back against its creator, but Batman had a secret weapon in Mister Terrific, whose powers made him invisible to machines. An adjustment to the satellite's engines sent Brother Eye into an orbital death spiral from which Batman himself narrowly escaped.

Fatal Decision

Alexander Luthor's scheme lay in ruins and Batman had the villain at his mercy. For an instant he considered using a gun to end the threat forever, but remembered his vow to never take a life. However, Alexander soon found himself cornered by the Joker, who sprayed his face with a jet of acid before putting a bullet in his head.

"You didn't let the Joker play." – Lex Luthor

MORTAL ENEMIES?

Batman is aware that a mind-controlling villain could turn Superman against him, and that he can't match the Man of Steel in a contest of strength. He has wisely prepared countermeasures for emergency use, including compact explosives to distract Superman and inner ear scrambling sonic screechers to disorient him. Batman's final line of defense is a ring containing a shard of Kryptonite.

ABSOLUTE POWER

With Batman's brain and Superman's muscle, the two could rule the world—that is, if their gallant natures didn't make such an act unthinkable. But in an alternate timeline where Bruce Wayne and Clark Kent experienced evil upbringings, they became dictators. A monument replaced the Statue of Liberty which read, "OBEY OR DIE."

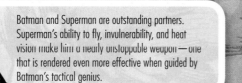

Batman and Superman are outstanding partners. Superman's ability to fly, invulnerability, and heat vision make him a nearly unstoppable weapon—one that is rendered even more effective when guided by Batman's tactical genius.

Batman and Superman were suspicious of each other at first, but over time they became fast friends who could act as a tightly synced fighting squad when needed. Because Gotham City and Metropolis are close neighbors, the two heroes will often collaborate when tracking down escaped members of their own rogues galleries. Batman and Superman are founding members of the Justice League, which gives them an international—and sometimes intergalactic—jurisdiction. Pitted against their many foes, the two heroes must use their individual skills as a combined force.

ALWAYS OUTNUMBERED

It is always a bad idea to challenge Batman and Superman, but this fact does not stop their enemies from trying to get the best of the formidable pairing. After Lex Luthor placed a one-billion dollar bounty on their heads, the two heroes found themselves cornered in Washington, D.C. by a dangerous group of villians which included Giganta, Black Manta, Cheetah, King Shark, and a whole host of other hopefuls with greed in their hearts.

BATWOMAN

"I've always felt that people should take responsibility for their actions, not excuse them."

BATWOMAN

Gotham City's criminals have learned to fear Kate Kane! With nearly unlimited resources to rival those of Bruce Wayne, the newest Batwoman has prevented the spread of the twisted Religion of Crime at great risk to her own life.

A traumatic kidnapping during their childhood forever changed the destinies of Kate and her twin sister.

Batman may originally have been her inspiration, but Batwoman has become a hero in her own right.

HONOR AND DUTY

Kate Kane grew up within the wealthiest Gotham family *not* named Wayne. As a child, she saw her mother and twin sister Beth gunned down during a botched kidnapping, and grew up under the heavy-handed influence of her father, a U.S. Army colonel. Kate studied at the United States Military Academy at West Point before she was asked to leave for refusing to hide her personal relationship with another woman from her superiors. She later began an on–off romance with Gotham City police officer Renee Montoya.

Kate found inspiration in Batman's example after the hero helped her during an encounter with a mugger. With assistance from her father, she undertook a two-year program of intense physical training. The Kane family fortune paid for her high-tech Batsuit and an arsenal of gadgets, and a bunker within the Kane manor became her secret headquarters.

During a period when Batman left Gotham City to pursue a spiritual journey overseas, Kate made her first patrol as the mysterious, flame-haired Batwoman. She faced her first foe in Bruno Mannheim, leader of the Religion of Crime. Mannheim's secret organization followed the evil doctrines of the Crime Bible, which prophesized the death of Kate Kane. After the cult attempted to sacrifice her, Batwoman escaped and teamed up with Renee Montoya—who had become the blank-masked hero the Question—to vanquish Mannheim and his fellow disciples.

The eerie woman known only as "Alice" replaced Mannheim as the head of the Religion of Crime. Batwoman's world shattered when Alice revealed herself as Beth Kane, Kate's own twin who had survived the childhood hostage raid but suffered deep psychological damage in the years since. Batwoman cut ties with her father for keeping the truth from her. Now armed with a new confidence as a member of the Batman family, Kate has softened her strict self-reliance enough to accept her cousin, Bette Kane, as her protégé in her war against crime.

With a knife throw, Batwoman took out Bruno Mannheim, the leader of the Religion of Crime. It was one of the first challenges she faced as a crime fighter in Gotham.

Batwoman's father urged her to ignore rumors of her sister's survival, but she was determined to discover the truth.

Kate's first serious romantic relationship was with G.C.P.D. police detective Renee Montoya. They continue to fight crime together.

The enigmatic Alice vanished in the waters of Gotham Harbor, leaving Batwoman with unanswered questions.

Batwoman has the same red hair as Batgirl, but thanks to their very different personalities they are seldom mistaken for one another.

KEY DATA

REAL NAME Katherine "Kate" Kane

OCCUPATION Adventurer, international operative, socialite

WEAPONS/POWERS/ABILITIES Batarangs, extendible staff, Utility Belt gadgets, military training in armed and unarmed combat

AFFILIATIONS Batman Inc.

RELATIVES Jake Kane (father), Gabrielle Kane (mother, deceased), Beth Kane (sister), Bette Kane (cousin)

FIRST APPEARANCE 52 #7 (JULY 2006)

Batwoman's crime-fighting suit contains a layer of impact-dispersing Kevlar weave, much like the Batsuit worn by Batman.

Every inch of Batwoman's costume is functional. Her no-slip, steel-toed boots provide both traction and kicking power.

TEACHER AND STUDENT

Though Bette Kane had previous crime-fighting experience as the costumed Flamebird, she didn't share Kate's disciplined military upbringing and found it hard to win her approval.

THE WEEPING WOMAN

Batwoman faced a deadly challenge in the form of a supernatural spirit that targeted Gotham's children and dragged them to watery graves. While stopping the spirit, known as the Weeping Woman, Kate began a relationship with Maggie Sawyer of the G.C.P.D.

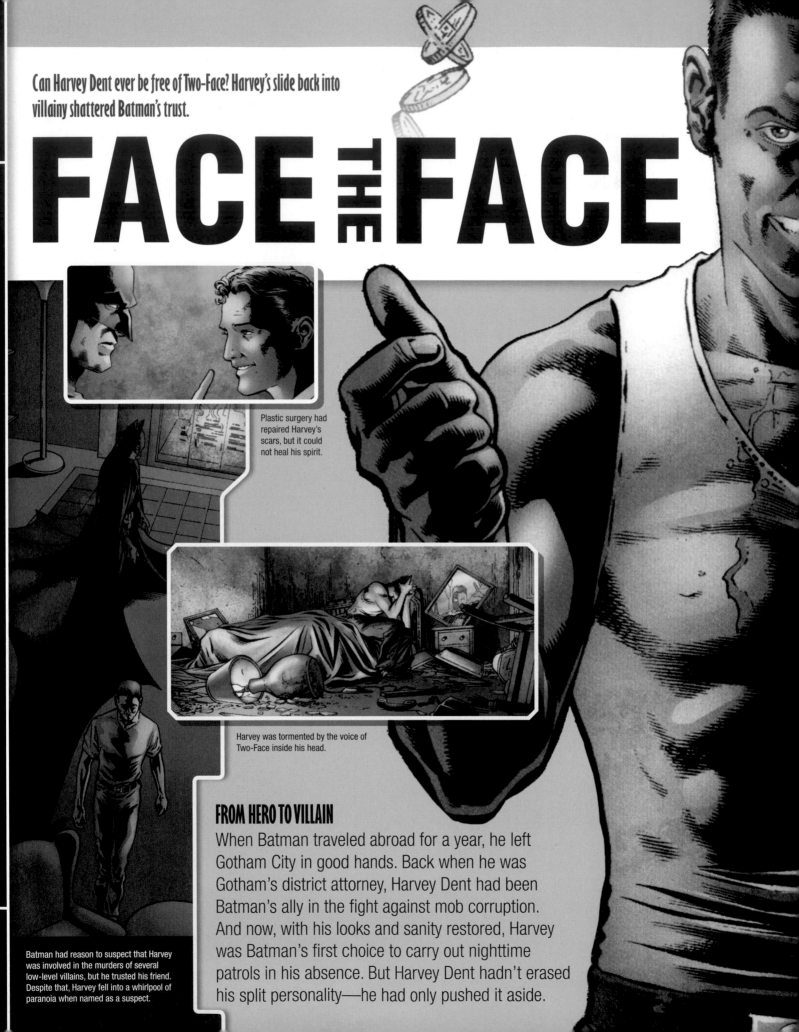

Can Harvey Dent ever be free of Two-Face? Harvey's slide back into villainy shattered Batman's trust.

FACE THE FACE

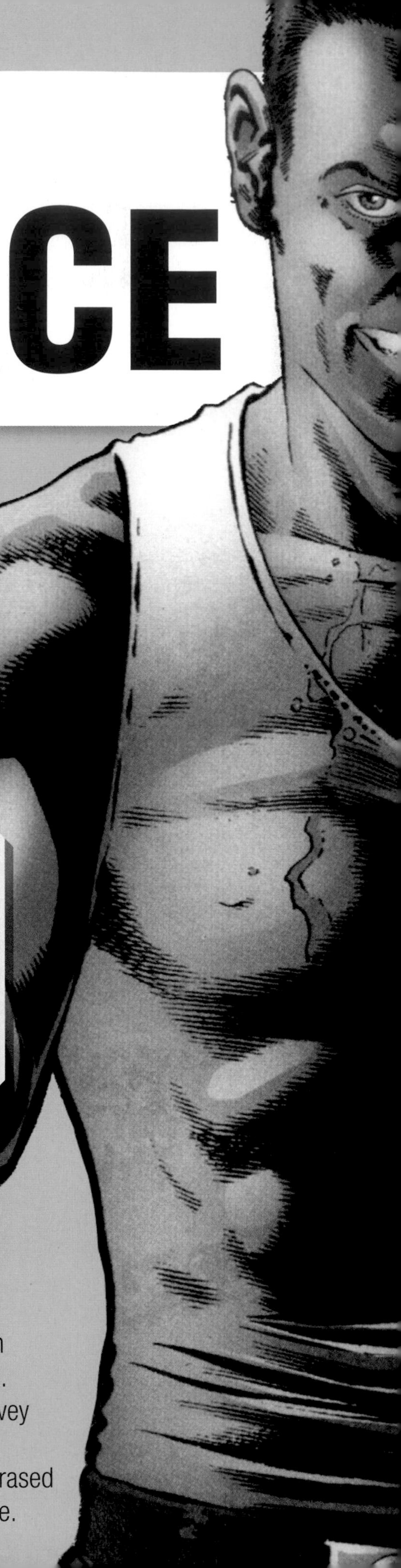

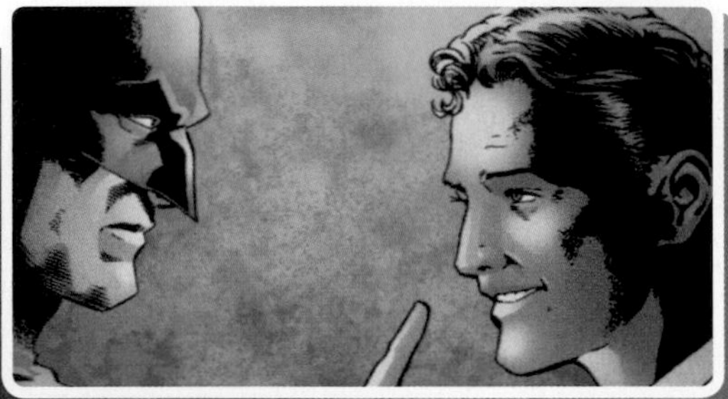

Plastic surgery had repaired Harvey's scars, but it could not heal his spirit.

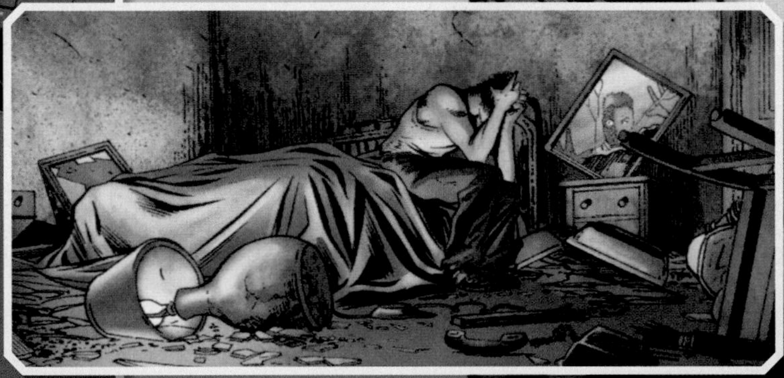

Harvey was tormented by the voice of Two-Face inside his head.

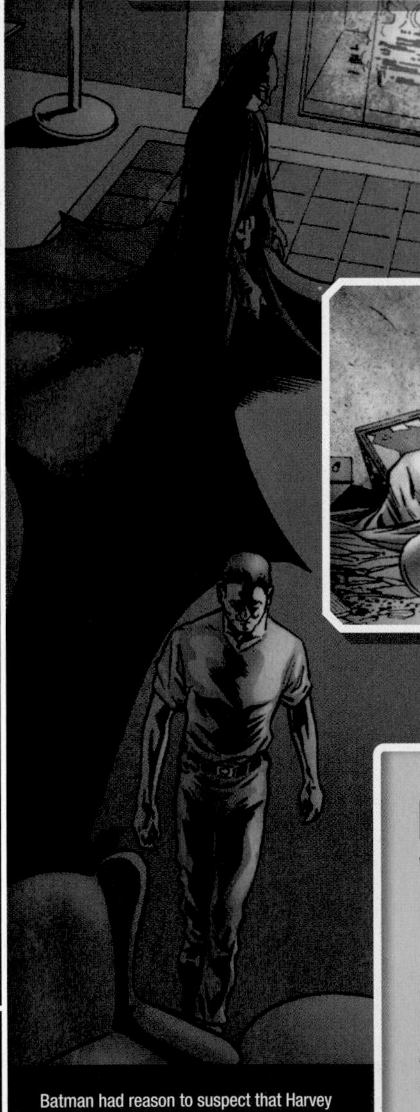

Batman had reason to suspect that Harvey was involved in the murders of several low-level villains, but he trusted his friend. Despite that, Harvey fell into a whirlpool of paranoia when named as a suspect.

FROM HERO TO VILLAIN

When Batman traveled abroad for a year, he left Gotham City in good hands. Back when he was Gotham's district attorney, Harvey Dent had been Batman's ally in the fight against mob corruption. And now, with his looks and sanity restored, Harvey was Batman's first choice to carry out nighttime patrols in his absence. But Harvey Dent hadn't erased his split personality—he had only pushed it aside.

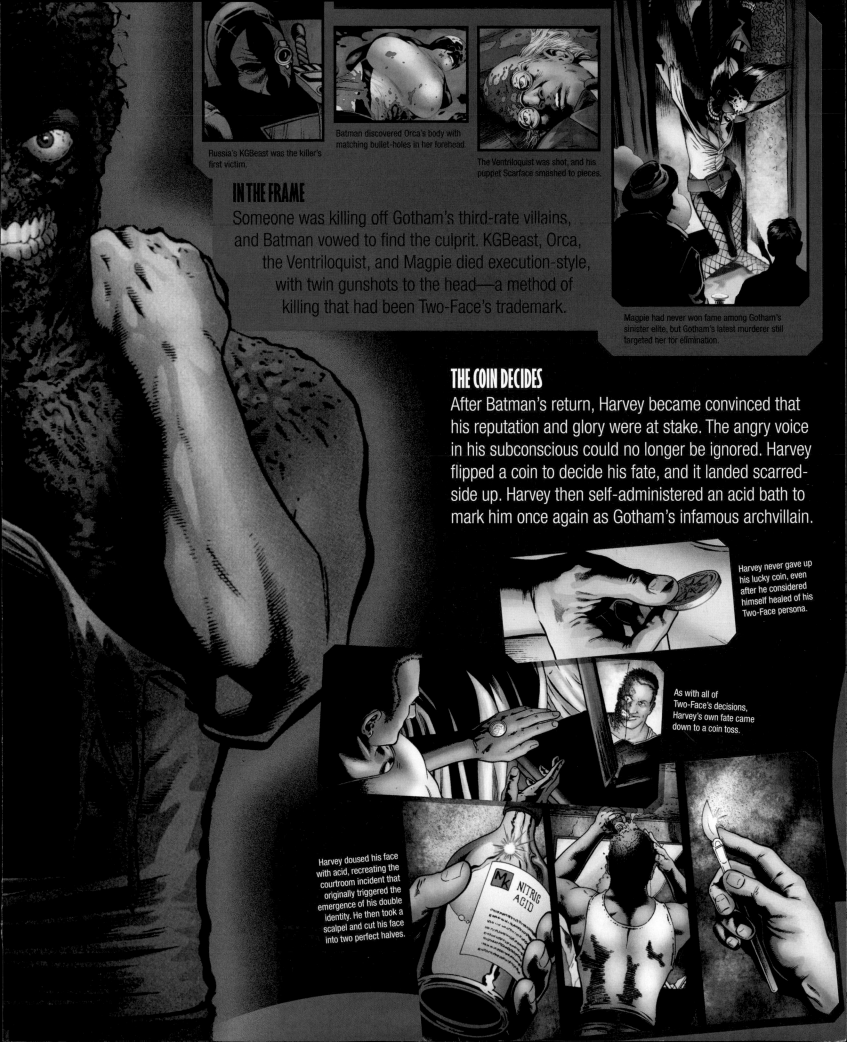

Russia's KGBeast was the killer's first victim.

Batman discovered Orca's body with matching bullet-holes in her forehead.

The Ventriloquist was shot, and his puppet Scarface smashed to pieces.

IN THE FRAME

Someone was killing off Gotham's third-rate villains, and Batman vowed to find the culprit. KGBeast, Orca, the Ventriloquist, and Magpie died execution-style, with twin gunshots to the head—a method of killing that had been Two-Face's trademark.

Magpie had never won fame among Gotham's sinister elite, but Gotham's latest murderer still targeted her for elimination.

THE COIN DECIDES

After Batman's return, Harvey became convinced that his reputation and glory were at stake. The angry voice in his subconscious could no longer be ignored. Harvey flipped a coin to decide his fate, and it landed scarred-side up. Harvey then self-administered an acid bath to mark him once again as Gotham's infamous archvillain.

Harvey never gave up his lucky coin, even after he considered himself healed of his Two-Face persona.

As with all of Two-Face's decisions, Harvey's own fate came down to a coin toss.

Harvey doused his face with acid, recreating the courtroom incident that originally triggered the emergence of his double identity. He then took a scalpel and cut his face into two perfect halves.

MK NITRIC ACID

UNDER THE RED HOOD

The Red Hood is someone Batman never expected to see again.
Jason Todd is back from the dead!

Regeneration

After miraculously coming back to life in a strange cosmic fluke, Jason required the restorative waters of a Lazarus Pit to bring him back to full health.

KRAAK AAK

Batman has a strict rule against the use of firearms, but Jason Todd uses every advantage, no matter the price. Armed with a rapid-fire cannon, he cut down a gang of street dealers without thinking twice about the body count.

> "Death will come to those who deserve death."
>
> – The Red Hood

AAK AAK

BACK WITH A VENGEANCE

Though he died at the hands of the Joker, Jason Todd—who had fought alongside Batman as the second Robin—returned to life. Jason remembered everything that had been done to him by the Joker, and he blamed Batman for not stopping his murderer when he had the chance. With a dangerous edge and a complete disregard for Batman's "no killing" rule, Jason returned to Gotham and assumed the identity of the Red Hood. His target for extermination was the gangster Black Mask, whose criminal gang controlled most of Gotham City's underworld.

In the Crosshairs

Black Mask had clawed his way to the top of Gotham's underworld, but the Red Hood spoiled his triumph by killing his aides. Black Mask hired mercenaries like Mr. Freeze to tackle the Red Hood, hoping to eliminate the newcomer before he threatened Black Mask himself.

In Batman's eyes, anyone who recklessly uses deadly force to fight their cause is no hero. Batman moved to shut down the Red Hood's crime-fighting operation long before he discovered the secret of the vigilante's identity.

Jason took pleasure in delivering brutal payback to the man who had killed him. He beat the Joker with a crowbar—just as the Joker had done to him when he was Robin—and left him close to death.

Prodigal Son

Batman could read the subtlety in the Red Hood's fighting style. He immediately suspected that the fallen Robin had returned. After Jason was unmasked, Batman hoped he could bring his former pupil back from the brink. But in his failure, he knew he had made a new enemy.

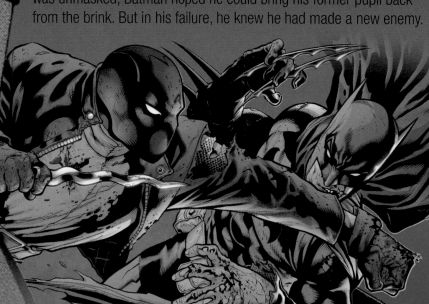

TRINITY

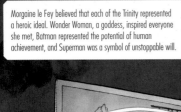

In their civilian identities, Diana Prince, Bruce Wayne, and Clark Kent kept a low profile when they met to discuss the disturbing dream they were all having. They concluded that they were under some kind of attack.

CORNERSTONES

Three heroes, three villains, and all of reality hanging in the balance. The stakes couldn't have been higher when the wicked sorceress Morgaine le Fey teamed with the alien powerhouse Despero and the riddle-spinning Enigma to usurp the roles of Wonder Woman, Superman, and Batman. Morgaine had discovered that they were the legendary Trinity—the foremost three among the heroes protecting Earth—and that the planet sat at a locus of power within the multiverse. By harnessing the fortune-telling abilities of the novice psychic Tarot and the cosmic energies of the imprisoned god Krona, she could create a new world in which her Dark Trinity held all the cards.

Jose Delgado, who once adventured as the Gangbuster, returned to action to rescue Tarot from the powerful forces moving against her.

TAROT

Marguerita Covas, also called Tarot, never suspected she had a destiny that would take her far beyond her Los Angeles neighborhood. Possessed with a natural gift for reading the fates of others by casting the cards of the mystical tarot, Marguerita attracted the malevolent attention of Morgaine le Fey. The centuries-old spellcaster dispatched her agents to kidnap Tarot, and then exploited the young woman's connection to the mysterious "worldsoul" to explore potential outcomes of her grand plan.

Morgaine le Fey believed that each of the Trinity represented a heroic ideal. Wonder Woman, a goddess, inspired everyone she met, Batman represented the potential of human achievement, and Superman was a symbol of unstoppable will.

DARK TRINITY

Morgaine le Fey prepared a spell to create a new reality in which her Dark Trinity would replace the true Trinity. She would play the part of Wonder Woman, and Enigma — an alternate-universe copy of the Riddler — would replace Batman. They enlisted Despero to fill Superman's role, not realizing that he was the alien conqueror Kanjar Ro in disguise. The Dark Trinity enslaved half-human, half-animal monsters called Howlers and sent them to raise havoc and distract the heroes while branding them.

Occult runes were inflicted on the Trinity during combat. When the last member was marked, Morgaine's spell took effect and the world changed to one where the Trinity had never existed.

New villains Sun-Chained-In-Ink, Primat, the Trans-Volitional Man, and Swashbuckler served the Dark Trinity as members of a team called the Dreambound.

The Riddler investigated the thefts of items used in Morgaine's rituals and identified himself as the culprit! He failed to detect the existence of Enigma, his mirror-universe twin.

"...WHO SAID WE CAME ALONE?"

Even on an Earth that never knew the Trinity, the spirit of heroism remained strong. Champions from all over the planet joined forces against Morgaine le Fey and her minions.

World-changing magic was not enough to eradicate memories of the Trinity. Already weakened by Kanjar Ro's treachery and met with worldwide opposition, Morgaine le Fey's spells came undone.

ENTERING THE BATCAVE

Batman's ten-year-old son Damian grew up in the cruel care of the League of Assassins. A lethal killer, he was heralded since birth as successor to the world-conquering legacy of his mother, Talia, and his grandfather, Rā's al Ghūl. Batman didn't know if he could fully overcome Damian's indoctrination, but he brought his son to the Batcave to begin his training.

Talia al Ghūl is one of Batman's deadliest foes. To Batman's surprise, she also turned out to be the mother of his son, Damian!

BATMAN AND SON

Surrounded by colorful sculptures and pop art prints, Batman foiled a horde of sword-wielding Man-Bat warriors. But he wasn't prepared for the surprise that Talia al Ghūl had in store.

MAN-BAT ARMY

Talia re-entered Batman's life when she attacked an art museum with a commando squad of ninjas, who had been mutated into flying freaks by Dr. Kirk Langstrom's Man-Bat serum. It was one step in Talia's plan for global domination. When Batman stopped her, Talia seized the chance to introduce her unruly son to his unwitting father. Damian was in need of discipline, and Talia knew Bruce Wayne was the man to teach it to him.

Tim Drake only wanted to be friends, but Damian was conditioned to see him as a rival—and a threat.

TRIAL BY COMBAT

Following the traditions of the League of Assassins, Damian believed he had to earn his father's respect by defeating the current Robin, Tim Drake. Damian donned his own version of the Robin costume and headed into Gotham to join Batman's crusade against crime. He killed a low-level crook known as the Spook to demonstrate his commitment, but only proved how much he still had to learn: his father's mission is one of redemption, not punishment.

The Spook may have been a professional crook, but he didn't deserve the punishment Damian dished out. His career was ended with a horrific beheading.

Doctor Hurt and the Club of Villains tried to send the Dark Knight to an early grave.

BATMAN R.I.P.

BREAKING DOWN BATMAN

Years ago, Batman spent ten days in a sensory-deprivation tank to sharpen his mind. The researcher in charge of the treatment, Doctor Simon Hurt, had secretly planted the subliminal phrase "Zur-En-Arrh" in his patient's mind. When communicated, the phrase would leave Batman delirious and vulnerable. Now, together with the Club of Villains—which included Le Bossu, Charlie Caligula, King Kraken, Scorpiana, and El Sombrero—Doctor Hurt planned to push Batman past breaking point. However, the Dark Knight had his own psychological countermeasures in place.

Incapacitated by Doctor Hurt's hypnotic "trigger phrase," Batman lay helpless as Doctor Hurt and the Club of Villains infiltrated the Batcave. They beat Alfred senseless, then drugged Bruce Wayne before dumping him, dazed and confused, onto the streets of Gotham to fend for himself.

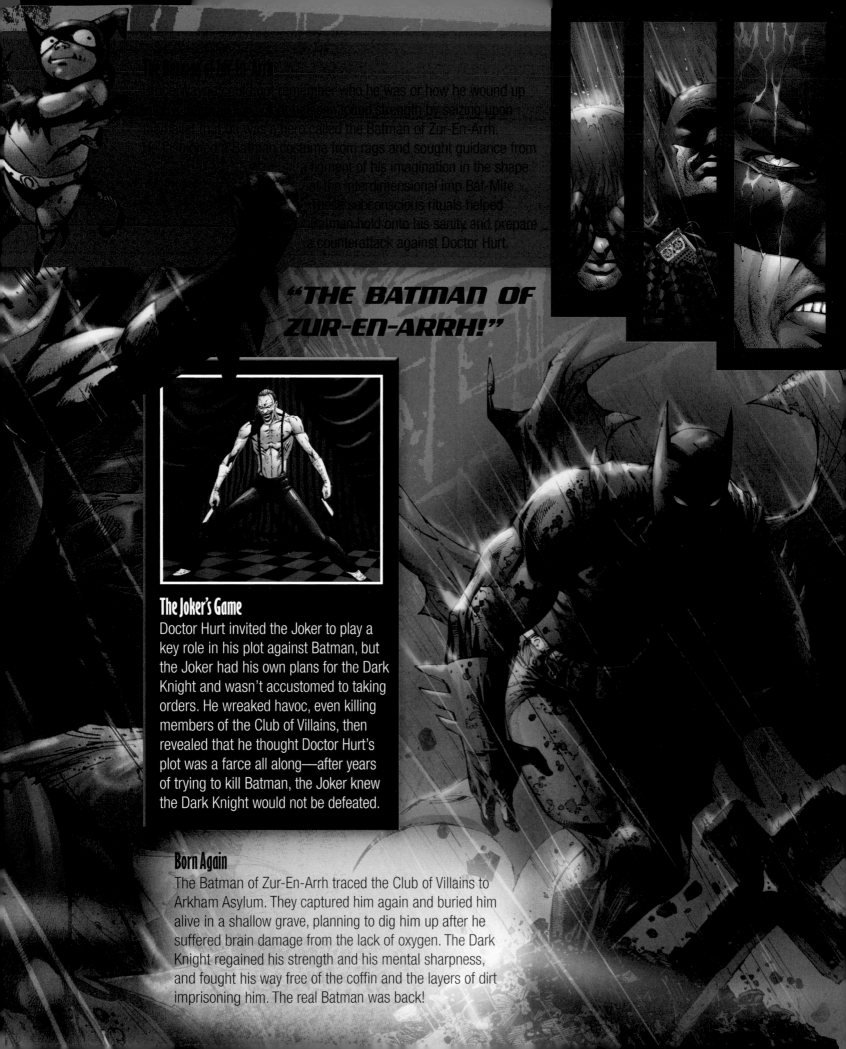

The Dark Knight couldn't remember who he was or how he wound up ... He recovered good strength by seizing upon ... and reinvented himself as the hero called the Batman of Zur-En-Arrh. He created a Batman costume from rags and sought guidance from ... a figment of his imagination in the shape of the interdimensional imp Bat-Mite. These subconscious rituals helped Batman hold onto his sanity and prepare a counterattack against Doctor Hurt.

"THE BATMAN OF ZUR-EN-ARRH!"

The Joker's Game

Doctor Hurt invited the Joker to play a key role in his plot against Batman, but the Joker had his own plans for the Dark Knight and wasn't accustomed to taking orders. He wreaked havoc, even killing members of the Club of Villains, then revealed that he thought Doctor Hurt's plot was a farce all along—after years of trying to kill Batman, the Joker knew the Dark Knight would not be defeated.

Born Again

The Batman of Zur-En-Arrh traced the Club of Villains to Arkham Asylum. They captured him again and buried him alive in a shallow grave, planning to dig him up after he suffered brain damage from the lack of oxygen. The Dark Knight regained his strength and his mental sharpness, and fought his way free of the coffin and the layers of dirt imprisoning him. The real Batman was back!

FINAL CRISIS
ISSUE #6

"I made a very solemn vow about firearms. But for you, I'm making a once-in-a-lifetime exception."

BATMAN

MAIN CHARACTERS: Batman, Darkseid, Superman
SUPPORTING CHARACTERS: Wonder Woman, Green Arrow, Supergirl, Mary Marvel, Flash, Black Racer
LOCATIONS: Legion of Super-Heroes arsenal, Blüdhaven, Darkseid's singularity

BACKGROUND

From the 1980s onward, DC drummed up sales for its interconnected comics with special crossovers. These events often had "crisis" in the title and starred a time-controlling villain able to rewrite history. The 2008-2009 crossover *Final Crisis* shocked readers by offering up what appeared to be Batman's dying act in his crusade against crime.

The Dark Knight uncharacteristically packed a futuristic firearm to defeat the godlike Darkseid. Batman wounded the villain before appearing to perish under Darkseid's counterattack: the lethal beams of the Omega Sanction.

After Final Crisis, Batman's presumed death kicked off a race to find his successor. It also gave his allies an occasion to memorialize the man who had given his life to alter events on a cosmic scale.

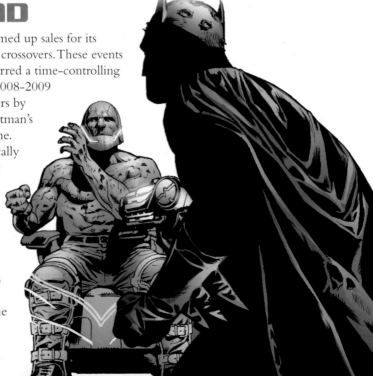

PUBLICATION DATE
January 2009

EDITOR
Eddie Berganza

COVER ARTIST
Carlos Pacheco

WRITER
Grant Morrison

PENCILLERS
J.G. Jones, Carlos Pacheco, Doug Mahnke

INKERS
Marco Rudy, Christian Alamy, Jesus Merino

LETTERER
Rob Clark Jr.

The Story...

The fate of the universe hangs in the balance as the Dark Knight of Gotham City takes on the might of the terrifying Fourth World god, Darkseid.

The entirety of time and space had been thrown into turmoil in the cataclysmic struggle known as the Final Crisis, and the planet Earth had become its battlefield. As the cornerstone of the multiple universes and timelines that constituted reality, Earth had attracted the attention of Darkseid, the all-powerful Fourth World god of Apokolips.

It was left for Earth's protectors to stand against him, led by the trinity of Superman, Wonder Woman, and Batman. But the heroes' ranks were broken. Darkseid had dragged the planet's population under his spell by eliminating free will. Wonder Woman had already become Darkseid's slave, with Green Arrow and others also joining the cause of evil.

While Superman sought the Legion of Super-Heroes' "miracle machine" in the 31st century **(1)** and Supergirl sparred with Mary Marvel in the streets of Blüdhaven **(2)**, the Flash tried to battle Darkseid by harnessing the power of the deity of death, Black Racer **(3)**. Batman, however, chose the direct path. He penetrated the walls of the singularity that shielded Darkseid's inner sanctum, relying on stealth to approach the god's throne.

But an immortal being could not be fooled by the clumsy footfalls of a mere human. Calling on Batman to reveal himself **(4)**, Darkseid gloated that the Dark Knight would soon be forced to embrace the brainwashed "peace" of anti-life. To Darkseid, there was no outcome but victory.

However, like countless mere-mortal criminals before him, Darkseid had underestimated the Dark Knight. Throughout the events of the Final Crisis, Batman had applied his knowledge of forensics to solve the case of the Fourth World god Orion, who had fallen victim to an assassin's bullet. Batman had reached two conclusions: Darkseid had orchestrated Orion's death to usher in the current crisis, and the bullet fired from the murder weapon had been cast from pure radion—the only substance in the universe with the power to kill a god.

Armed with a firearm of Fourth World manufacture loaded with the radion bullet recovered from the Orion crime scene, Batman held in his fist the means to end Darkseid's reign. "A gun and a bullet, Darkseid," he said "It was your idea." **(5)**

Faced with his imminent annihilation, Darkseid remained defiant. "Can you outrace the Omega Sanction?" he challenged Batman, as he prepared to fire his eye-beams and condemn his victim to the "death that is life."

Batman remained resolute in the face of Darkseid's awe-inspiring power. Ever since the mugger's gunshots in Crime Alley that had made him an orphan, he had kept his distance from guns and done everything in his power to stop their spread. During the previous Infinite Crisis, he had refused to give in to temptation and use a handgun to end a super-villain's life. But when the fate of the universe hung in the balance, the Dark Knight was forced to make a one-time exception. Batman and Darkseid fired at the same time **(6)**, with Batman's radion bullet hitting Darkseid in the shoulder **(7)**. Seeing his handiwork, Batman whispered "gotcha"—just before Darkseid's lethal Omega beams tore him to atoms **(8)**.

An enraged Superman **(9)** later recovered what was believed to be Batman's corpse **(10)**. The fallen hero was laid to rest near the graves of Thomas and Martha Wayne. But it was soon revealed that Darkseid's action had not killed Batman: instead, it had caused him to become unstuck in time.

Black Lantern symbol

BLACKEST NIGHT

The Green Lantern Corps is one of seven interstellar forces, including the Red Lanterns of rage and the Blue Lanterns of hope, that represent different colors and emotions. The absence of color once had a champion too, in the death-obsessed Black Hand. He sought to raise fallen heroes as Black Lanterns, and the key to his scheme was the freshly buried body of Batman!

Though living, Wonder Woman, Superman, and Green Arrow were all overpowered by Black Lantern rings. They were made vulnerable by their past experiences of death and resurrection.

White Lantern

The colors of the seven Lantern Corps combined to make white light, ending the Blackest Night and activating a White Lantern ring that Batman would briefly control.

GRAVE ROBBER

Black Hand lacked the power to create an entire Black Lantern Corps by himself, so he enlisted the help of Nekron, the Lord of Death. From an unmarked grave near the tombstones of Thomas and Martha Wayne he dug up the remains of Bruce Wayne, who had been laid to rest after his apparent death at the hands of Darkseid. The body would later be revealed as a cloned fake, but this did not spoil Black Hand's plan. He only needed to stir the emotions of those who remembered Batman.

The Dead Rise

Thousands of Black Lantern rings activated by Nekron resurrected dead heroes and villains as hateful shells of their former selves. Batman's living allies, including Commissioner Gordon, Barbara Gordon, Nightwing, and Robin fought off their advance, while the seven Lantern Corps joined forces against Nekron.

Using Batman's skull as a talisman, Black Hand forged an empathic link with those who had known Batman best. Ragged strips of flesh suddenly reanimated Batman's body, turning the hero into an undead horror. Confronted with their friend's transformation, Superman and other defenders dropped their guard and became mindless agents of Nekron.

Batman was dead—or so the world believed. Who would carry on the Dark Knight's crime-fighting legacy?

BATTLE FOR THE COWL

GOTHAM NEEDS BATMAN

With Bruce Wayne supposedly laid to rest beside the graves of his parents, the members of Batman's inner circle were torn over what to do next. Having served as the original Robin, Dick Grayson was the obvious choice to don the cape and cowl of his fallen mentor—but being Batman was an honor he didn't feel worthy of accepting. Others had their own designs on the cowl, including two more Robins. Jason Todd believed Gotham needed a ruthless Batman that acted as judge, jury, and executioner, and Tim Drake was forced to grow up before he was ready in order to stop him. As Black Mask plunged the city into chaos, Gotham's citizens called out for a savior. Where was Batman?

Black Mask

A Gotham with no Batman was an easy target for a criminal with no conscience. When Black Mask arrived, he freed the city's worst villains from Arkham Asylum and Blackgate Penitentiary, reveling in the madness that ensued.

Jason Todd

Back from the grave and angrier than ever, Jason Todd had convinced himself that Batman's "no killing" rule was what prevented the original hero from achieving true greatness. Jason geared up in a modified Batsuit and set out to frighten Gotham's crooks into submission—even if he had to leave behind a few bodies as examples to others.

Dick Grayson grew up in the shadow of Batman and never considered what it would mean to step into his mentor's shoes. He was the obvious choice, but becoming Batman seemed an almost overwhelming responsibility.

Determined to stop Jason Todd, Tim Drake donned an old version of Batman's costume and followed clues to a trash-strewn lair that Jason has been using as his own Batcave. In the brawl that followed, the two opponents seemed evenly matched, having both experienced similar training regimens under Batman's watch. But Jason's ruthlessness gave him the upper hand and he defeated Tim, leaving him bloodied but alive.

Nightwing

Dick Grayson never set out to become Batman. For years he had adventured as Nightwing, earning respect for his own accomplishments rather than the reputation of his mentor. But he soon learned that Gotham wasn't safe without a Batman to watch over it, and that Jason Todd couldn't be allowed to tear down everything Bruce Wayne had built.

Dick Grayson soon realized that to leave Batman's legacy in the wrong hands was to shame it. He finally accepted the cape and cowl, becoming the new Batman of Gotham City.

Superman, Booster Gold, Green Lantern, and the time-traveling Rip Hunter searched for Batman through time.

THE RETURN OF BRUCE WAYNE

Bruce Wayne was thought dead but he was actually lost in time. His journey home took him through the past, present, and future.

Witch Hunter

A time-skip sent Bruce to Puritan-ruled Gotham in 1640, where he took the name "Mordecai" and investigated accusations of local witchcraft. He was unable to save a woman from death by hanging before another time-skip moved him forward once again.

Bruce's ancestor, Nathaniel Wayne, gave orders for the accused witch Annie to be hanged.

A young warrior of the Miagani became Bruce Wayne's prehistoric Robin-like squire.

Caveman

After arriving in prehistory, in the territory that would one day become Gotham City, Bruce Wayne led a persecuted tribe to victory over his immortal enemy Vandal Savage and a band of Neanderthals. He left the people of the Miagani tribe with a story that would echo throughout the ages.

Chasing Time

When Darkseid blasted Batman with his Omega beams, he sent him through time—an act meant to kill the Dark Knight slowly. Each time-skip would infuse Batman with Omega energy until it had built up to such a degree that it threatened the universe itself.

Gotham Gunslinger

In the late 19th century, and a Wild West Gotham, Bruce again crossed paths with the immortal Vandal Savage. Another time-skip saved Bruce from what would have been a fatal gunshot wound.

Noir Detective

Dropped into Gotham City decades before the present, Bruce came to a woman's aid as a private investigator. She soon revealed herself as a cultist of the Black Glove organization, which planned to sacrifice Bruce Wayne in exchange for immortality.

The Black Glove's agents tried to sacrifice Bruce to the Miagani gods.

The notorious bounty hunter Jonah Hex signed on as a hired gun in Vandal Savage's cowboy posse.

Deep in a cave once used by the ancient Miagani, Bruce found relics dating from his time with the tribe.

The Black Pirate

Finding himself in 1718, an age when Blackbeard terrorized the seas, Bruce posed as the fabled Black Pirate to frighten Blackbeard away from the hidden treasures of the Miagani tribe.

By merging with the Hyper-Adaptor, Bruce was able to destroy it.

Back to the Present

Arriving at the end of time, Bruce Wayne defeated Darkseid's agent, the Hyper-Adaptor, and purged his body of Omega energy. He returned to Wayne Manor, ready to reclaim the title of Batman.

BATMAN INCORPORATED

"Batman is everywhere." – Bruce Wayne

BATMAN GOES GLOBAL

Bruce Wayne shocked the public when he announced Wayne Enterprises' plans for Batman, Inc.—an international initiative to install licensed Batman agents across the planet. What the original Batman had done for Gotham City, Wayne argued, the legend of Batman could do for the entire world. As the program took hold, investors threw their support behind Wayne Enterprises, but an enemy soon emerged with a similar goal of worldwide expansion. Batman needed every member of Batman, Inc. to fight back against the mysterious cabal known only as Leviathan.

Bruce Wayne's public role as Batman, Inc.'s financial backer helped to dispel rumors that *he* was secretly the Batman of Gotham City.

Flanked by a squad of Batman-like robots, Bruce Wayne demonstrated that automated agents could play a valuable role in stopping street-level crime.

BATMAN (DICK GRAYSON)

Origin: U.S.
Bio: After the formation of Batman, Inc., Dick Grayson continued wearing the Batman costume he had first put on during Bruce Wayne's absence. The presence of *two* Batmen helped underscore the ever-vigilant mission of Batman, Inc.

ROBIN

Origin: U.S.
Bio: Damian Wayne, the current Robin, signed on to his father's newest project as a loyal operative. He chased down leads concerning the evil Leviathan organization, but the revelation of Leviathan's true mastermind came as a shock.

RED ROBIN

Origin: WORLDWIDE
Bio: As Red Robin, Tim Drake has broadened his crime fighting jurisdiction on an international scale. Within Batman, Inc., Red Robin leads a team of Outsiders consisting of Metamorpho, Looker, Katana, Halo, and Freight Train.

BATGIRL

Origin: U.S.
Bio: Stephanie Brown filled the role of Batgirl during the early missions of Batman, Inc., while Barbara Gordon assisted as the computer expert Oracle. After the history-changing Flashpoint event, Stephanie departed the team.

BATWOMAN

Origin: U.S.
Bio: The military-trained Batwoman fits in well within Batman, Inc.'s hierarchy. She assisted the team on a mission to the Falkland Islands, where she investigated the sinister Doctor Dedalus and his ties to the Leviathan syndicate.

KNIGHT AND SQUIRE

Origin: U.K.
Bio: Knight and Squire are high-profile heroes in the UK, with a long history of working with Batman. The Knight is Cyril Sheldrake, who succeeded his father in the role, and his Squire is the scrappy Beryl Hutchinson.

THE HOOD

Origin: U.K.
Bio: George Cross works for the British intelligence service MI5 and models himself after Robin Hood, taking from the rich and giving to the poor. The Hood played a key role in helping Batman, Inc. neutralize the villainous Doctor Dedalus.

EL GAUCHO

Origin: ARGENTINA
Bio: A founding member of the now-defunct Batmen of All Nations, El Gaucho is a prominent Argentinean hero whose signature weapon is the bola. In his other identity of Santiago is a wealthy and respected landowner.

BATWING

Origin: DEMOCRATIC REPUBLIC OF CONGO
Bio: David Zavimbe is a police officer in the city of Tinasha in the Democratic Republic of Congo. He also coordinates Batman, Inc.'s operations throughout Africa in his role as Batwing. His jet-powered suit allows him to fly.

BLACKBAT

Origin: HONG KONG
Bio: With combat skills honed by the League of Assassins and extensive field experience as a former Batgirl, Cassandra Cain is Batman, Inc.'s agent in Hong Kong. She currently adventures under the identity of Blackbat.

NIGHTRUNNER

Origin: FRANCE
Bio: A new recruit into Batman, Inc., Bilal Asselah is a French Muslim who lives in suburban Paris. His advanced parkour free running skills make him a nimble guardian of the city's people.

MAN OF BATS AND RED RAVEN

Origin: U.S.
Bio: This father/son duo operates from a Sioux reservation in South Dakota, U.S.A. Man of Bats was once a proud member of the Batmen of All Nations. His son, Red Raven, has expressed a desire to emerge from his father's shadow.

MR. UNKNOWN

Origin: JAPAN
Bio: For decades one of Japan's leading costumed heroes, Mr. Unknown lost his life in battle with his arch-enemy Lord Death Man. Mr. Unknown's sidekick and stand-in, Jiro Osamu, volunteered to fill his role within Batman, Inc.

JIRO OSAMU

Origin: JAPAN
Bio: As the sidekick of Mr. Unknown, Jiro Osamu had stood in for his aging mentor when situations called for physical combat. Jiro helped Batman avenge Mr. Unknown's death and agreed to join Batman, Inc. in his boss's place.

DARK RANGER

Origin: AUSTRALIA
Bio: Johnny Riley is Batman, Inc.'s Australian representative and the second-generation successor to the country's original Ranger. The Dark Ranger's jetpack allows him to fly and he carries a pulse weapon to fight off attackers.

BATMAN OF MOSCOW

Origin: RUSSIA
Bio: The Russian representative of Batman, Inc. died after facing rival crime fighter Morgan Ducard, who is otherwise known as Nobody. Ducard "erased" the Batman of Moscow by submerging him in a vat of acid.

FLASHPOINT

The Flash awoke to a world in which his late mother lived, a global super hero war raged, and Dr. Thomas Wayne crusaded as Batman!

Wayne Manor had fallen to ruin, but it still held Batman's secrets.

BROKEN TIMELINE

After waking up in a strange new timeline, the Flash struggled to make sense of things. Some super heroes did not exist, others were at war, and he himself had lost his powers. Inside his ring, the Flash found not his own costume but that of his enemy, the Reverse-Flash. He was convinced that the Reverse-Flash had altered history. Enlisting the aid of Batman—in this world, Bruce Wayne's father—the Flash rallied other heroes for a final showdown with the Reverse-Flash.

Entering the Batcave

The world might have been turned upside down, but the Flash believed that there was one person he could trust in any reality—Batman. Inside the Batcave, however, he encountered a Dark Knight he no longer recognized. The shifting Flashpoint timeline had caused Dr. Thomas Wayne to become Batman, and he scoffed at the Flash's description of a world where his

Looking into Batman's eyes, the Flash saw just how deep the changes to history went.

son Bruce had lived and become a hero to all. Yet eventually, Dr. Wayne put aside his doubts and began to listen. Somehow the Flash's tale rang true. Finally convinced, Batman generated an artificial lightning strike to restore the Flash's speed powers.

Hooked to an electrical rig, the Flash received a jolt that mimicked the accident that had originally blessed him with super-speed.

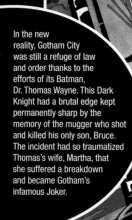

In the new reality, Gotham City was still a refuge of law and order thanks to the efforts of its Batman, Dr. Thomas Wayne. This Dark Knight had a brutal edge kept permanently sharp by the memory of the mugger who shot and killed his only son, Bruce. The incident had so traumatized Thomas's wife, Martha, that she suffered a breakdown and became Gotham's infamous Joker.

Subject 1

Batman hoped that a secret prisoner held by the U.S. government's Project Superman might be able to help them. Joined by the hero Cyborg, he and the Flash penetrated the Project Superman vault to find Subject 1, a young Kryptonian named Kal-El who had never felt the energizing rays of Earth's yellow sun.

Despite a lifetime spent in solitary confinement, Subject 1 had a kind heart and helped his rescuers escape the facility. However, once outside the vault he panicked and flew away.

Reverse-Flash Revealed

As the war escalated, the Reverse-Flash made himself known. Gloating, he revealed that the Flash himself had created the Flashpoint Earth by accidentally damaging the timeline and only the Flash could repair it. The Reverse-Flash tried to kill his arch-enemy, but Batman stopped him by running him through with an Amazonian war sword.

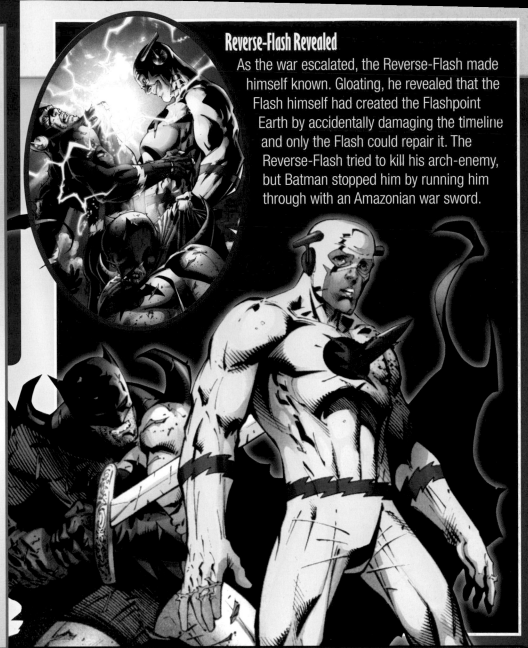

The Return

To mend the timeline, the Flash would have to undo everything that had led to this moment, erasing the only world Dr. Thomas Wayne knew. Nevertheless, Batman urged him to go ahead. The Flash raced back through the timestream, carrying a letter for Bruce from the father he would never know.

"Love always...your father, Thomas"

BATMAN
ISSUE #1

"Gotham is Batman. Gotham is Batman's city. Gotham is the Bat. All answers I'm partial to, myself."

BATMAN

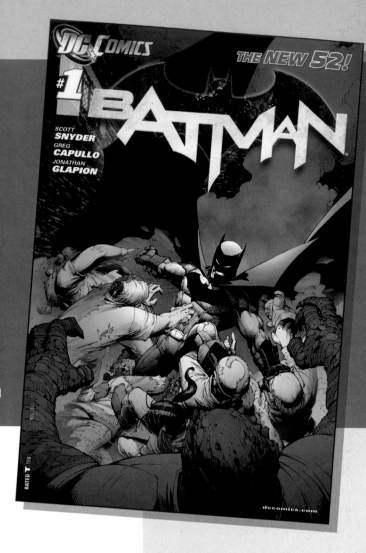

MAIN CHARACTERS: Batman, Nightwing (Dick Grayson), Commissioner Gordon
SUPPORTING CHARACTERS: Mr. Freeze, Scarecrow, Clayface, Robin (Damian Wayne), Red Robin (Tim Drake), Vicki Vale, Lincoln March, Harvey Bullock
LOCATIONS: Arkham Asylum, Police headquarters, the Batcave, Wayne Manor, Gotham slums

BACKGROUND

The *Flashpoint* crossover event in 2011 gave DC the opportunity to make some changes. From a business standpoint, a move to same-day digital distribution for tablets and e-readers made sense. The move had the potential to attract all-new audiences and get them hooked on DC's brand of serialized storytelling. In a clean break that demonstrated DC's commitment to the move, every comic ended its run with the issue that bore a cover date of October 2011. The following month, DC launched 52 comic book series. Some of them were all new, and others were relaunches of titles that had long histories of their own.

Two of the "New 52" marquee titles were *Detective Comics* and *Batman*. For the first time in over seven decades, both comics restarted with new #1 issues, jumping right into the action with a de-emphasis on past continuity.

In *Batman* #1, writer Scott Snyder drew parallels between Batman and Gotham, with the city becoming a character in its own right as the story unfolded.

PUBLICATION DATE
November 2011

EDITOR
Mike Marts

COVER ARTIST
Greg Capullo

WRITER
Scott Snyder

PENCILLER
Greg Capullo

INKER
Jonathan Glapion

LETTERERS
Richard Starkings, Jimmy Betancourt

The Story...

A new era dawns for Batman in an adventure through the key locations of the Dark Knight's legend, including Arkham Asylum, the Batcave, and the mean streets of Gotham City.

While putting down a riot at Arkham Asylum **[1]**, Batman found his thoughts drifting toward a feature frequently printed in the *Gotham Gazette*: "Gotham Is." When citizens were asked to fill in the next word, some likened their hometown to its famous villains: Gotham is Two-Face, Gotham is Killer Croc. But the most frequent answer—and the one that the Dark Knight had tried to prove through his actions—was Gotham is Batman.

His mental preoccupation was a sure sign that Mr. Freeze, the Scarecrow, Clayface, and the other participants in the breakout were not a great challenge to his crime-fighting abilities. The sudden appearance of the Joker threatened to turn the tide in the villains' favor **[2]**, until he inexplicably started fighting on Batman's side! **[3]**

Later, Batman regrouped with Commissioner Gordon on the rooftop of the G.C.P.D. headquarters. Gordon revealed that an Arkham guard may have unlocked the cells to trigger the evening's bedlam. On his return to the Batcave **[4]**, Batman found the Joker was there waiting for him! All became clear when Dick Grayson dropped his holographic disguise **[5]**.

As Bruce discussed the Arkham case with his former ward— and current Nightwing—he demonstrated some of his new technology upgrades. The Batcave's central computer could now beam data directly onto a contact lens over Bruce's right eye, permitting remote analysis, real-time lip reading, and other clever tricks.

Bruce took the lens upstairs to Wayne Manor for a test run at a Wayne Enterprises press conference and donor reception arranged by Alfred. Damian Wayne and Tim Drake were present **[6]**, and Bruce's eyewear automatically updated with a facial-recognition readout that confirmed Tim's alternate identity of Red Robin and Damian's role as the latest person to don Robin's costume. Bruce Wayne proudly announced Wayne Enterprises' plans to revitalize Gotham's dilapidated downtown infrastructure **[7]**, but prudently omitted the fact that the construction would hide the installation of secret "bat bunkers" throughout the city.

Among those present at the benefit was Vicki Vale of the *Gotham Gazette*, who introduced Bruce to mayoral candidate Lincoln March **[8]**. March hinted that he had equally big plans for the city, but Bruce excused himself from further mingling. His covert eyewear surveillance had been able to piece together the content of a murder investigation call between Commissioner Gordon and G.C.P.D. detective Harvey Bullock. Now it was time for Bruce to help Gotham as the Batman **[9]**.

Detective Bullock was unfazed by the Dark Knight's sudden appearance at the crime scene in the city's slums. Accustomed to Batman's comings and goings, Bullock brought his visitor up to speed. The victim, skewered by razor-tipped throwing knives which avoided major arteries, had died after a drawn-out ordeal. The handle of each knife was shown to bear the mark of an owl, a traditional symbol of Gotham. Batman detected the smell of linseed oil **[10]**, and borrowed Bullock's lit cigar to ignite a spill on the wall. There, written in flame, were the words "BRUCE WAYNE WILL DIE TOMORROW."

One more clue remained. Batman analyzed a tissue sample found beneath the victim's fingernails, and Alfred calculated a DNA match at the Batcave that pointed to Dick Grayson **[11]**. But the real killer was still out there, and Batman's investigation would soon throw a light on the ultra-secretive Court of Owls.

THE NEW 52

The events of Flashpoint brought about a new status quo, and reaffirmed Batman's role as a central figure of the heroic age. With his son Damian serving as Robin, Batman has redoubled his commitment as the protector of Gotham City despite opposition from unfamiliar enemies and the emergence of a centuries-old secret society known as the Court of Owls. The Dark Knight's influence can be seen close to home in the vigilance of Batgirl, Batwoman, and Nightwing, and on a global scale through the actions of Batwing and even those of Red Hood and the Outlaws.

BATMAN

Bruce Wayne might be one of Gotham City's most prominent citizens, but even he dismissed the mysterious Court of Owls as nothing more than a nursery-rhyme fantasy. But the secret society was all too real. Batman discovered that its members had murdered Bruce's ancestor, Alan Wayne, nearly a century before. Now, in the modern era, they sent their assassin Talon to kill Bruce. After restarting his investigation into the clandestine organization, Batman uncovered secret thirteenth-floor "owls' nests" concealed in skyscrapers across Gotham where the well-armed Talon could rest and resupply. The sheer scale of the operation forced Batman to confront the truth: the city he thought he knew so well was a stranger to him.

DETECTIVE COMICS

A new villain joined Batman's Rogues Gallery when the Dollmaker sliced his way into the Gotham City headlines. The Dollmaker's father, a serial killer, had died years ago when G.C.P.D. officer James Gordon shot him in the line of duty. Now the son had taken up the family's gruesome business, becoming a serial killer whose trademark was to sew new skins onto his tortured victims, turning them into "dolls." The Dollmaker delivered on his long-delayed vengeance by sending his minions to kidnap Police Commissioner Gordon, then subjected him to twisted experiments. As he raced to save the commissioner's life, Batman discovered disturbing evidence that the Joker had undergone the Dollmaker's treatments to gain an unrecognizable new face.

BATMAN: THE DARK KNIGHT

Most of Gotham's problems begin at Arkham Asylum. When Batman arrived to quell an uprising of inmates at the hospital for the criminally insane, he found the beautiful White Rabbit haunting the corridors. Like her *Alice in Wonderland* namesake, the White Rabbit urged her pursuer to follow—but a monstrously muscled Two-Face blocked Batman's way. Analysis of Two-Face's mutated condition revealed a bloodstream contaminant that appeared to be the White Rabbit's calling card. As he followed the newcomer across the city, Batman encountered opposition from other bulked-up villains including Mr. Zsasz and the Ventriloquist. To stop the White Rabbit, Batman would need the help of all the city's heroes.

BATMAN AND ROBIN

Batman had already trained four Robins, but his experience counted for little when his son Damian became the fifth to carry the name. Damian's upbringing among the League of Assassins—a group of killers headed by his mother, Talia al Ghūl—gave the latest Robin a ruthless streak and a cocky arrogance. At first, he sought to control these qualities under the guidance of his father. But when the crimefighter Morgan Ducard, also known as Nobody, tried to lure Damian away from his father and teach him to mete out "true" justice as both judge and executioner, Ducard's approach appealed to Damian's ingrained killer instincts. Ducard's actions succeeded in driving a wedge between father and son—and Batman and Robin.

BATWING David Zavimbe is Africa's protector within Batman, Inc.

CATWOMAN Selina Kyle has sharpened her claws battling with the Russian mob.

BATWOMAN Kate Kane makes an impact in Gotham as its newest hero.

TEEN TITANS As Red Robin, Tim Drake fights alongside Superboy and Kid Flash.

RED HOOD AND THE OUTLAWS These outcasts operate internationally.

BIRDS OF PREY Black Canary, Katana, Poison Ivy, and Starling are the new team.

NIGHTWING Dick Grayson protects Gotham in the role he has made his own.

BATGIRL Barbara Gordon is back in the Batgirl costume and better than ever.

JUSTICE LEAGUE Batman is a core member of this mighty super-group.

JUSTICE LEAGUE INTERNATIONAL A second team follows Batman's example.

COMRADES IN ARMS

From the alleys of Gotham to the peaks of the Himalayas, Batman's colleagues and protégés continue to carry out their own crusades against crime.

GOTHAM BY GASLIGHT

After witnessing the deaths of his parents at the hands of a coach robber, Bruce Wayne became the Batman of the year 1889. Though he was successful at stopping street-level smash-and-grabs, Batman faced a challenge when Jack the Ripper's arrival in Gotham City took things to a terrifying new level. The police arrested Bruce as a suspect in the Ripper murders but he managed to deduce the killer's true identity from behind bars. After breaking out of jail and apprehending the Ripper himself, Batman was able to resume his role as Gotham's industrial-age protector.

BATMAN & DRACULA: RED RAIN

Vampires ruled Gotham from behind the scenes, with Dracula as their unholy lord. Initially incredulous, Batman was forced to accept the truth after he suffered a wound that turned him into a member of their undead clan. Despite his transformation, Batman remained committed to law and order, and teamed up with a vampire hunter to track down Dracula and put an end to his centuries-long reign. Batman, now possessing supernatural strength, vampiric fangs, and leathery bat-like wings, soared above Gotham City as its immortal guardian.

BATMAN BEYOND

After Bruce Wayne retired from crime fighting, the mantle of Batman fell to high-schooler Terry McGinnis. Wearing a sleek black interpretation of the famous costume, Terry became the new face of heroism for the people of Neo-Gotham. Yet the past didn't stay quiet. Bruce Wayne's new role as Terry's mentor proved critical when the Joker reappeared on the scene, and when a mystery villain took up the role of competitive rogue Hush. By working alongside Police Commissioner Barbara Gordon, Terry became the Batman of a new generation.

ALTERNATE REALITIES

BATMAN: YEAR 100
One hundred years after the first reported sightings of Batman in 1939, a familiar hero stood up to an oppressive governmental regime. The Gotham City of 2039 was a police state with its citizens under constant surveillance—the kind of place where an urban legend like the Batman was not supposed to exist. But the Batman of this era had friends, including a new Robin and a G.C.P.D. officer descended from James Gordon. Playing up to the myths, Batman wore ceramic teeth that made him resemble a monster and used fear to uncover a conspiracy to bioengineer a worldwide pandemic.

ALL-STAR BATMAN
The Batman of this world was a reckless and profane vigilante who reveled in violence, but whose methods got results when compared to the only partly effective measures of Green Lantern or Superman. After Batman rescued Dick Grayson from the gangsters who shot his parents and the clutches of the corrupt G.C.P.D., he gave the boy a drill sergeant's instruction in dirty fighting and urged him to take revenge on his parents' killers. Opposed by both the Justice League and the Joker, Batman and sidekick Robin meted out their own brand of morality.

KINGDOM COME
After a new crop of vigilantes won praise for their bloodthirsty approach to peacekeeping, Earth's original heroes felt they were no longer needed. But after the American heartland was destroyed by a nuclear bomb, Superman was prompted to assemble an old-guard Justice League to rein in the new extremists. Batman believed that Superman's actions edged dangerously close to fascism and gathered his own team in response. Lex Luthor appeared to share Batman's concerns but betrayed him at the last minute, leading to a three-way battle against a backdrop of imminent nuclear annihilation.

In the past, the future, and on other versions of Earth, Batman is still a significant figure. The different incarnations of Bruce Wayne might lead unfamiliar lives, but a childhood tragedy always steers them toward dark vigilantism. Later generations of Batmen are inspired by Bruce Wayne's example and endeavor to carry on his work.

AFTERWORD

"Starting this issue: The amazing and unique adventures of the Batman!"

That's how Batman was introduced to readers in 1939, in a blurb printed on the cover of *Detective Comics* #27. The story inside was a tight action mystery that starred a Batman who would be instantly recognizable to modern audiences, the key pieces of his legend already in place. Looking at it with fresh eyes, it's striking how little Batman has changed since 1939.

But of course, Batman has changed, evolving through the Golden, Silver, Bronze, Dark, and Modern Ages up to DC's "New 52" rollout in 2011. Batman might be timeless, but times change. And here's where it gets tricky. DC's super hero comics are a self-contained fictional universe, in which characters arrive, depart, and evolve. But Batman and other famous heroes need to exist outside that universe, in forever-young incarnations that can be reinterpreted for movies, video games, and t-shirts. After all, if the comics had tried to tell an uninterrupted Batman biography starting with that first adventure in 1939, their star would now be around one hundred years old!

So, DC doesn't tell an uninterrupted biography. Instead the company has periodically pushed the reset button on their fictional universe, introducing timeline-altering "crisis" events to bring its heroes into the modern era. The most recent of these resets, *Flashpoint*, occurred mere months before I started writing this book. Therefore I didn't always have a clear picture on whether something from Batman's past "really happened" in current continuity.

Ultimately I decided it didn't matter. This book isn't only a guide to the Batman of the comics, but also a history of those comics from a publishing perspective. Hence the focus on the Golden Age, Silver Age, and beyond, and the inclusion of storylines that fans remember fondly. Continuity sticklers — and I consider myself one of them — have to concede that all of these events really happened to our fictional Dark Knight Detective, even if some of them were overwritten by updated timelines.

Big thanks to DK Publishing for putting together a visual and informational tour de force, particularly to Hannah Dolan, Robert Perry, Catherine Saunders, Nathan Martin, Clive Savage, Toby Truphet, Julia March, Pamela Afram, Emma Grange, and Neil Kelly. At Warner Bros. Consumer Products I want to thank Benjamin Harper and Joshua Anderson, and at DC Entertainment thanks go to Kevin Kiniry, Patrick Flaherty, Adam Schlagman, and Roger Bonas.

With our hero starring in a newly invigorated array of comics titles — not to mention the blockbuster movie *The Dark Knight Rises* and the award-winning *Batman: Arkham City* video game — there's never been a better time to be a Batman fan.

DANIEL WALLACE
MARCH 2012

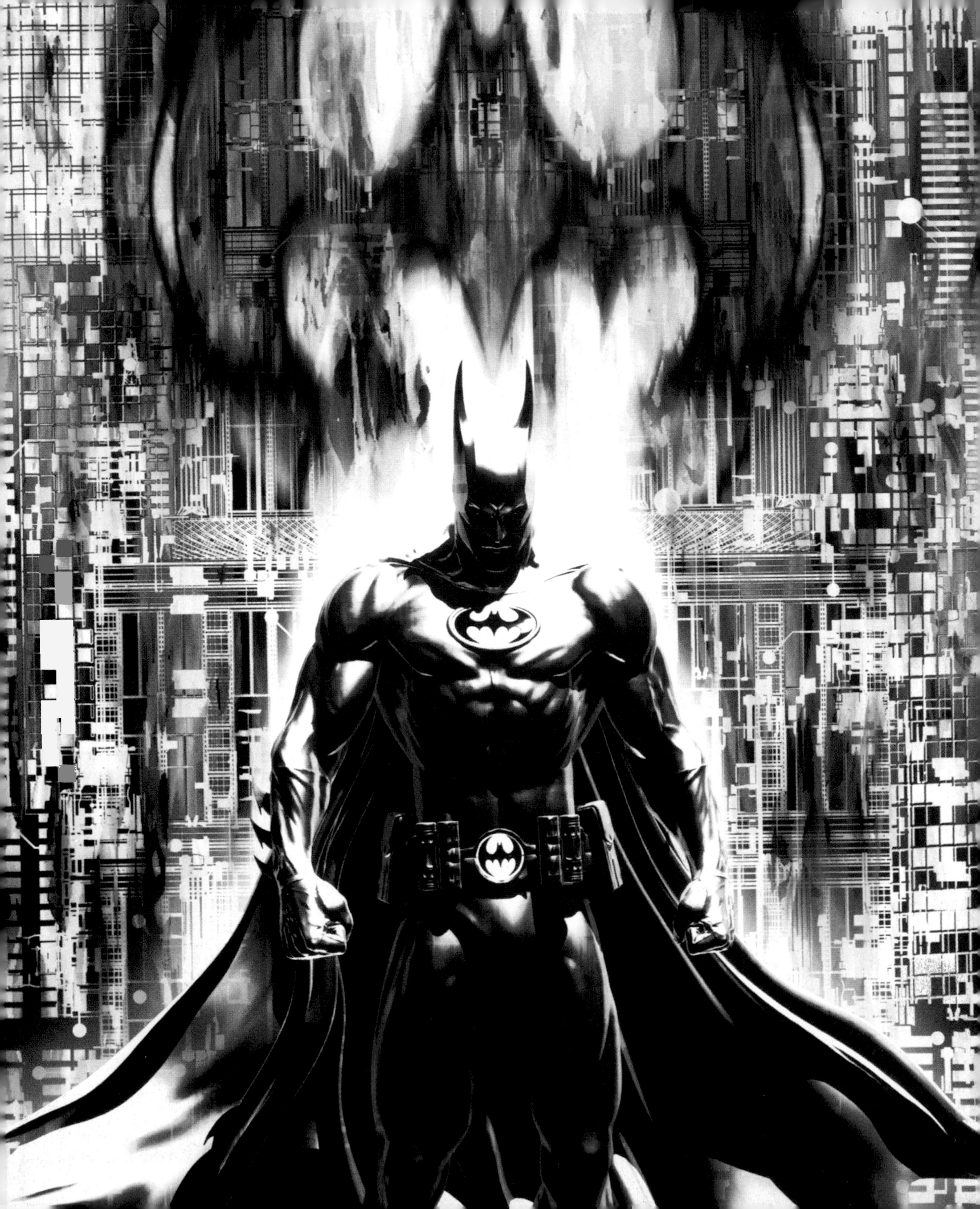

Index

Acknowledgments

Artists, Inkers, and Colorists: Neal Adams, Christian Alamy, Oclair Albert, Mario Alquiza, Murphy Anderson, Jim Aparo, Aspen Studios, Terry Austin, Tony Avina, Ramon Bachs, Mark Bagley, Michael Bair, Jim Balent, Matt Banning, David Baron, Eduardo Barreto, Eddy Barrows, Chris Batista, Moose Baumann, David M. Beaty, Ed Benes, Ryan Benjamin, Joe Bennett, Liz Berube, Shannon Blanchard, Blond, Brian Bolland, Brett Booth, Doug Braithwaite, Norm Breyfogle, Bob Brown, Steve Buccellato, Mark Buckingham, Rick Burchett, Chris Burnham, Jack Burnley, Sal Buscema, Jim Calafiore, Robert Campanella, Greg Capullo, Claudio Castellini, Keith Champagne, Richard Chasemore, Chris Chuckry, Vicente Cifuentes, Scott Clark, Andy Clarke, Gene Colan, Kevin Conrad, Will Conrad, Jeromy Cox, Andrew Dalhouse, Rodolfo Damaggio, Carlos D'anda, Tony S. Daniel, Alan Davis, Shane Davis, Mike DeCarlo, Luciana Del Negro, Edgar Delgado, John Dell, Jesse Delperdang, Mike Deodato, Tom Derenick, D'Israeli, Rachel Dodson, Terry Dodson, Dale Eaglesham, Nathan Fairbairn, Mark Farmer, Wayne Faucher, Raul Fernandez, David Finch, Walt Flanagan, Sandu Florea, John Floyd, Francesco Francavilla, Derek Fridolfs, Richard Friend, Lee Garbett, José Luis García-López, Stefano Gaudiano, Noelle Giddings, Joe Giella, Keith Giffen, Dick Giordano, Jonathan Glapion, Patrick Gleason, Mick Gray, Sid Greene, Mike Grell, Paul Gulacy, Ian Hanin, Scott Hanna, Ed Hannigan, Jeremy Haun, Doug Hazlewood, Hi-Fi Design, John Higgins, Matt Hollingsworth, Richard Horie, Tanya Horie, David Hormung, Sandra Hope, Adam Hughes, Rob Hunter, Carmine Infantino, Frazer Irving, Klaus Janson, Georges Jeanty, Phil Jimenez, Jock, J. G. Jones, Kelley Jones, Malcolm Jones III, Ruy Jose, John Kalisz, Bob Kane, Gil Kane, Stan Kaye, Karl Kesel, Leonard Kirk, Don Kramer, Andy Kubert, Michel Lacombe, Julia Lacquement, Andy Lanning, Michael Lark, Stanley Lau, Ian Laughlin, Bob Layton, Jim Lee, Pat Lee, Richmond Lewis, Kirk Lindo, Kinsun Loh, Aaron Lopresti, Lee Loughridge, Doug Mahnke, Guy Major, Alex Maleev, Guillem March, Laura Martin, Marcos Martin, Shawn Martinbrough, Marcos Marz, Ron Marz, Jose Marzan, Francesco Mattina, J. P. Mayer, Randy Mayor, David Mazzucchelli, Ray McCarthy, Tom McCraw, Scott McDaniel, Ed McGuinness, Dave McKean, Jamie McKelvie, Mark McKenna, Bob McLeod, Shawn McManus, Adriana Melo, Jaime Mendoza, Jesus Merino, Mike Mignola, Danny Miki, Al Milgrom, Brian Miller, Frank Miller, Steve Mitchell, Sheldon Moldoff, Shawn Moll, Rags Morales, Tomeu Morey, Win Mortimer, Patricia Mulvihill, Dustin Nguyen, Tom Nguyen, Graham Nolan, Mike Norton, Phil Noto, Irv Novick, Kevin Nowlan, Ben Oliver, Ariel Olivetti, Glen Orbik, Jerry Ordway, Andy Owens, Carlos Pacheco, Jimmy Palmiotti, Peter Pantazis, Yanick Paquette, Charles Paris, Sean Parsons, Allen Passalaqua, Bruce D. Patterson, Jason Pearson, Andrew Pepoy, George Pérez, Pere Perez, Rich Perotta, Sean Phillips, FCO Plascencia, Paul Pope, Howard Porter, Joe Prado, Bruno Premiani, Javier Pulido, Frank Quitely, Stefano Raffaele, Pamela Rambo, Rodney Ramos, Norm Rapmund, Fred Ray, Brian Reber, Ivan Reis, Rod Reis, Chris Renaud, David Roach, Darick Robertson, Jerry Robinson, Roger Robinson, Kenneth Rocafort, Alex Ross, George Roussos, Stephane Roux, Adrienne Roy, Joe Rubinstein, Marco Rudy, Neil Ruffino, P. Craig Russell, Matt Ryan, Tim Sale, Amilton Santos, Joe Shuster, Damion Scott, Nicola Scott, Trevor Scott, Mike Sekowsky, Jerry Serpe, Bill Sienkiewicz, Alejandro Sicat, Walt Simonson, Alex Sinclair, James Sinclair, Paulo Siqueira, Cam Smith, J. D. Smith, Pam Smith, Ryan Sook, Aaron Sowd, Dick Sprang, Chris Sprouse, John Stanisci, Joe Staton, Peter Steigerwald, Brian Stelfreeze, Cameron Stewart, Dave Stewart, Chic Stone, Karl Story, Lary Stucker, E. J. Su, Ardian Syaf, Pat Tan, Philip Tan, Romeo Tanghal, Art Thibert, Marcus To, Anthony Tollin, Dwayne Turner, Michael Turner, George Tuska, Ethan Van Sciver, Lynn Varley, José Villarrubia, Dexter Vines, Matt Wagner, Brad Walker, Lee Weeks, Chris Weston, Bob Wiacek, Wildstorm FX, Freddie E. Williams II, J. H. Williams III, Scott Williams, Ryan Winn, Stan Woch, Walden Wong, Wally Wood, Pete Woods, Gregory Wright, Jason Wright, Patrick Zircher, Tom Ziuko

Writers: Brian Azzarello, Mike W. Barr, Don Cameron, Paul Dini, Chuck Dixon, Bill Finger, Ed Herron, Kyle Higgins, Geoff Johns, Jeph Loeb, Brad Meltzer, Frank Miller, Alan Moore, Denny O'Neil, Frank Robbins, Greg Rucka, Jerry Siegel, Gail Simone, Scott Snyder, Peter J. Tomasi, Len Wein, Judd Winnick

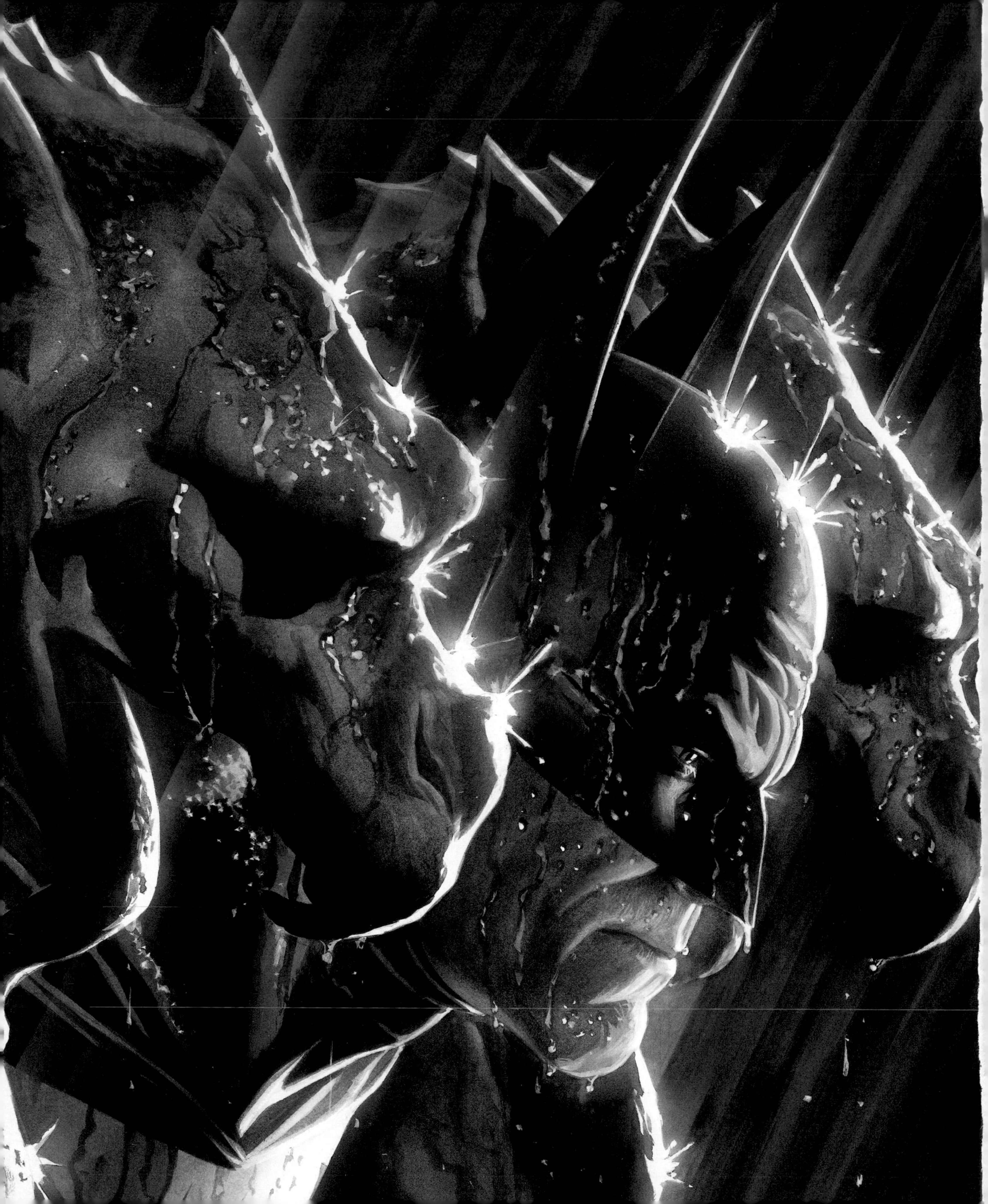

J 741.5973 WAL

Wallace, Daniel, 1970-

Batman

9-10-12

WATCHING LIBRARY
12 STIRLING ROAD
WATCHUNG, NJ 07069